COMMENTARY
ON
ECCLESIASTES

by

Ernest W. Hengstenberg

Wipf & Stock
PUBLISHERS
Eugene, Oregon

Wipf and Stock Publishers
199 West 8th Avenue, Suite 3
Eugene, Oregon 97401

Commentary on the Book of Ecclesiastes
By Hengstenberg, E.W.
ISBN: 1-57910-143-7
Publication date 8/3/1998
Previously published by James and Klock Christian Publishing Co., 1977

INTRODUCTION.

IT is of great importance accurately to determine the circumstances of the time at which this Book was written. In this way, not only will a sure foundation be laid for investigations respecting its authorship, but a point be secured from which we may start in endeavouring to unfold its meaning. For this latter purpose the inquiry is a specially pertinent one, inasmuch as the book evidently, in the first instance, took its occasion from passing events, was addressed to a particular generation of men, and intended for their admonition and comfort.

The Author has studiously maintained a certain tone of reserve in respect of the circumstances of his time; and of design rather glanced at them, than entered into details. This explains why so many false views have been entertained of the situation of affairs, to the great prejudice of the interpretation and practical application of the book. He had two reasons for restricting himself to bare allusions to the events of his time. In the first place, he felt that though writing primarily for his own generation, his book was destined to form part of the Canonical Scriptures, and, consequently, to be of service to the Church of God in all ages. This consciousness he gives express utterance to in chap. xii. 11: "The words of the wise are as goads, and as nails fastened by the masters of assemblies, which are given from one shepherd." This being the case, the writer would naturally endeavour to give prominence to that which was general and eternal in its character, over that which was special and temporary, only lightly glancing at the latter, in order that his teachings might be easier of universal application. The Psalms were generally composed on the same principle. Though connected with, and owing their origin to certain historical events, as a general rule they allude so sparingly and gently to actual occurrences, that a microscopical investigation is required to bring them out with any degree of clearness, precision and fulness. A second reason for his reticence is expressly assigned by the Author himself in chap. x. 20 : "Curse not the king, no not in thy thought: and curse not the rich in thy bed-chamber : for a bird of the air shall carry the voice, and that which hath wings shall carry the matter." According to this, it would seem to have been dangerous for the Hebrews to use plain language concerning things, because of the numerous spies and informers employed by their tyrannical heathen rulers. Despite this reserve, however, by gathering up and combining scattered traits we may form a tolerably accurate and complete picture of the period to which the book of Ecclesiastes owes its origin.

First of all, let us bring into view the detached and fragmentary hints which the work itself gives relative to the external circumstances of the people of God at the time of its composition.

Evidently they were in a state of deep misery, and had fallen a prey to vanity ; for in chap. i. 2-11, the writer holds up to the view of his nation the worthlessness of this entire earthly existence, intending thus to bring his fellow-countrymen to regard the wretched lot under which they were groaning in a more favourable light. If misery is the destined portion of man, if man is born to evil, as it is said in Job v. 7, it surely cannot be of great consequence whether his lot be a shade brighter or a shade darker. For one whose sufferings are peculiarly severe, there is sweet consolation in the thought, that to a certain extent, or rather, that in all the essential characteristics of his condition, all men are his associates. If all is vanity, why need we vex ourselves so much about having a handful or so more of it ?

This was a time when all the splendour of the age of Solomon had passed away : for, from chap. i. 12, to the end of chap. ii., the writer labours to show that that also was vanity, hoping thus to console and tranquillise under their loss, the minds of those who were consuming themselves with looking back upon, and yearning for bygone glories. Vanished also was the radiant wisdom of the generation of Solomon; for in chap. i. 12-18, those are cheered who were bewailing the past : vanished, according to chap. ii., were its great works and projects, its rich possessions, its brilliant relations, its glorious and joyous life, for the author takes the greatest pains to show that it was all " vanity and vexation of spirit," to the end, that the people might feel less keenly its present lack of wealth and enjoyment.

From chap. iii. 1-15, we learn that for Israel there had begun a time of death, of the uprooting of what was planted, of the breaking down of what was built up, of mourning, a time when God had gone far away from them and withdrawn His help and grace. The nation was persecuted, was being tried in the furnace of affliction, was under the dominion of heathen rulers.

Chap. iv. 1-3, teaches us that the earth was then a scene of injustice and of violence : the times were such as to force on men's minds the thought that it is better to die than to live, nay more, that it had been best never to have been born. In chap. iv. 4-6, the writer seeks to console his miserable fellow-countrymen by the consideration that, at all events, they have not to bear the heavy burden of envy. This consolation implies of course, that they were in anything but an enviable condition. According to chap. iv. 7-12, Israel was then a poor people in contrast with their rich heathen tyrants. The object of the author in pointing this out was to lead his nation to form a just estimate of that which the heathen possessed, and of which they were destitute, to counteract the envy of the riches of the world to which their own circumstances rendered them so liable. From the 7th to the 12th verse, he consoles the people in their beggary for the loss of their possessions ; from the 13th to the 16th verse, in their bondage for their loss of liberty.

The heathen tyranny under which the people of God lay groaning, constitutes the point of departure for chap. v. 7-8. According to ver. 7, the Inheritance of the Lord, destined originally to universal dominion, but now degraded to the rank of a mere province, was the scene of oppression of the poor and of perversion of justice and judgment.

In chap. v. 9-19, and chap. vi., the nation, sighing beneath the extortions of the Gentiles, is again comforted for the loss of earthly good ; the rich man represents the Gentile, the poor man Israel.

According to chap. vii. Israel was then in the house of mourning, the heathen, on the contrary, sat in the house of feasting (ver. 2), in the house of mirth (ver. 4), had the upper hand, and were floating on a sea of pleasures and delights (ver. 5). The times were such as to incline men strongly to deem the day of death better than the day of birth (ver. 1). These were times when men asked, "What is the cause that the former days were better than these?" (ver. 10)—when Israel was compelled to listen to the rebukes of the wise, who took occasion from their misery to reproach them for their sins (ver. 5)—when the temptation to cherish a bitter and discontented spirit lay especially near (ver. 9)—when there was abundant opportunity of exercising the virtue of patience (ver. 8)—when no signs were discernible of the victory over the world promised to the Church of God, but in that respect it was left entirely to faith and hope (ver. 6, 8). According to verses 11, 12, Israel was then without possessions, and had fallen into the hands of death. Every other portion which should belong, and once had belonged to the people of God, was now taken away, and it was reduced to the one inheritance of the wisdom coming from above—an inheritance, however, the author teaches, which must bring all other blessings in its train, inasmuch as it was itself the good of chief value at that time. In verses 19 and 20, also, power is represented as being entirely on the side of the heathen, whilst to Israel there remained only its inalienable prerogative and birthright of wisdom. Verses 15-18 complain that Israel is unfortunate, despite its righteousness, and that, on the contrary, the heathens, or the heathen tyrants, are fortunate, notwithstanding their wickedness. According to verses 21 and 22 Israel was forced to listen without reply to the curses and slanders heaped upon them by the Gentiles ; and those held the upper hand who, of right, and by God's ordination, should have been the bondsmen of the nation which, from its very commencement, was exalted to the throne of the world.

From chap. viii. 9 we learn that it was a time when "one man ruled over other men to their hurt"—when the wicked had in their possession Jerusalem, "the place of the holy"

(ver. 10)—when this state of things had already lasted long
(ver. 12)—when the earnestly expected decree of their heavenly
king against the usurpers had been long delayed (ver. 11).
(Throughout the entire book no other king than the heavenly
one is spoken of as their own ; and it is a very characteristic
feature that He is without hesitation designated "*the king*"
(viii. 2). Everywhere the Gentiles are introduced as holding
external earthly rule over the people of God.)

The commencement of chap. ix. gives us to understand
that the present position of affairs proved a serious stumbling-
block in the way of faith, and caused men to err in respect
to God and the righteousness of His rule in the earth, as they
saw how the lot of the righteous was interwoven and con-
founded with the lot of the wicked. So truly hopeless and
forlorn did the condition of the covenanted people appear to
those who looked on it with eyes of flesh alone that they
were in danger of utterly despairing. Whilst in other and happier days the men of God regarded it as their bounden duty
to counteract frivolity, and to draw attention to the earnestness
of life, the author of this work strives, on the contrary, with all
diligence to impress on his readers the lesson, " Eat thy bread
with joy, and drink thy wine with a merry heart" (ix. 7)—
a plain proof that his generation was in great danger of yielding to a gloomy and discontented spirit, and that their life
was threatened with the loss of all that made it desirable and
joyful. The desperate nature of their circumstances is clear
also from the earnestness with which the writer warns them
against listless inactivity (ix. 10 ; xi. 4-6). Sluggish hands
are to be found wherever men's circumstances seem hopelessly
bad ; see Isa. xiii. 7 ; xxxv. 3 ; Ezek. vii. 17 ; Job. iv. 3.

Characteristic of the posture of affairs are the words of
chap. x. 6, 7 : "Folly (which is everywhere set forth in the
book as the soul of Heathendom) has been set on great heights,
and the rich (*i.e.*, those who, according to God's word and promise, should be rich) sit in a low place. I saw servants (*i.e.*,
those who by right, and by God's law, ought to be servants)
on horses, and princes (*i.e.*, members of the nation whose
vocation it is to rule over the world, Exod. xix. 6), walking
on foot like servants." The condition of the power which
then ruled the world is depicted in chap. x. 11-20. It pre-

sented a spectacle at once of wickedness and folly (iv. 11-15);
the king and his nobles had surrendered themselves to rioting
and drunkenness (iv. 16, 17); nowhere had morality any
hold; rottenness, wantonness, and gold prevailed everywhere,
consequently ruin was inevitable.

Now, the picture thus drawn corresponds to no period but
that when the Persians held dominion over the people of God.
During the time embraced by the canonical books of the Old
Testament, this was the only power to whose tyranny the
people of God was subjected in its own land, the temple at
the same time standing, and the worship thereof being kept
up (compare chap. v. 17).

The time of the Persian rule corresponds to the descriptions given in this book, not only as respects the external,
but also as respects the internal condition of the people. Considerable importance must be attached to the fact, that idola-
try, the temptation to which had beset the nation so strongly
from the days of Solomon to the Babylonish exile, never
appears in the delineation of internal evils. During the residence in Babylon false gods seem to have lost their attrac-
tions for Israel. On the other hand, however, we find them
assailed by enemies and dangers which, from other sources, we
know to have been peculiar to the time which succeeded the
exile. Malachi, the last of the prophets, delivered his prophecy during the Persian dominion, and in particular during
the reign of Artaxerxes, and his warnings and attacks are
directed to the same evils as those set forth in this book.
Israel's temptation, then, was to Pharisaism — to a resting
contented with a hollow righteousness which sought to supply the lack of living fear of God and spiritual devotion by
beggarly outward works, sacrifices (iv. 17), long prayers, and
the like. We encounter here, as in Malachi, that moroseness
which ever accompanies unspiritual religion and soulless morality, when the expectations on which they were based prove
to be a delusion, and when painful experience teaches the
lesson that godliness is not an affair of gain. Covetousness
also is here, which can only be uprooted in a soul that rises
steadily and truly towards God, and which a Pharisaical piety,
instead of destroying, stimulates and fosters. By this sin
men are especially tempted, in times of distress; then we fall

very easily into a habit of scratching and scraping for gain. Finally, in chap. viii. 11, our attention is drawn to the existence of a power tempting men to utter apostacy from God and law, to transgress into the way of the wicked ; and from this also we should judge the period to have been one of heavy misfortune.

If such were the external and internal circumstances of the people of God, the idea cannot for a moment be entertained that the book dates from the time of Solomon, and that he was himself the author. For a long time this opinion prevailed both in the Jewish and Christian Church. The true interpretation of the work thus suffered serious detriment, for its practical significance depends in great measure on our clearly and distinctly understanding the historical circumstances to which it owed its origin, and in adaptation to which it was written. The first step towards the overthrow of this prejudice was taken by the Chaldee Paraphrast. It is true, he holds to the opinion that Solomon was its author, but at the same time supposes that through the spirit of prophecy he was transported to, and described the time when, Jerusalem was destroyed and the nation was carried away into exile.* We may remark also in passing, that those who start with the groundless prejudice that David composed all the Psalms, resort to a similar mode of explanation in regard to several whose contents it is plainly impossible to understand from the events and circumstances of that particular period. To Grotius belongs the merit of having first clearly recognised the invalidity of the opinion that Solomon wrote this book.† He failed, however, to enter into a closer discussion of the main argument for his view, namely, the hints given by the book itself regarding the historical circumstances in the midst of which it was composed. The only ground urged by him was the character of the style and language, which indicated a later period. But he erroneously maintained that

---

* He gives the following pharaphrase of chap. i. 2: Cum videret Salomo rex Israel per spiritum propheticum, regnum Roboam filii sui divisum iri cum Jeroboam, filio Nebat, Jerusalem etiam domumque sanctuarii destructum iri, et populum filiorum Israel exulaturum, dixit in verbo suo, " vanitas," &c.

† Ego tamen Salomonis non esse puto, sed scriptum serius, sub illius regis tanquam pœnitentia ducti nomine. Argumenta ejus rei habeo multa vocabula quæ non alibi quam in Daniele, Esdra et Chaldæis interpretibus reperias.

it was written under the name of Solomon as the Penitent.
In this respect he followed too closely in the footsteps of the
older commentators of the Church, who looked upon Ecclesiastes
as the fruit of Solomons repentance.   Grotius found an ad-
herent of his view in the marvellous Hermann, v.d. Hardt
(*de libro Coheleth*, 1716), who, however, was quite incom-
petent to bring convincing evidence of the correctness of his
opinion.   Both these men were justly a scandal to the theology of the Church, and, in respect of this question as well as
of others it has maintained an attitude of coolness towards
them.   The Church should take shame to itself for having
left Rationalism to make good the truth as to the composition
of this book, especially as its very commencement is decidedly
against the prevalent prejudice ; to its honour, however, be it
said that on its revival it gave willing ear to the truth, and
since then only a few isolated and unimportant attempts have
been made to return to the lower position.   In the present
work, by more carefully examining the historical relations of
the book, we have endeavoured to lay a firmer foundation for
the more correct view, and hope thus to render impossible a
revival of the old prejudice.

The only argument which is urged with any force in favour
of the authorship by Solomon, is the one drawn from the fact
that he is named as the author in the title, and is introduced as speaking in the work.   The nullity of this argument
we shall endeavour to show at chap. i. 1.   We shall prove
that Solomon is not only not the direct author of the book,
but that it does not even profess to be by him, that, on the
contrary, the very first words indicate him not to have written it.

Evidence against the authorship of Solomon has been improperly drawn from chap. i. 12-16, ii. 7, where it is said
that the fictitious character of the work is for the moment
thrown aside ; see the remarks on the passage.   On the other
hand, it is inconsistent with the composition of the book by
Solomon that he is represented in chap. ii. 3, 9, as prosecut-
ing his search after sensual enjoyments, possessions, and
renown, in the manner of a philosophical experimenter.   Solomon is evidently here introduced, not in his actual historical
character, but as an ideal person, as the ideal of wisdom.

The tacit allusion in chap. ii. 12, 18, 19, to Solomon's evil successor, would lead also to the conclusion we are advocating. Besides, the author, in designating himself "a wise man" (chap. xii. 9), gives up any pretence of being personally identical with Solomon.

Hand in hand with the evidence against Solomon drawn from the historical circumstances of the work, goes that which is derived from peculiarities of style and language. These are undeniably not those of the time of Solomon, but of the later post-exile period, as we shall show in specific instances in our commentary. Compare, for example, our observations on רעות and רעיון, chap. i. 14; חרץ מן, in the sense of "besides" chap. ii. 25; on מדינה, chap. v. 7; on על דברת, in the sense of "in order that," chap. vii. 14; on פשר, chap. viii. 1; on שלטון, chap. vii. 4; on בכן, chap. viii. 10; on פתגם, chap. viii. 11; on נומץ, chap. x. 8; on מדע, chap. x. 20; and on בטל, chap. xii. 3.

Finally, the position the book occupies in the Canon is a proof that Solomon was not its author—it stands, namely, separated from the writings of that period, and is placed after the "Book of the Lamentations" of Jeremiah, with which last of all the poetical books it is directly associated. It comes also immediately before those writings whose history and prophecy find their explanation in the circumstances of the time succeeding the exile. Had the collectors of the canonical books regarded this as the work of Solomon they would certainly not have given it a place between "Lamentations" and "Esther." For remarks on the arrangement of the third part of the Canon and the Hagiographa, see the "Christology of the Old Testament," pt. iii.

If we may consider it proved that the book originated within the period of the Persian dominion, our next duty is to examine whether we can determine more exactly the precise date of its composition. In doing this we must be principally guided by the fact that the nation which held the supremacy is represented as deeply deteriorated, as having fallen a prey to folly (chap. x. 1), as demoralised by the exercise of despotic power (chap. vii. 7), as sunk in sloth, luxury, debauchery, and mammonism, and as everywhere exhibiting symptoms of the speedy downfall of the entire edifice of the state (chap. x. 18 - 19, vii. 1 - 6). These representations do not permit us to think of the time of Cyrus, but at the same time do not necessitate us to look beyond Xerxes, during whose reign internal corruption and external decay had made the mightiest advances. In these historical circumstances we find then a significant *point d'appui* for the conviction running through the entire book, that a terrible catastrophe was shortly to befal the Persian empire. From looking beyond the period of Xerxes and Artaxerxes we are prevented by the consideration that then the collection of the canonical scriptures was finally completed ; and no book or part of a book can be shown to have had a later origin. Another circumstance also leads us to fix on this time, namely, that this book has strong points of affinity with other productions which then appeared, especially with the prophecies of Malachi, who flourished during the reign of Artaxerxes. The peculiar resemblance between Ecclesiastes v. 5, and Malachi ii. 7, is in itself startling. But of much more decided importance is their agreement in reference to the inner condition of the people. Both writers draw attention to the superficial and external spirit, the self-righteousness, and to the germs of Pharisaism which were then in operation, so that in this respect no two others stand so nearly related to each other as these. With the remarks we have made in reference to Ecclesiastes compare our observations on Malachi in the " Christology," part iii., which are to the following effect : " Immediately after the reproaches uttered by the Prophet follows regularly an inquiry on the part of those who are upbraided as to how they have merited such treatment : and then comes the Prophet's further and fuller exposition. To regard punishment in this light is essentially the tendency of that Pelagian blindness which knows neither God nor itself. No better delineation of the constancy with which this tendency remains true to itself could be given than that which is afforded by the repetition of the same question through the whole book. Pharisaism, in its main features, was already in existence when Malachi spoke. Consider only the predominance of the priestly order, the total want of deeper knowledge of the nature of sin and righteousness, the boasting of external obedience to law, the thirst after judg-

ments on the heathen, who are alone regarded as the object
of divine retribution, and, lastly, the murmurs against God,
and the truth of our remarks will be apparent." The words,
"Be not righteous overmuch" (chap. vii. 16), find their
proper comment in Malachi iii. 7, where the people are represented as replying to the summons, "Return to the Lord,"
and saying, "Wherein shall we return?" on which Abar-
banel remarks—*impudenter dicitis acsi nesciatis peccatum
aut iniquitatem*. In Malachi the people consider themselves
clear as to their own performances, it is only God who is
behind-hand in His. To the reproach (chap. v. 3-5) regarding the bad fulfilment of vows—a thing perfectly natural in
such a condition, seeing that a dead orthodoxy can never
overcome a living selfishness—corresponds what Malachi says
chap i. 8. "And if ye offer the blind for sacrifice, is it not
evil? and if ye offer the lame and sick, is it not evil?"
i. 14, also, "Cursed be the deceiver which hath in his flock
a male, and when he hath a vow sacrificeth unto the Lord a
corrupt thing." Moroseness and discontent with the arrangements of God's providence we encounter in Malachi ii. 17,
"You weary the Lord with your words: yet ye say, wherein
do we weary Him? In that you say,—every one that
doeth evil is good in the sight of the Lord and He delighteth
in them; or, where is the God of judgment?" How strong
a hold avarice had taken of their souls is clear from Malachi
iii. 8, where they are accused of having cheated God in the
matter of tithes and offerings. Finally, with the unfavourable picture of the internal condition of the nation drawn
from the book of Ecclesiastes accords perfectly the super-
scription to the prophecies of Malachi—"This is the burden
which the Lord utters against Israel by Malachi:" a super-
scription which would not be at all appropriate to those of
Haggai and Zechariah, the immediate predecessors of Malachi.
In equal accordance also is the circumstance that Malachi so
emphatically announces the approaching judgment.

Ewald has advanced a twofold argument *against* assigning
the composition of this book to the time of Ezra and Nehemiah, and in *favour* of, "the last century of the Persian
dominion." The first is, that the writer complains, "in an
entirely new and unheard of manner, of an excess of book-

making and reading." It cannot, however, be shown, that a difference in this respect existed between the last century and the last but one of the Persian rule: and to a time subsequent to this, it is by no means allowable to look. For further remarks, we refer to our comments on chap. xii. 12. The second reason urged, is that " such harrowing pain, and desperate cries of agony did not characterise the earlier period of the Persian rule." It must have become, Ewald thinks, in its last years, more oppressive and violent. On this matter, however, history furnishes no authentic information. Nor must we allow ourselves to be led away by the special mention made, in the canonical records of the time, of occasional brighter spots in the history of the nation whilst subject to the Persian yoke ;—such as, for example, the permission given by Cyrus to rebuild the Temple, and that accorded by Artaxerxes for the building of the wall of the city. It was rather in accordance with the peculiar purpose of these books, to lay stress on such things, in proof that the Jews were still the chosen people, and that God's grace continued to watch over them. If we keep in mind that what is said in chap. x. 20, indicating that writers were obliged to maintain a certain degree of reserve, holds true also of other works composed during the time of the Persian dominion ; and if we carefully gather up scattered hints, it will appear that the people were from the commencement in an extremely oppressed position, that they led a cramped existence, that deep sadness filled all hearts, and that to sink themselves in God was the only remedy against despair.

The characteristic tone of those " Pilgrim Songs," which belong to the time immediately subsequent to the deliverance from exile, to the years when the building of the Temple was interrupted, is one of deep sadness, which has found consolation in God. In Psalm cxxiii. 3, 4, we read, " Have mercy upon us, O Lord, have mercy upon us ; for we are exceedingly filled with contempt. Our soul is exceedingly filled with the scorning of those that are at ease, and with the contempt of the proud." The proud and such as live in security, are no other than their Persian tyrants. Again, in Psalm xxv. 3, we read, " For the sceptre of wickedness shall not rest on the lot of the righteous, lest the righteous put forth their hands unto iniquity." The sceptre of wickedness is the Persian dominion, which was so pertinacious and cruel in its outrages and provocations, that the chosen people were sorely tempted to fall into utter perplexity about God's dealings, to apostatise from Him their Lord, and to become partakers in the wickedness of the wicked. The very same temptation presents itself to our notice in chap. viii. 11 of this book. In Psalm cxxvi. 5, 6, it is said, " They that sow in tears shall reap in joy. They who go forth weeping bearing the seed-train come again with rejoicing, bringing their sheaves with them." Those who sow in tears are themselves. The present has only tears : joy belongs to the future, to the region of hope. Finally, Psalm cxxx. begins with the words, " Out of the depths do I cry unto thee, O Lord." Not without cause has the Church set this apart as a funereal Psalm. It is the cry for help sent up by Israel when encompassed with the bands of death.

The words of chap. vii. 7, " a gift destroyeth the heart," and of chap. x. 19, " Money answereth all things," find their explanation and justification in chap. iv. 5 of the book of Ezra, where the Persian officials are clearly charged with being open to bribes ;—" and hired counsellors against them to frustrate their purpose, all the days of Cyrus King of Persia, even until the reign of Darius,"on which Michaelis remarks, " *mercede conducebant, qui pecunia a Cuthæis accepta auctoritate sua effecerunt ne Judæis nunc pergere liceret.*" And in chap. ix. 7, of the same book, the state of the Jews under their heathenish oppressors, which still continued, is described as one of extreme wretchedness :—" they were delivered over to spoil and confusion of face ;" through the mission of Ezra they received a little life in their bondage. " We are bondsmen," it is said in ver. 9, " but our God has not forsaken us in our bondage."

According to Nehemiah i. 3, news is brought to Nehemiah from Jerusalem, " that the remnant in the country are in great affliction and reproach." What utter poverty was the result of the oppressive tribute, from which, according to Ezra vii. 24, only the Priests and Levites were exempt, is plain from Nehemiah v. 4, where such as had been reduced to personal bondage by the usurers, address Nehemiah in the words, " We have borrowed money for the king's taxes on our lands and vineyards ;"—their produce consequently was not sufficient to pay the high imposts. In chap. v. 15, Nehemiah relates that "the former governors who had been before him" —who were without doubt Gentiles, for, as it appears, Serubabel and Nehemiah were the only Jews who had held that office—"had been burdensome to the people, and had taken from them bread and wine, besides forty shekels of silver, (daily ;) their servants also had used violence towards the people : but so did not I because of the fear of God." שלטו העם על compare Ecclesiastes viii. 9, "a day when one man exercises power over another to his hurt." In chap. v. 18, Nehemiah says, "The bread of the governor have I not required, because the service was heavy upon this people :" it was already heavily enough burdened with the taxes which it had to pay to its tyrant rulers. At the solemnization of the Feast of Tabernacles under Nehemiah, we read (chap. viii. 9,) that Ezra said to the people, "this day is holy to the Lord your God : therefore mourn not, nor weep." For all the people, it is observed, wept "when they heard the words of the law,"— words which had found such a sad fulfilment in their present misery. The description given in Nehemiah ix. 36-37, is of itself a sufficient proof that the circumstances alluded to in Ecclesiastes are in no respect more sad and gloomy than those of the time of Ezra and Nehemiah. There the existence of the people appears to be entirely precarious : they have only so much as is left them after the utterly lawless, unjust and arbitrary exactions of their oppressors. Not only does the produce of their lands stand at their disposal, but the cattle, and even the men themselves must do service whenever their heathen tyrants please to claim it : "and over our bodies do they rule, and over our cattle, as they please, and we are in great distress." In consequence of their wretched condition, religious indifference had gained ground amongst the people ; the spirit of sacrifice had died out ; and the portion of the Levites was not given to them, so that they fled, every man to his own lands, and the house of God was forsaken, (Neh. xiii. 10-11 ;) the Sabbath was in many ways desecrated (xiii. 15-22,) and an usurious disposition gained the upper-hand amongst the people, in that every man believed himself forced to care for himself, (chap. v.)

The Book of Esther presents a picture of the Persian Empire in a state of deep moral degradation, the direct result of which was "oppression," (Eccles. vii. 7,) and violence. Everything was dependent on the humours of the king and his great officers. All moral considerations were disregarded ; and there was recognised no higher standard than the pleasure of the king. The Book of Esther furnishes vouchers for the complaints in Ecclesiastes of the drunkenness of the tyrants, of the unbounded influence of money : Haman urged as a reason for the destruction of the Jews, that it would bring ten thousand talents of silver into the treasury.

The arguments brought forward by Ewald to prove that this book was written towards the close of the Persian rule, are thus shown to be untenable, unsound. On the other hand, even Ewald himself is compelled to acknowledge that "of all biblical books Malachi's prophecies bear the closest resemblance to Ecclesiastes."

What are we to say now regarding the plan of the book, which under such circumstances was meant to exercise an influence on the people of God ? Herder has given the right answer to this question. "Theologians," says he, "have taken great pains to ascertain the plan of the book ; but the best course is to make as free a use of it as one can, and for such a purpose the individual parts will serve." A connected and orderly argument, an elaborate arrangement of parts, is as little to be looked for here as in the special portion of the Book of Proverbs which begins with chapter x., or as in the alphabetical Psalms. Such matters of plan and connection have been thrust into the book by interpreters who were incapable of passing out of their own circle of ideas, as by degrees became evident from the fact that no one of these arrangements gained anything like general recognition, but that on the contrary each remained the sole property of its originator and of his slavish followers. Carpzov betrays a narrow estimate of Inspiration when, in his "Introduction," he speaks of it as necessarily implying and producing the "ordo concinnus." The same limitation of view is chargeable also upon certain more recent writers, who think that a definite plan must be found in the book in order to save the credit of the author. It is a part of the peculiarity of

the book to have no such plan : and this characteristic greatly
conduces to the breadth of its views and the variety of its
modes of representation.   The thread which connects all the
parts together is simply the pervading reference to the circumstances and moods, the necessities and grievances of the
time.   This it is that gives it unity : and its author sets a
good example to all those who are called to address the men
of our own generation in that he never soars away into the
clouds, nor wastes his time in general reflections and com-
mon-places, but keeps constantly in view the very Jews who
were then groaning under Persian tyranny, to whose sick souls
it was his first duty to administer the wholesome medicine
with which God had entrusted him : by ever fresh strokes
and features he depicts their condition to them, little by little
he communicates the wisdom that is from above, and in the
varying turns of his discourse sets before them constantly
the most important and essentially saving truths.   It is quite
misleading to represent the work as occupied with a single
narrow theme, as for example Knobel does when he says that
" the affirmation of the vanity of human life and human endeavours forms the subject of the book."   Such also is Keil's
mistake, who says (see Havernick's " Introduction,") " The
aim of the book is to teach how to enjoy life truly, that is,
how to realise in life that solid pleasure of which contentment and piety are constituent elements."   A superficial
glance at its contents will amply show that they are of far
too rich and varied a nature to be comprehended under one
such single theme.   And if we are determined that the book
shall have one leading topic, we must give it as wide and
general a scope as the author himself does in the words of
chap. xii. 13, " Fear God."   To further the fear of God and
life in Him is the great purpose of the writer in all that he
advances : hence his assertion of the vanity of all earthly
things, for he alone can fully appreciate what a precious
treasure man has in God, who has learnt by living experience the truth, " Vanity of vanities, all is vanity."

Let us now pass to a more careful examination of the contents of the book.   Written in the midst of circumstances
such as have been just described, its tone is partly one of
consolation, and partly one of admonition and reproof, so that

in it may be discerned "the rebuke of the wise," (chap. vii. 5.)
Nor is it by accident that the author girds himself first of all
to the discharge of his office as a comforter, using therein all
diligence.   His prime object was to turn the hearts of the
people again to God, for notwithstanding its great weaknesses
it was still God's heritage, and in its midst God had His
dwelling-place.   Only when this end had been attained could
a hearing be gained for admonitions and reproofs.   The people
had fallen into error regarding God and His ways, and this
was the real root of their moral corruption,—on this account
were the hearts of the children of men fully set to do evil,
(chap. viii. 11.)

The manner in which the author opens his mission of consolation may at first sight strike us as somewhat singular:
from all sides there rose the complaint, " vanity of vanities,"—
how evil are our times compared with earlier ones, especially as
compared with the glorious days of Solomon?   Then the
writer breaks in with the proclamation, that the life of man is
altogether vanity, that this world is a vale of tears, that the
difference between happy and troublous times is much less
decided than it appears on a superficial examination, (chap. i.
2-11.)   The cross is much easier to bear when it is seen to be
the universal destiny of man.   From chap. i. 12, to the end
of chap. ii., Solomon, whom the writer introduces as the
speaker, shows from his own example and experience, the
emptiness of everything earthly.   He begins with wisdom.
This was one of the splendid possessions of the age of Solomon,
upon which the after-world looked back in astonished admiration and with painful yearnings : and all the more earnestly,
because this had been imposing, even in the eyes of that Gentile world, beneath whose contempt and scorn they now sighed.
From wisdom, Solomon then turns to the possession and enjoyment of the good things of this world.   Everywhere the
author discovers the hollowness which lies concealed beneath
glitter and show, the pain which is covered by the mask of
pleasure.   In this way, he tears up envy and discontent by
the roots, and exhorts his fellow countrymen to seek elsewhere
their happiness, to draw it from those inexhaustible eternal
fountains, which even at that time were open to all who chose
to come.

In other places also the author offers to his unhappy contemporaries the consolation which is derivable from a just estimate of earthly possessions. He exhibits most earnestness and keenness in unmasking the hollowness of those riches for the sake of which the Gentile world was an object of envy. " Man's life consisteth not in the abundance of the things which he possesseth," is the theme of which he treats in chap. vi. 4 ;—" Riches expose to envy and involve in uneasiness" is the text of chap. iv. 7-12, chap. v. 9-19, and of the whole of chap. vi. Here are to be found the properly classical passages of Holy Scripture, on which may be based a true estimate of riches. Nowhere else is the vanity of riches exposed with such depth of penetration, with such fulness of detail, with such caustic pungency. After laying bare the vanity of riches, he proceeds to show the prevalence of folly and falsity in the government of kingdoms, (chap. iv. 13-16.)

Hand in hand with the exposure of the vanity of what was mourned as lost, attention is directed to sources of joy still remaining open to the people of God, even in its poverty-stricken state, and out of which it is bound thankfully to draw. Life itself is a noble possession, (chap. xi. 7, 8 ;) and the godly heart may still always find in it a multitude of lesser joys, of which it is its duty, living only for the present moment, to avail itself in freedom from care and covetousness, (chap. ii. 24 ; iii. 12, 22 ; viii. 15 ; xi. 9, 10.) Despite all their losses in wealth and power, they may continue to " eat, drink and be glad."

But that consolation which springs from setting a true value on earthly happiness and earthly endowments is not sufficient by itself. For on the one hand, however little importance is to be attached to earthly good in itself, God gave a pledge to His people in the earliest days of its existence, that He would never forsake nor neglect it, even as regards external matters, and it must therefore give rise to doubts of God's omnipotence and love if no evidence can be adduced of the fulfilment of His promises. And, on the other hand, it was not a question here merely of lower blessings and possessions. The real sting of the grief was the prostrate position of the people of God, the crying contradiction existing between its inward idea and its outward manifestation, between the word of God and the realities around them. Koheleth must therefore open up new fountains of comfort if his mission of consolation is to be satisfactorily fulfilled.

In chap. iii. 1-15, he comforts the poor and wretched who seek water and find it not, by directing their thoughts to the all-superintending providence of God, "who maketh everything beautiful in its time," who even in days of suffering has thoughts of peace, from whom it behoves to accept everything without reluctance because whatever He does is done well, whose beneficent hand is upon us even when we fail to see it, and who will at last bring all things to a glorious termination. The writer exhorts men also in chap. vii. 13, 14, to commit themselves to the fatherly care of God who proceeds ever on the wisest method.

So repeatedly and emphatically does the author refer to an exaltation of Israel impending in the immediate future, to the revelation of the retributive righteousness of God, to the change of relative positions which their king was about to introduce on a large scale, that we may regard it as one of the prominent ideas of the book. In chap. iii. 16, 17, he expatiates on the thought that so certainly as there is a righteous God in Heaven, who watches over the maintenance of His laws and order upon earth, so certainly must the disorder which characterised the tyrannies of heathendom come to an end, and Israel, which, notwithstanding the false seed that had been mixed up with it, was still God's people, the congregation of the "righteous" and "upright," lift up its head amongst the nations. In chap. v. 7, 8, he teaches that the heavenly King and Judge will bring all things again into order at the proper time. According to chap. vii. 5-10, the prosperity of the world is the precursor of impending destruction : the people of God on the contrary will receive its best portion at the end, if it only exercise patience and wait on the leadings of divine providence. According to chap. viii. 5-8, and 9-13, God will one day deliver His own, punish their oppressors, and no power in the world will be able to interrupt the course of His judgments. According to chap. ix. 7-10, God takes pleasure in the works of His own people, and therefore at the proper time the now failing recompence will be effected. In chap. ix. 11, 12, we are reminded that sudden catastrophes very frequently cast down to the ground that which had exalted itself. In chap. x. 5-10, it is foretold that at some future day God will take away the reproach which is offered by the humiliation of His own people, and by the triumph of the world. Several passages hint still more definitely at the imminent downfall of the Persian Empire : as for example, chap. vi. 2, where the stranger who will consume the wealth of the rich man, is the successor of the Persian on the throne of the world ; and chap. vi. 3, where the words "and he shall have no burial," set before the Persians the prospect of a mighty and bloody overthrow ; and chap. vii. 6, where the prosperity of the Persians is compared to a fire of crackling thorns which blazes violently up, but is quickly extinguished; and ver. 7, where the lemoralization of the Persians, a result of their exercise of tyrannical power, is represented as the herald of their speedy destruction. Of the same tendency are chap. x. 1-3, where the writer dwells on the thought, that whenever folly prevails as it did at that time amongst the Persians, ruin cannot be far off : also chap. x. 11-20, where the moral decay of the Persians, which had now reached its extreme point, is conceived to portend a swift extinction ; and lastly, chap. xi. 3, which teaches that the storm of divine wrath will soon uproot and cast down the haughty tree of the Persian Empire : "When the clouds are full of rain, they empty themselves upon the earth ; and if a tree falls, be it in the south or be it in the north, in the place where it falleth there shall it be."

That a great change would at some future day take place in the position of affairs, the people of God might hope with the greater confidence, because they continued to possess the wisdom which is from above—not the glittering and brilliant wisdom of the age of Solomon, but the secret and hidden wisdom peculiar to the children of God, of which they alone amongst all the nations of the earth were the depositaries. This advantage over others was of itself a pledge of their future victory over the world. The Gentile nations are foolish because they are left to the guidance of their own reason, and are cut off from the source of all wisdom. But in the midst of Israel, on the contrary, the nation of revelation, to which God had made known His nature and will, thus delivering it from the sophistries by whose chains the natural man has been completely bound ever since the Fall, wisdom has established its abode. At the fitting time, too, power must certainly follow in the footsteps of wisdom. According to chap. vii. 11, 12, wisdom and life go hard in hand. On this ground, Israel may comfort itself even in death. According to chap. vii. 19, 20, wisdom is the only defence against divine judgments, because it alone preserves from sins which inevitably draw judgments in their train. In chap. ix. 13-18, the theme is discussed,—wisdom, the treasure that remains, is nobler than the strength which is lost: "wisdom is better than weapons of war, and one sinner destroys much good."

Still, to point attention merely to a future reconciliation to be brought about between realization and idea, between the destiny assigned to the people of God and its actual visible condition, was not a full discharge of the writer's mission of consolation. His business was further to open to his fellow-countrymen an insight into the causes of the temporal disturbances of the true and normal relations of things, for until it was shown to have an adequate ground and reason, it would be impossible to look forward with any confidence to a final restoration. If God is capable in any sense or degree of being unrighteous and hard towards the people of His choice, towards those whom He had pledged himself to love, the fear that He might continue so to the end would present itself again and again with fresh force.

The first thing to be learnt is to recognise in temporal afflictions the ordainments of that divine *righteousness* which cannot leave even the sin of its own children unpunished;— nay more, which must discover itself especially in its treatment of them, as those who by God's grace "know how to walk before the living," (chap. vi. 8.) This is as certain as that the servant who knows his Lord's will and doeth it not shall be beaten with many stripes; as that God will fulfil what is said in Leviticus x. 3: "I will be sanctified in them that come nigh me;" as that it is said (Amos iii. 2): "You only have I known of all the families of the earth, *therefore* I visit upon you all your iniquities," and "Judgment must begin at the house of God." The author leads his sorrowing and afflicted people to this at once painful and consolatory point of view in chap. vii. 21, 22. He works also indirectly

towards this end whenever he lays bare their sins before the
eyes of the people. Their duty was to be content with God,
to see light and justice in His providential arrangements, in
the same degree in which they were dissatisfied with themselves. When the writer, in chap. iv. 17—v. 6, reproaches
the nation with a superficial piety, which sought to satisfy
God by sacrifices instead of honouring Him with obedience
to His laws, which endeavoured to substitute high sounding
words for the lacking devotion, and which acted frivolously
in respect of vows: and when further, in chap. vii. 15-18, he
demonstrates that the pretended "righteousness" of Israel,
that foundation of its proud claims, when more closely examined proves to be but another form of godlessness, and
points to the open apostacy of which they were at the same
time guilty, he furnishes the people with the key to their
troubles, and throws light upon the arrangements of God,
which hitherto through the want of self-knowledge had been
enshrouded in darkness. He thus treads in the footsteps of
Moses, who drew an exalted picture of such a Theodicy in
Deut. xxxii, where his theme was: "God is faithful and
without iniquity, just and upright is He. Hath He acted
corruptly towards His people? The blot is on His sons, a
perverse and corrupt generation."

The second thing to be learnt is to recognise in suffering
an ordainment of *divine love*—to see that it is grace concealed
under the form of severity, that there dwells in it a reforma-
tory virtue for all those who love God, that it is an indispensable means of progress of which God cannot without cruelty
deprive His children. "Whom the Lord loveth, He chastiseth."
Where is there a father who does not chastise his son?
Koheleth directs the attention of his sorrowing people to this
sweet kernel which lay hidden within the bitter husk of
affliction, in chap. vii. 2-4: "It is better to go to the house of
mourning than to the house of feasting. Sorrow is better
than laughter, for by the sadness of the countenance the heart
is made better. The heart of the wise is in the house of
mourning, but the heart of fools is in the house of mirth."
Suffering gives the peaceable fruit of righteousness to such as
are exercised thereby. The same purpose is subserved by
chap. iii. 18, "I said in my heart, For the sake of the children

of men such things happen, in order that God may purify them, and in order that they may see that by themselves they are beasts." Suffering is a means of refinement to the people of God, serving especially to strip them of all pride and to lead them to humility. Purification is the general aim of tribulation: but special mention is here made of *pride* as the root and foundation of sin. That such is its character is evident even from the words which the Old Serpent whispered in his temptation of our first parents : " In that day ye shall be as God;" and by which he caused them to fall. The greater the privileges vouchsafed by God to the nation to which He specially revealed himself, the more liable was it to this particular form of sin. From the same point of view, namely, as a means of " hiding pride from man," (Job xxxiii. 17) are afflictions regarded also in chap. vii. 13, 14. God permits evil days to alternate with good, " in order that man may not find anything behind himself;" in order that he may not be able to fathom in any measure that which lies behind his present condition, and still less arrange any part thereof according to his own will ; and finally, in order that thus he may be fully conscious of his dependence, may become a little child and thoroughly humble.

In this manner did the writer of Ecclesiastes fulfil his mission as a comforter. Many things may be missed here, specially any definite reference to Christ, the central point of all consolation, and to that future glory with which the sufferings of this present time are not worthy to be compared, but which the Lord will bestow on his own followers. We must bear in mind, however, that the Scriptures are an organic whole consisting of very different members, and that it is therefore preposterous to expect to find the same thing everywhere. To " wisdom," in the narrower sense of that word, but a limited sphere was assigned amongst the Israelites. Its business lay not with what was hidden but with that which was manifest, not with the proper mysteries of the Faith, which, under the Old Covenant, belonged to the domain of prophecy, but with the truths which had already become thoroughly a part of the consciousness of the community. With these the mind of thoughtful Israelites occupied itself ; these it sought to make clear, and bring home to the under-

standing and the heart.* The prophecies of Daniel, and of
the three post-exile prophets, Haggai, Zechariah and Malachi,
constitute the nearest supplement to Koheleth.

The human side of this book, as to which it belongs to the
sphere of sacred philosophy,—for the writer does not profess
himself to be an organ of immediate divine revelations,—is
brought to view especially in chap. vii. 23-29, where the
author himself reflects on the way and manner of his acquaintance with higher truth. Compare particularly verse 25: "I
applied myself with my heart to know and to search and to
seek out wisdom and thoughts," and verse 27: "Lo, this
have I found, said Koheleth, one by one, finding thoughts."
His method he describes to have been that of taking separately single thoughts, and by meditation drawing out their
fulness and significance. This is the reflective and speculative
method, not that of direct intuition. That there is a higher
degree of wisdom in its more general sense, the degree to
which a Moses or an Isaiah arose, who received truth by
direct revelation, the writer himself confesses in chap. vii. 28.
But he does not for this reason relinquish the claim to be
inspired: his inspiration must be conceived specially as pre-
serving, purifying, and heightening the natural powers of his
mind. In chap. xii. 11, he expressly co-ordinates his work
with the sacred writings, the distinguishing characteristic of
which in relation to all other literary productions is, as he
himself states, "that they are given by the one shepherd,"
who ever relieves the wants of his people, who feeds them in
green pastures, and leads them by the fresh waters, and in
consequence are living and mighty, laying hold of heart and
spirit in their inmost depths. With this expression of the
author all will agree whom God's Spirit has qualified for
forming a judgment in this sphere. What Picus of Mirandola

---

* Oehler, in his "Prolegomena zur Theologie des Alten Testaments," justly
characterises most of the Hagiographa as "the product of the Israelitish mind,
partly, when endeavouring, by feeling, to penetrate into the depths of the divine
revelation and the experiences to which that revelation gave rise in life, and
partly when musing on the same," (page 92) and deduces their origin (pages
88, 89) "from the struggle of Hebrew intellect to enter into the task assigned
to, and the view given of, life by Mosaism, the effort to appropriate inwardly,
and to attain to a thorough understanding of, the substance of revelation, and
by reflection to solve its enigmas and contradictions."

says of the entire sacred Scriptures, holds perfectly true of this book: "Nothing so strongly affects both heart and judgment as the reading of Holy Scripture, and yet they are but simple words without art, which thus overpower us. These words, however, are full of life, soul, and fire,—they penetrate deeply into the spirit, and transform the whole man."* In agreement with the circumstances of the time wisdom walks here in the form of a servant, and in the utterly unadorned garment of poverty; but its words are as goads and nails, and there dwells in them a power to refresh and sanctify the spirit and heart.

The writer's peculiar use of the name of God furnishes a noteworthy indication that he deliberately purposed to confine himself to a circumscribed sphere of thought. Amongst the Hebrew names of God Elohim had the most general signification : and this name occurs in the book no fewer than thirty-nine times, seven times with, and thirty-two times without the article. Nowhere do we meet with another designation; especially, be it remarked, we do not find the name Jehovah, which answered to the fully developed religious consciousness, and the use of which absolutely predominates in the Prophets who preceded and were contemporary with Koheleth. The writer thus emphatically shows that he makes no pretensions to be an organ of direct revelations from God, but that his purpose is to unfold a sacred philosophy.

That the author refrains from employing the designation Jehovah has been ascribed by some to the superstitious fear which the later Jews had of giving utterance to that name. Such dread, however, belonged to the post-canonical period : within the canon itself there is nowhere a trace of it. Within the canon the use of the names of God is everywhere determined by their inherent difference of signification, and it was a matter for the free choice of the several writers which of the two names was employed. It is so in the Pentateuch : it is so in the Psalms.† To the use of these names here, that of the book of Job bears the nearest resemblance : and with it

* v. Raumer, *Geschichte der Pædagogik*, p. i., s. 49.
† Compare my Commentary, part iv.

Koheleth was without doubt well acquainted.* In the Prologue to the book of Job יהוה is generally used ;—as also in the Epilogue and in the historical remarks which are interspersed. In the discourses of Job and his friends, on the contrary, the general names of God, Eloah, El, &c., are employed, with the single exception of chap. xii. 9, where we find Jehovah. The problem before the writer is considered from the point of view of Natural Theology with the aid of experience, and of reason as purified by the Spirit of God. If the author's intention was to treat his subject from the point of view afforded by that consciousness of God which is common to men in general, then it was perfectly natural that he should confine his speakers to the corresponding divine name. Once only does he permit Job to break through this rule, and then in order that the avoidance elsewhere of the name Jehovah might be more distinctly seen to be intentional, and might not be traced to any merely external reasons. The Book of Nehemiah, which was nearly contemporaneous with Ecclesiastes, also furnishes an analogy. The facts of the case are presented as follows by Kleinert in the Dorpat *Beiträge zu den Theologischen Wissenschaften,*" 1. §. 132. "In the entire Book of Nehemiah," (*i.e.,* in chapters i.-vii. and xi.-xiii.; for chapters viii.-x. were written by Ezra, and only adopted into his work by Nehemiah), "the name Jehovah occurs only once, namely, in chap. i. 5, in conjunction with Elohim : besides, Adonai occurs only twice : and elsewhere Nehemiah always designates God by the term Elohim." In the Book of Ezra, on the contrary, and in chapters viii.-x. of Nehemiah, which, as was observed before, are by Ezra, the name Jehovah predominates. Nehemiah wrote as a layman, as a politician mixed up with the affairs of the world. His humility did not permit him frequently to take God's holiest name upon his lips. In all these cases, and in Ecclesiastes as well, there was no absolute necessity for abstaining from the use of the name Jehovah ; other reasons might have decided for its employment ; but the authors

---

* Hitzig remarks in his Commentary, "The Book of Job, which, as to its general views and tendency, is so nearly related to Ecclesiastes, must undoubtedly have been read by Koheleth," v. 14, vii. 28. (The other passages adduced by Hitzig, viz., vi. 3, vii. 14, 16, are less certain).

were guided by such considerations as seemed to them to favour their abstinence.

It being the purpose of the writer to expound a sacred philosophy, and not to touch upon the sphere of the mysteries of the faith, we might thence explain why nothing was said about immortality and eternal life, if this were actually the case, as Rationalistic interpreters with one voice affirm. In the course of our Commentary we shall plainly show that such is not the case. According to chap. iii. 11, God has put eternity into the heart of man: according to chap. iii. 21, the spirit of man rises upwards at death, whilst the souls of beasts perish with their bodies; according to chap. xii. 7, the spirit of man returns at death to God who gave it, in order that it may receive that which its deeds have deserved (chap. xii. 14). It is, however, so far correct that the author maintains a gentle reserve in respect of this doctrine, limiting himself to slight though distinct and unambiguous hints, in order thus not to pass the boundary line which separates "wisdom" from prophecy. The comparison of Isaiah xxv. 7, 8, xxvi. 19, and of Daniel xii. 2, 3, will throw light on this distinction.

Thus far we have occupied ourselves only with the consolatory part of the mission of Koheleth: let us now turn our attention to its admonitory and punitive aspect.

Several of the admonitions of the Preacher are so general in their character, that they are equally well adapted to all times. In chap. xii. 13, he exhorts to the fear of God and the keeping of his commandments. This he describes as a duty universally binding upon men, and as the only preservative from the judgments of God who cannot permit that man, whom He made in His own image, should emancipate himself from Him. That, says he, is the conclusion and sum of the whole matter; this is the Alpha and Omega of an upright life, the starting-point and basis of all the special teachings and exhortations of the book. "Fear God"—in these two words he sums up, in chap. v. 7 also, all that he has to say to his readers. Hand in hand with this goes another brief saying which applies to the faithful of all times, namely, "Do good," (chap. iii. 12, with which compare chap. vii. 20). "Remember thy Creator:" such is the writer's exhortation in chap. xii. 1, and the strongest motive he can urge for the following of his advice is, that those who refuse to listen to it, being separated from God, the source of all health, will have to mourn in this world a misspent existence, and after death will fall under Divine judgment. The author makes repeated and emphatic reference to the judgment of God both in this life and in that which is to come, which visits inevitably every deed however secret; and he shows himself to be most livingly penetrated by the thought that God will recompense to every man according to his works (compare chap. vii. 16, 17, xi. 10, xii. 7, 14).

Along with general exhortations like these we find such as have a special bearing on the circumstances and tendencies of the time. The writer lays bare the evils of the time, and seeks to effect their removal, not after the manner of the Prophets by raising his voice in trumpet tones against them, but by calmly reasoning and exposing their preposterous character.

At all periods in which the powers of this world have weighed oppressively on the people of God, the temptation has been peculiarly strong to approve and adopt the worldly wisdom which prevailed amongst the surrounding heathen nations. The danger lay very near of coming, in that manner, to terms with the world, and seeking thus to be on equal footing with it. Against this false heathenish wisdom, which seeks out many inventions, (chap. vii. 29,) and which should be regarded as the great foe of their welfare and safety, the writer utters his warning in chap. vii. 25, 26 ; he further admonishes the Israelites to offer energetic resistance to its attacks upon themselves. In chap. xii. 12, he warns them against familiarising themselves with worldly literature. In opposition to the false foreign wisdom he sets before them the genuine, viz., their own native wisdom, which " knows the meaning of things," which leads men to a knowledge of their true nature, and thus affords the basis for a right practical conduct in relation to them. With the manifold divisions of heathendom which though ever learning never comes to a knowledge of the truth, he contrasts their own book of books, (chap. xii. 11,) which, whilst seeming to have many authors had in reality but one, even the Shepherd of Israel, and the words thereof are consequently as goads and nails, penetrating heart and spirit and laying hold of their inmost depths.

Hand in hand with the temptation to adopt the wisdom of the heathens went that of falling into their sinful way of life. Those who saw misery weighing heavily on the people of God, and on the contrary all things going well and happily with the heathen in their life of sin : those who saw how these latter "tempted God and escaped," and how the "doers of crime were established," (Mal. iii. 15,) must have felt a strong temptation to doubt and despair of God, and to let the evil desires of the heart have full and free play. Against this danger the author warns men in chap. viii. 1-4, 11 ; vii. 17.

Still even these temptations were by no means the most dangerous. The most critical and suspicious elements of the present condition of the Jews, were those which prepared the way for the later Pharisaism.

The prime evil of the time, was that righteousness which owed its origin to speculations on the advantages it would bring, which was full of claims, full of merits, and full of murmurs against God, who refused to honour the drafts drawn on Him. In chap. vii. 15-18, he enters the lists against this destructive tendency, which at a later period grew so much more hardened and decided that the Lord was driven to utter, against those who in His day were its representatives, the terrible words : "ye serpents, ye generation of vipers, how can ye escape the damnation of hell?" This counterfeit righteousness which then gave itself such pretentious airs, he describes as but another form of ungodliness, running parallel with open apostacy ; and he shows, that so far from ensuring salvation, it involves us in the divine condemnation : for God cannot allow himself to be put off with such a hollow and heartless piety, but demands, and must have genuine fear and faith.

In chap. viii. 14, 15, the book speaks out against the hireling spirit which was bound up with such an evil righteousness. Godliness ought not to be a question of gain, nor righteousness to originate in speculations of future good. Therefore are the ways of the recompensing God quite darkened : and things go very differently from men's fancies. If they went according to men's thoughts, that is, in other words, if for every work really or apparently good, and for every evil deed, the reward were forthwith weighed and measured out piece by piece, there would soon be no genuine uprightness left on earth, for true righteousness is the daughter of hearty and unselfish love. The happiness of life must not then be regarded as a hireling regards his wages ; it must not have this basis. Our duty is rather cheerfully to enjoy in the present what God graciously bestows, to use the present moment and not to speculate on the future.

Moroseness also is inseparably conjoined with false righteousness, as was clearly shown in the example of Cain at the very commencement of the human race. The punishment inflicted on sin, where there is defective knowledge of the sin itself, produces dark despondency, and discontent with God's arrangements, (Isaiah lviii. 3 ; Malachi iii. 14.)

With this spirit of gloom, dejection and ill humour the self-righteous had more or less infected the whole people. This too was the one amongst the chief evils of the age, which even the really righteous were least able to resist. To the healing of this disorder the author has directed his special attention. See chap. ii. 24 ; iii. 12, 22 ; viii. 15 : "Then I commended mirth because a man hath no better thing under the sun, than to eat and to drink and be merry:" compare also chap. ix. 7 ; xi. 8-10. Koheleth is from his heart an enemy to extravagant mirth and sensual feasting. He says to laughter, "thou art mad, and to mirth, what doest thou?" (chap. ii. 2.) "The heart of fools is in the house of mirth," (chap. vii. 4.) Indeed the entire book, and in particular chap. vii. 1-5, breathes the intensest earnestness. In chap. xii. 1, he points out how *devotion* is the foundation of all happiness, of all joy, and in chap xi. 9, warns the extravagant and dissolute that God will bring all their doings and ways into judgment. At the same time, he recommends that cheerful confidence in God which does not allow itself to be led astray by the aspect of affairs at the present moment, but waits joyfully in hope of a better future : and enjoins an unbroken courage which can proceed steadily forward in the path of duty, and can calmly wait until the actual arrangements of this world are once more brought into agreement with the word and nature of God. He warns against thanklessly despising that which God graciously offers. The Saviour set His seal of confirmation to the utterances of this book, when, with a reference to it, he said, " the Son of man is come eating and drinking." And the offence which the Pharisees took at His manner of life, proves that in them was still perpetuated the tendency against which the author of this book directs his observations.

In conjunction with this morose and melancholy spirit were found a slothful feebleness and timidity. Men had no courage or pleasure in doing anything, because they regarded it all as useless. Against such conduct the author raises his voice in chap. ix. 10, and again in chap. xi. 4-6. Precisely in dark and troublous times ought we to be the more earnest in fulfilling the vocation wherewith God has called us : we should sow incessantly in tears that we may reap in joy.

The religious superficiality of the age, the want of a living fear of God, manifested itself not only in self-righteousness, and in the gloomy discontent and hopeless inactivity which it produced, but also in a disposition to put off God with soulless sacrifices instead of honouring Him by obedience, in the efforts made to cover the absence of a heart which constantly seeks and supplicates God by the show and pretence of offering long prayers, and finally, in the extreme readiness to vow vows in the fulfilment of which they showed little conscientiousness, and the obligations of which they thought themselves able to discharge by a mere formality. Against such things the writer speaks in chap. iv. 17 ; v. 6.

It is not a superficial piety that can give in arduous circumstances the precious pearl of peace of soul, and preserve from that irritability, whose inevitable result is a heightening of our suffering. Only a deep and hearty godliness, which sees in all, even in the most afflictive events a Father's hand, and submits itself with quiet resignation, can do this. Against that dangerous enemy *irritability* the author warns his fellow-countrymen in chap. x. 4. Side by side with this we may place his recommendation of *patience*, (chap. vii. 8.)

The Pharisees, as the New Testament says, were covetous. Covetousness flourishes most luxuriantly where a religiousness which is merely external, and changes not the heart, presents it with a covering of fig leaves. When men conclude a peace with God by means of services which do not flow from the

heart, their darling inclinations come all the more freely into
play.   In battling with this enemy of the divine life, the book
displays peculiar zeal—a plain proof that it was then specially
dangerous.   They are the same passages as those in which the
author opposes the prevalent envy of the riches of the heathen ;
and envy has the same root as avarice, (chap. iv. 7-12 ; v. 9-
19 ; vi.)

The preacher rightly discerned the signs of the times.   He
saw that a great catastrophe drew nigh, that a time approached
when the "the peoples will rage and the kingdoms be moved"
(Psalm xlvi. 7).   Whilst teaching how men should make pre-
parations for this, so that they may feel that they have a
gracious God through it all, he sets in opposition to the bosom
sin of the age, namely, covetous narrow-heartedness, that
generous-minded liberality which is closely allied with a true
love of God and is a proof that we are his children (chap.
xi. 1-3).

In this manner has the writer discharged the mission of
reproof and admonition, with which, as well as with that of
consolation, he was intrusted.

Various judgments have been passed upon this book.   As
the representative of the theology of the Church let us hear
what Luther says about it.   He styles it—"This noble little
book, which for good reasons it were exceedingly worth
while that it should be read of all men with great carefulness
every day."   "The main point (or more correctly, a main
point) in this book," says he, "is, that there is no higher
wisdom on earth under the sun than that every man should
fill his post industriously and in the fear of God, not troub-
ling himself whether or no his work turn out as he would fain
have it, but contenting himself, and leaving the ordering of
all things great and small entirely to God.   In fine, that he
be contented, and abide by that which God gives him at the
present moment, taking for motto the words, 'The Lord's
behest will turn out best.'   And thus a man should not
worry and question and trouble himself how things will or
should turn out in the future, but think within himself—
God has entrusted me with this office, with this work, and I
am resolved to discharge it diligently : if my counsels and
plans do not succeed as I expected, let God dispose, ordain,

and rule as He will." Even on profounder minds, who held a freer position in relation to Holy Scripture, this book has exercised an attracting influence. Herder, for example, says —"No ancient book that I am acquainted with describes more fully, impressively, and concisely the sum of human life, the uncertainty and vanity of its business plans, speculations and pleasures, along with that in it which is alone true, lasting, progressive, and compensatory." On the contrary, the soulless, spiritless, vulgar Rationalism has been capable of little sympathy with the book. A. Th. Hartman gave most open expression to his antipathy to it.* He describes it as "the work of a morose Hebrew Philosopher, composed when he was in a dismal mood, and in places thoroughly tedious."

Even at an early period objections were raised against this book amongst the Jews. In the Talmud, in Tractate Schabbath, f. 30, b., it is said that the wise men wished to suppress the book of Koheleth, because it contains contradictions. "But why have they not suppressed it? Because its beginning and its end are words of the law." According to the Midrasch, the wise men wished to suppress Koheleth, because all its wisdom ended in the injunction of chap. xi. 9 : "Rejoice, O young man, in thy youth, and let thy heart cheer thee in the days of thy youth, and walk in the ways of thine heart, and in the sight of thine eyes," which passage contradicts Numbers xv. 39. Inasmuch, however, as Solomon has added, "But know thou that for all these things God will bring thee into judgment," therefore, they said, "Solomon has spoken well," שלמה יפה אמר. Jerome has reported similar words as uttered by Jews ; for which see the quotation given at chap. xii. 14.

Some have supposed that by the "wise men" are meant the collectors of the Canon—but wrongly. Had these been meant they would have been more distinctly designated. We have before us reflections on the book as one which had already had its place assigned to it in the Canon. A distinction should further be drawn between the thoughts and their dress, between the mode of saying and the thing said. The thought is, that examining the book only super-

---

* Linguistical Introduction to the Book of Koheleth in "Winer's Zeitschrift," 1 s., 29 f.

ficially it awakens hesitations, but these vanish after deeper consideration. The opinion is not, that we should be content to put up with the offensive passages for the sake of such as are of an edifying nature, but that the latter should be our guide in investigating and understanding the former.

The assertion which Augusti, Schmidt, and, in part also, Knobel have ventured to make, that the author of the "Book of Wisdom" attacks Koheleth in chap. ii., has so little foundation that it is not worth the trouble of examining and refuting.

Early in the Christian era also single individuals raised their voices against this book. Philastrius in his "*Hær.* 130" speaks of heretics who reject Solomon's *Ecclesiastes*, because, after having declared all things to be vanity, he leaves but one thing worth caring for, namely, to eat, drink, and gratify one's own soul.

Knobel has, last of all, summed up the rationalistic attacks, bringing against the book the reproach of fatalism, moral scepticism, and moral Epicureanism. "All the moral lessons and admonitions of Koheleth," he maintains, "end in recommending ease and enjoyment in life." Ewald has already given a partial, though a very striking refutation of this assertion : a complete one is contained in the investigation of the contents which has preceded, and in the commentary which follows. Such charges it would be impossible to advance but for the low state to which exegesis has been reduced. But in face of such attacks we feel ourselves able confidently to say, "Come and see."

Against any such profane view of the book as brings it into conflict with the remaining Old Testament canonical literature one fact is by itself a sufficient argument, viz., that the author stands in a most friendly relation thereto. The passage of most importance in this respect is chap. xii. 11, where the writer incorporates his work with the other canonical Scriptures of the Old Testament, ascribes to it a deeply penetrating influence, and finds its origin in that divine inspiration which constitutes the boundary line between the literature of revelation and the literature of the world, against which latter, moreover, he gives an emphatic warning in the following verse. In chap. xii. 7 and in chap. v. 3, 4, he refers to the Pentateuch; to the book of Job in the passages already adduced; to Psalm cxviii. 12, in chap. vii. 6; to Psalm cxxxix. 15, in chap. xi. 5; probably to Psalm xli., in chap. xi. 1-3; to Proverbs xxii. 1, in chap. vii. 1; to Zechariah iv. 3, in chap. xii. 6.

A guide to a true estimate of the book may be found in the numerous links of connection between it and the New Testament—especially in the frequent allusions made to it in the discourses of our Lord. Amongst the passages adduced from the New Testament by Carpzov in his *Introd.* ii., p. 212, which he supposes to have reference to Koheleth, only one will bear examination, namely John iii. 8, with which compare Eccles. xi. 5, "As thou knowest not the way of the wind." There are, however, other undeniable references which he overlooked. Compare with chap. i. 1 of Koheleth, Luke xiii. 34; with chap. ii. 1-2, Luke xii. 16-21; with chap. ii. 24, and its parallels, Matthew xi. 19; with chap. iii. 1, John vii. 30; with chap. iii. 2, John xvi. 21; with chap. iv. 17, Luke xxiii. 34; with chap. iv. 17, v. 1, James i. 19; with chap. v. 1, Matthew vi. 7, 8; with chap. v. 5, xii. 6, James iii. 6; with chap. vii. 18, Matthew xxiii. 23; with chap. ix. 10, John ix. 4.

Through a too great dependence on exegetical works such as that of Knobel, a respectable and esteemed representative and upholder of the theology of the church, Dr Oehler, has allowed himself in his *Prolegomena to the Theology of the Old Testament,* and in his *V. T. sententia de rebus post mortem futuris,* to be led into views of this book which in reality do endanger its canonical dignity, however strongly he may disclaim any such intention. According to his opinion the writer is involved in a conflict between faith and knowledge. "The contradiction between the divine perfection and the vanity of the world (more correctly, the sufferings of the people of God) is set before us without any reconciliation being effected. The latter is treated as a matter of undeniable experience: the former is assumed as a religious postulate. The only real wisdom, therefore, in life is *resignation,* which enables a man to use this vain and empty life as well as he can, and at the same time leaves all at the disposal of God." On the one hand, the author teaches that there is a providence and a retribution, and on the other hand, *omnia vana et consilii experta esse.* From the point of view of faith, he teaches, in chap. xii. 7, that there is an eternal life: from the point of view of reason, he judges that the soul perishes with the body (chap. iii. 19), that between the good and evil in and after death there is no difference (chap. ix. 2 f.) On this view the book of Koheleth would be the work, and present us the picture, of a distracted heart, of a divided spirit, ἀνὴρ δίψυχος, such as are produced in masses in our own time; and the Holy Scriptures themselves would thus be involved in the conflict they were destined to heal.

Against this we would observe, that it is not correct to say that the book presents to us an unadjusted discord between faith and knowledge, idea and experience. There is of course no denying that, just as in the Psalms, the writer lets scepticism have its say. So far there is truth in the view which distinguishes in the work two voices: but wherever that of scepticism is allowed to speak, it is only for the purpose of at once overcoming it. Nowhere, as a sort of model for the Theology of a de Wette, do doubt and faith stand in front of each other, as forces equally entitled to hearing and existence, but everywhere when the voice of the flesh has spoken, the voice of the Spirit replies in confutation. Such is precisely the case in Psalm xxxix. This is most remarkably evident just in that passage, (chap. ix. 1-10,) in which scepticism pours itself forth like a mighty stream. The expression of "the mood of scepticism and of discontent with life" goes there only as far as ver. 6: in verses 7-10, it is vanquished by the sword of faith. The pretended dualism in regard to the doctrine of eternal life is set aside by the observation that in chap. ix. 2, the voice of the flesh is allowed to be heard in order that immediately afterwards it may be judged and convicted. Chap. iii. 21, when interpreted on correct philological principles, so far from containing a denial, is an express affirmation of eternal life.

Nor is it just to maintain that the author knows of no higher wisdom in life than resignation. Without doubt he teaches that human life often presents difficult enigmas, that it is very hard to understand God's arrangements, and that not unfrequently we find ourselves reduced to blind faith. In chap.

iii. 11, for example, he says : " Man cannot find out the whole of the work which God doeth, neither beginning nor end ;" in chap. vii. 24 : " far off is that which was made, and deep, deep, who can find it ?" in chap. viii. 17 : " Man cannot find out the work that is done under the sun ;" in chap. xi. 5 : " As thou knowest not what is the way of the wind, like the bones in the womb of her that is with child, even so thou knowest not the work of God, who doeth all." But who does not see that these are truths which apply still even to those who live in the light of the Gospel ? It was not in vain and for nought that the Lord pronounced those blessed who see not and yet believe. The Apostle recommends it to our consideration that we walk by faith and not by sight.[*]

To recognise everywhere the causes of the divine arrangements, to thread the ways of God so often intricate, demands an eye clearer than the clearest possessed by man. Ever afresh is attention called to the fact that all our knowledge is but fragmentary. In the times of the writer of this book, it was specially important to give prominence to this side, for there were too many who were destitute of clearly seeing eyes, and above all, of that knowledge of sin which gives the key to the sanctuary of God to all those who desire to find there the solution of the problem of this earthly life. But he has not the slightest intention of leaving us altogether to blind faith. The idea never occurs to him of handing over the region of knowledge to unbelief. "Who is as the wise man," he exclaims in chap. viii. 1, " and who knoweth the interpretation of things ?" He believes, therefore, that there exists a wisdom which introduces men into the essence of things, which especially throws light into the dark depths of the cross, and justifies the ways of God. The consciousness that he himself, in struggling for wisdom, has attained to important results is expressed in chap. vii. 25, 27 : according to chap. xii. 9, he is, by God's grace, a wise man, and competent to instruct the people in a wisdom which harmonises with what was taught

---

[*] Even the Christian Poet sings—
" Da werd' ich das ː ː Licht erkennen
   Was ich auf Erde . dunkel sah
   Das wunderbar und heilig nennen
   Was unerforschlich hier geschah."

by the wise of former ages, who were all sent by the one Shepherd, (chap. xii. 11.)   How far the writer's counsels are from ending in simple "Resignation," to which none are limited but those whom God, because of unbelief, has forsaken, and to whom the gates of the sanctuary do not stand open, (Psalm lxxii. 7,) is plain from the long series of passages in which he announces a termination to the sufferings of the people of God and their approaching victory, at the same time laying bare the causes of their present depression, and justifying it as ordered of the ordering of divine love and righteousness.

COMMENTARY.

THE SUPERSCRIPTION, CHAPTER I. 1.

The words of the Koheleth, the Son of David, the King in Jerusalem. It is not a question of words in general, but of *the* words. There exist no other words spoken by Solomon to the generation then existing. Only in virtue of this mission did he bear the title Koheleth, (compare under chap. xii. 9.) There can be no doubt whatever that Koheleth properly signifies—" The Assembler," (in the feminine.) The Kal form of קהל does not occur otherwise. The participle in Kal must be employed here for the participle in Hiphil—a thing which might the more easily take place as it stands for the noun. The verb is always used of persons, never of things. It is the standing form employed for the calling together of the whole Israelitish community, of the entire people of God. Compare Deut. iv. 10, where we read—" On the day that thou stoodest before the Lord thy God in Horeb, when the Lord said unto me, *gather* me the people *together,* and I will make them hear my words that they may learn to fear me :" Exodus xxxv. 1, —" And Moses *gathered together* all the congregation of the children of Israel, and said unto them, these are the words which the Lord hath commanded that ye should do them : Leviticus viii. 3,—" and *gather* thou all the congregation *together* unto the door of the Tabernacle," (Numbers viii. 9 ; x. 7 :) 1 Kings viii. 1, " then Solomon assembled the elders of Israel, &c." The fact of the person who speaks bearing the name Koheleth—which name was as to essentials correctly explained even by Jerome*—indicates the ecclesiastical

---

* Coeleth, id est Ecclesiastes. Eccl. autem Græco sermone appellatur, qui coetum, id est ecclesiam congreget, quem nos nuncupare possumus *concionatorem,*

character of the book, and its high significance in relation to the entire church of God. In this respect it accords with the commencement of Psalm xlix.: "Hear this all ye people, give ear all ye inhabitants of the world: both low and high, rich and poor together. My mouth shall speak of wisdom, and the meditation of my heart shall be of understanding." The wisdom of the Israelites was animated by a spirit moving its possessors to become witnesses of its excellence: it had a thoroughly popular character, it belonged not to the narrow limits of the school but to the spacious courts of the temple: it was a leaven intended to leaven the whole lump. Wisdom, within the Church, was to address itself not merely to a few peculiarly gifted individuals, but has something of importance to communicate to all alike. It is full of compassion like the God who is its fountain: it delights to seek out those who are lost: whereas the wisdom of this world cannot find a bridge over to the simple and ignorant, and has no disposition to interest itself in them. The tendency to association, which has its root in the wisdom coming from above, belongs only to the Church, and therefore, outside its pale, and where its path has been forsaken, we find only isolation and infatuated dissolution. The world is compelled to make the confession, "we all go astray like sheep, we turn, every one of us, to his own way." The name Koheleth occurs three times in the first chapter, namely, in verses 1, 2, 12, three times in the last chapter xii. 9, 10: once in the middle, where it is joined with the feminine, whereas elsewhere it is joined always with the masculine. In chap. xii. 8, the article is joined with it: in the other places the word stands without article as an ideal proper name. That Solomon is intended to be designated by it is plain from the addition of the words, "Son of David, King in Jerusalem," the purpose of which evidently is to anticipate and prevent all doubt in this respect. But in what sense is this applied to Solomon, seeing that in reality it can signify nothing more than "The Assembler" (feminine)? This is a matter of controversy; but there can be no doubt whatever that the title, an explanation of which is given in chap. xii. 9, "Moreover Koheleth was a wise man, and *taught the people knowledge*,"

eo quod loquatur ad populum, et sermo ejus non specialiter ad unum, sed ad universos generaliter dirigatur.

was applied to Solomon, because through him wisdom spake to the people of God, because he was regarded as wisdom personified, besides being its mouth and organ. It is precisely on this ground that his discourses have so decided a significance and importance : for this reason do they bear a canonical character; just as the words of the prophets derived their weight from the presence of the Spirit of Christ in them, (1 Peter i. 11,) from their speaking as they were moved by the Holy Ghost, (2 Peter i. 21,) and as the Apostles also, according to Acts xv. 28, were organs of the Holy Spirit. By his employment of this title, the author indicates that Solomon is not here regarded by him in the light of a philosopher, but as the representative of a higher spirit than his own—of that mind which is alone capable of uttering such things as are of thorough and lasting importance for the people of God. For this, as the only correct explanation of the term, the passage chap. vii. 27, is plainly decisive. There, a contrast is drawn between the Koheleth and the stranger, the foreigner, i. e., philosophy and wanton seduction : and the evidently intentional construction of Koheleth with the feminine, can only be explained by its being descriptive of the wisdom which is from above. A further proof of the correctness of this view is afforded by a comparison with the first nine chapters of the Book of Proverbs, where in fact we have the true key to the designation. The writer would never have chosen this title had he not been able to calculate on readers who would look to those chapters of Proverbs for its meaning, or the solution of his enigma—for with an enigma we evidently have to do here. Those chapters form a kind of porchway or introduction, and before an exposition was given of the particular doctrines of the wisdom which, by God's grace, had fixed its seat in Israel, they were intended to exhibit its real nature, and to kindle a love of it in the hearts of the readers : they were further meant at the same time, to unmask and stir up hatred of its rival false wisdom, the foreigner, which, by its seductive arts, was trying to gain admittance amongst the people of God. Wisdom is then introduced as a person, and as speaking to men.* In its character as Kohe-

* Ch. B. Michaelis on Chap. viii. Quod sapientia hic non ut qualitas sed ut persona inducatur, non inde solum liquet, quod vox, labia, os aliaque, quæ per-

leth, as the Assembler, it is clearly brought forward in chap.
i. 20, 21, "wisdom crieth without, she uttereth her voice in
the streets. She preacheth in the chief place of concourse :
she utters her words in the gates of the city :" further also
in chap. viii. 1, ff. From such a personification of wisdom
there is but a step to its becoming as it were personal in an
individual, as in this Book of Ecclesiastes. To assume such an
embodiment of wisdom in a person here is matter of less difficulty, seeing that the like thing occurs undeniably in the New
Testament. A comparison of Luke xi. 49, 50, with Matthew
xxiii. 34, will leave no room to doubt that in the first passage
Christ represents himself as the personal embodiment of wisdom. That there is a connection between these passages and
Solomon's appearance as Koheleth, was recognised already by
Bengel in his time, and that the two stand in a certain
measure on the same line. He says in his Gnomon, on Luke
xi. 49, ἡ σοφία τοῦ θεοῦ, *sapientia dei*. *Suave nomen*. Koheleth
congregatrix. Chap. xiii. 34, ποσάκις ἠθέλησα ἐπισυνάξαι τὰ τέκνα
σου. In these words from Matthew xxiii. 37, quoted by Bengel,
Christ appears to allude to himself as the true Koheleth. The
objections which have been urged against the explanation now
given of the name Koheleth, especially of the feminine form of it,
are untenable. Those who affirm that the author must have
expressed himself much more distinctly had he intended to
apply to Solomon the title Koheleth because of his standing
as the representative of wisdom, overlook the fact that this
explanation is involved in the relation existing between this
book and the exordium of the book of Proverbs ; and further
that we are driven to it by chap. vii. 27. When it is objected
that a multitude of expressions do not at all correspond to
what we might expect from the lips of Wisdom, as, for example,
when the person speaking is represented as having contem-
plated, sought to obtain, and actually gained possession of,
wisdom, there is an overlooking of the consideration that
Koheleth is not wisdom absolutely, but only so far as it has
found an embodiment in Solomon : or, in other words, that

---

sonarum potius quam rerum sint, ei tribuuntur, v. 1 sqq., sed maxime ex consideratione illorum characterum, qui, v 22 sqq. expressi sunt, ad quos in prologo
evangelii Johannis, ubi divina Christi natura adseritur, respectum fuisse, vix
quisquam negabit.

Solomon is designated Koheleth from the principle by which he was animated. We have thus also met the objection that Solomon always comes on the scene in the distinctest manner as an actual person, and not as the personification of an idea, and that accordingly reference is made to the experiences of a living person, to the fortunes of a definite individual. Koheleth is not, like Wisdom in the book of Proverbs, a "personified idea," but Solomon himself, who is regarded as the representative, or so to say, as the incarnation of wisdom. The usual course has been to assume without further proof that Koheleth is a sort of surname of Solomon's. " He undertakes the office of a public teacher of truth, and the word Koheleth is intended to point out that he enters here on this definite vocation." A decisive ground against this notion is, that the name is conjoined with the feminine in chap. vii. 27. The assumption that Solomon bears the title Koheleth as the representative of wisdom furnishes the only satisfactory explanation of the alternating conjunction of the word with the masculine, which plainly predominates, and with the feminine. Moreover, on the view above mentioned the feminine form cannot be satisfactorily accounted for. Some appeal to the frequent employment in titles of office, of the abstract word, for persons. " The official is *totus* in the business assigned to him in life, and receives its name as his title." קהלת signifies properly "*preaching*," the office and business of a public speaker: it is then used also of the public speaker himself. So some argue. There are however many difficulties in the way of this position. The feminine termination does undoubtedly serve for forming abstract names (see Ewald, s. 166), but this never takes place with an active participle, and for a very simple reason. From עוּר " blind," we may indeed form עורת " blindness;" from הטא " sinful," הטאת " sin, sinfulness;" but from קהל " the assembling one," we cannot form קהלת, in the sense of " preaching sermon." Then, no case can be actually adduced of a concrete word being made abstract, and afterwards again employed in a personal sense. For the question, who is the author of this book, it is of no little significance that Solomon does not appear here under his own name, but under that of Koheleth. All the other publications of Solomon bear his usual name on their title-page:

for example, "The Proverbs," whose inscription runs, "The Proverbs of Solomon, the Son of David, the King of Israel ;" the "Son of Songs;" Psalms lxxii., cxxvii.: and it is a perfectly natural thing that he who wishes himself to be regarded as the author of any work should employ no other designation than that by which he is already known. To use enigmas, and to play at hide and seek, would be little in place in such a matter. Consequently the writer of this work, in styling Solomon Koheleth pretty clearly indicates that it is only in an ideal sense he is introduced as the author, that he was concerned with the book only as a representative of Wisdom. The very name, which is strictly an impersonal one, shows that the person to whom it is applied belongs to the region of poetry, not to that of reality. Thus we find that the only argument, with any show of reason, for Solomon's authorship, changes sides altogether as soon as it is more carefully examined. The book of Ecclesiastes was not only not actually composed by Solomon, but does not even pretend to have been.*

CHAPTER I. 2-11.

Human life, according to the judgment pronounced on it in Genesis iii. 17-19, is at its best but brilliant misery. Our first parents felt this deeply even in their day. They named one of their two sons Hebel (Abel), that is to say, Vanity. The parents of Noah also confessed this, for they spake at his birth; "this shall comfort us in our toil and work upon the earth, which the Lord hath cursed," (Genesis v. 29). In Genesis xlvii. 9, Jacob says, "few and evil are the days of my life:" in Psalm xc. 10, Moses says, "the days of our years are threescore and ten, and if by reason of strength they be fourscore years, yet is their strength labour and sorrow:" and in Psalm xxxix. 6-7, David exclaims, "Only to utter vanity was every man ordained. Only as a vain show walketh

---

* What A. Fabricus says of the "Book of Wisdom" in the Bibl. Gr. 3, s. 736, holds quite good in the present instance, viz.: *Perinde ut Salvianus nunquam voluit existimari libros suos a Timotheo esse scriptos discipulo apostolorum, sed satis ipsi fuit sub nobili hoc persona delituisse.*

every man: surely they disquiet themselves in vain; he heapeth up and knoweth not who shall receive it." It is of great importance that this character of our earthly existence, depicted in so affecting a manner in the hymns, "Ah! how empty! ah! how fleeting!" and "alas! what is the life of man?" should become so distinctly a matter of consciousness, that men shall not seek to gild over their misery by vain fancies. Only thus can the vanity to which we are subjected have its right operation, answer its purpose, which is to drive us back to God whom we have forsaken, to bring us into the position of saying with entire truthfulness, "Thou alone, O Jehovah, remainest to me what thou art, in thee I put my trust." It is one of the principal aims of the extraordinary sufferings with which God visits His children, His whole church and individuals, to impress deeply on the mind this vanity of earthly things. It is, however, a difficult process: man proves herein a hard learner. He is ever slow to reconcile himself to the emptiness of earth; he is easily brought to fancy his lot a peculiarly hard one, and he does all in his power to put an end to a condition of things which he deems exceptional. And when he finds it impossible to accomplish his design, he falls a prey to despair. This book is unintelligible except on the historical presupposition that the people of God was in a very miserable condition at the time of its composition. They were bondsmen in their own native land: heathens ruled over them: everywhere reigned degradation and misery. When the foundation of the second temple was laid, the people were moved to bitter tears, as they contrasted the present with the past. Vanity of vanities was the universal cry: alas! on what evil days have we fallen! They said one to another, "How is it that the former days were better than these?" Ecclesiastes vii. 10. In particular did they look back on Solomon and his day with the desperate yearnings of a Tantallus. And then on the ears of the people in such a condition bursts the proclamation of our author, that human life is altogether vanity. Thus on the one hand he administered the consolation lying at the basis of the words, *dulce est solamen miseris socios habere malorum.* The cross is much easier to bear when we see that it is the universal destiny of mankind. And on the other hand, he

suggests powerful motives to a sincere return to God, whose
very name Jehovah or Jahve, signifying "the One who absolutely is, Pure Being," constitutes a perfect contrast to the
vanity with which every creature separated from Him is
justly chargeable.

Ver. 2. *Vanity of vanities, said Koheleth, vanity of vanities; all is vanity.* Ver. 3. *What profit hath man of all his
labour which he taketh under the sun?* Ver. 4. *One generation passeth away and another generation cometh, and the
earth abideth for ever.* Ver. 5. *The sun also riseth, and the
sun goeth down, and (goeth) to his place where he eagerly
riseth.* Ver. 6. *The wind goeth toward the south, and turneth
about unto the north, it whirleth about continually; and the
wind returneth again to its circuits.* Ver. 7. *All rivers run
into the sea, yet the sea is not full: unto the place whence the
rivers come, thither they return again.* Ver. 8. *All words
become weary, none can utter it; the eye is not satisfied with
seeing, nor the ear filled with hearing.* Ver. 9. *The thing
that hath been, it is that which shall be; and that which has
been done is that which shall be done, and there is nothing
at all new under the sun.* Ver. 10. *Is there a thing whereof
it may be said, see this is new? It hath been already of
old time which was before us.* Ver. 11. *No memorial have
they of old; nor shall they who are to come have any remembrance with those that shall come after.*

Ver. 2. That it was the mission of this book to impress on
the Church of God the vanity of all earthly things, to convince it that "the world is but a vale of tears, and that
everywhere are to be found only needs, troubles, and fears,"
is externally indicated with sufficient clearness by the fact
that the word הבל, "vanity," occurs in it thirty-seven
times, whilst in the entire remaining portion of the Old
Testament it occurs only thirty-three times. "Vanity of
vanities," according to the well known usage of speech, signifies "the utmost vanity." The word "all" is more precisely
defined afterwards as "all that is under the sun, whatever
belongs to the sublunary world, to this poor earth." It does
not include the Creator, whose very name Jehovah, signifying
"The self-existent One," "pure, true, absolute being," stands
in the completest opposition to vanity: nor does it refer to

union with Him and the joy which is sought in Him (compare chap. xii. 13), but to the poor creatures which since the time spoken of in Genesis iii. have been subjected to vanity (Romans viii. 20). The earth can offer nothing capable of affording true satisfaction and contentment to man. The assertion that "here at the beginning of the work its author gives strongest expression to the bitterness of his own spirit;" rests on an utter misunderstanding. If that were true in this case, it would be equally true in the case of Thomas a Kempis, who commences his "*de Imitatione Christi*" with the words: *Vanitas vanitatum et omnia vanitas præter amare Deum et illi soli servire. Vanitas igitur est divitias perituras quærere et in illis sperare. Vanitas quoque est honores ambire et in altum statum se extollere. Vanitas est carnis desideria sequi,* etc. There can be no word of *subjective* bitterness, for the simple reason that the vanity of all the possessions of this world, and of the efforts spent upon them, is an undeniable *fact*. To recognize this is of the utmost importance, and whosoever helps us to gain this knowledge is an excellent preacher, for he prevents us seeking any longer happiness where it is not to be found, he moderates the pain we feel at losing and being deprived of what is in itself really worthless, and makes us intensely eager to attain to the true source of joy. Negative wisdom is the condition and groundwork of positive. We cannot really see in God the highest good unless we have first of all discerned the vanity of that pretended good which is laid before us by the world. "Soul, why weariest thou thyself with the things of this world?"—such words constitute an admirable commencement when we wish to lead men to God. Vanity of vanities and all is vanity,—to know that is the preliminary condition of a true enjoyment of those pleasures which still spring up in the barren wastes of life. He who has given up making undue claims on life will be able to take with a contented and thankful spirit those joys which present themselves unsought on his path, he will be able to live for the present moment, free from cares and covetousness. "I have laid my account with possessing nothing, and therefore the whole world is mine."

Jerome asks the question how it is reconcileable with God's

having created all things good, to say that all is vanity?*
He did not find the proper answer to this question, nor did
Luther, who supposes that the writer "does not say this against
the creatures, but against the naughtiness of the human heart
which will not rest, but makes for itself all kinds of sorrow
and misfortune." He does not speak of God's works, "but of
those wretched objects beneath the sun with which men are
bound up as to their physical constitution, for whose sake they
give themselves so much fruitless unrest, trouble and labour."
To limit his words entirely to human efforts, contradicts the
subsequent carrying out of the thought. Besides, the vanity
of human efforts is specially grounded in the vanity of the
sphere in which they are put forth. And that vanity is pre-
dicable of the whole of that sphere in respect to which God
spake the words "very good," (Genesis i.,) is evident from the
sentence, "in the day thou eatest thereof thou shalt die,"
—die a death whose crowning point is Death personally so
designated. Other evidence to the same effect is borne by
Romans viii. 20, according to which the irrational creation is
subjected to vanity, and by James iv. 14, where our life is
described as ἀτμίς, the same word as that by which Aquila has
translated הֶבֶל. Not only, then, are human efforts vain,
but creation also, in its merely natural aspect, may be included
under the description "all is vanity." The true solution of the
problem lies here:—Between the words "and behold, everything was good," and those of our author, "all is vanity," the
fall of man has intervened. With that, an entirely new order
of things was inaugurated. To man in his degeneracy God's
creation, though good in itself, was no longer fitted. Hence
the complaint, "all is vanity," is not a charge against God,
but, on the contrary, when we carefully consider the nature
and constitution of man, rather a *praise* of God. It is just in
the decreeing of punishment, and the establishment of the
economy of the cross, that God specially manifests His glory
and greatness. The Berleburger Bible observes : "As it was
said in the beginning, *everything is good, everything is very*

* Si cuncta quæ fecit Deus valde bona sunt, quomodo omnia vanitas, et
non solum vanitas, sed etiam vanitas vanitatum ? Ut sicut in Canticis Canti-
corum inter omnia carmina excellens carmen ostenditur ita in vanitate vanitatum vanitatis magnitudo monstretur.

good, so also will it once again be said regarding the creature, everything is precious and new, everything is very precious, good, and glorious." "All is vanity,"—cannot be the end of God's ways: it can only be a point of transition. The end must correspond to the beginning. The words—"all is vanity,"—will lose the sad truth they have as respects the present course of the world, in the "regeneration" of which our Lord speaks in Matthew xix. 28, in that blessed age depicted by Isaiah in chap. xi. of his prophecies, and by Paul in Romans viii. As vanity is not the original, so can it not be the final character of the world's constitution and course. Death, the climax of vanity, entered into the world with sin, (see Genesis ii. 17; Romans v. 12.) And therefore when sin has been completely overcome, death also will cease, (1 Cor. xv. 54 f.) and as it is said in Revelations xxi. 4, "God shall wipe away all tears from their eyes; and there shall be no more death, neither sorrow nor crying, neither shall there be any more pain, for the former things are passed away." All the descriptions of this future contained in the Scriptures, pre-suppose what is expressed in the words, "All is vanity," for they are intended to give courage to those who sigh and groan under vanity, and to save them from despair. So, for example, Isaiah xxv. 6-8,—"And in this mountain the Lord of Hosts prepareth unto all people a feast of fat things, a feast of wines on the lees, of fat things full of marrow, of wines on the lees well refined. And He destroyeth in this mountain the face of the covering with which all nations are covered over. (The veil as the sign of sorrow.) He destroyeth death for ever, and the Lord God wipeth away the tears from all faces." Further, Isaiah xxxv. 1 ff.: "The wilderness and the solitary place will be glad, and the desert will rejoice and blossom as the rose. Then will the lame man leap as a hart, and the tongue of the dumb sing: for in the wilderness will waters break out and streams in the desert. The parched ground will become a pool, and the thirsty land streams of water. Then will the eyes of the blind be opened, and the ears of the deaf be unstopped." But a fundamental condition of our pa - ticipating in this future glory, is that we attain to a clear and deep insight into the significance of the saying, "All is vanity," that we do not gild over our present misery. Only as this

truth is distinctly understood and intensely felt, will its effect
be to drive us to God, who is our everlasting dwelling-place,
(Psalm xc.,) and to arouse us to repentance, in that we estimate
the extent of our guilt by the severity of the sufferings we
have to endure.   Such was the feeling of Perthes when he
wrote after the death of his beloved wife, "an immeasurable
load of guilt must rest on us, seeing we have to suffer such a
loss."   De Wette brought against St Paul the reproach, that
in his writings we encounter sometimes "the discordant tone
of contempt of the world."   He who with such eyes considers
the words "all is vanity," will not only retain his share of trouble,
—for say what we may, the world is, and continues to be a vale of
tears, notwithstanding that by our forced laughter we should
fancy we have changed it into a house of gladness,—but will
wantonly rob himself of the wholesome fruit of his sufferings.
The bringing in of the new covenant has effected no alteration
in that vanity of vanities which our author speaks of so emphatically.   The blessings which already accrue to us therefrom
belong to an order of things entirely different from that which
is here spoken of.   They spring not forth from the region
beneath the sun but from the kingdom of heaven.   The earth
meanwhile continues its existence of vanity, and in this its
character is a powerful motive pressing men to appropriate the
heavenly treasures offered by the Church.

Ver. 3. In ver. 3, is given the result which follows from
ver. 2.   If "all is vanity," what profit hath man ? or strictly
"the earthly one, (Geier, *cum aculeo terrenæ fragilitatis*) of
all the labour which he taketh under the sun ?"   There is
much ado about nothing.   One who has arrived at a knowledge of the true nature of this world receives a strange, yea
even a tragicomical impression when he sees men running to
and fro, and seeking to snatch the prey from each other's
grasp.   The results, too, are in the end of scarcely greater
compass and importance than those of the movements of an
anthill.   And then joined with all this, the airs of importance,
and the pompous phrases about progress and the like.   The
best commentary on this verse is furnished by the beautiful
hymn of Gryphius beginning—"The glory of the earth, must
at last become smoke and ashes."   Interpreting these facts
according to the mind of the Preacher the practical result

would be to "quit the world, and honour, fear, hope, favour and learning, and to follow only the Lord, who will ever rule, whom time cannot change, and who can confer upon us eternal blessedness."

Ver. 4. The subject of discourse in the context is the vanity of everything earthly, and the consequent fruitlessness of human efforts. Ver. 4. would not at all suit the connection in which it stands, unless the earth be regarded as the scene of vanity and misery which it really is. The generations of men are continually changing, ceaselessly do fresh ones appear on the scene, but O! misery! the earth, against which the curse recorded in Genesis iii. 17-19 was pronounced, on which it is impossible to realise permanent results, or to arrive at abiding happiness, and where men find themselves hemmed in on all hands—that remains. The new generations are compelled always to begin where the old ones ended. That old fable, the rolling of the Sisyphus-stone, is illustrated ever afresh.*
לעלם does not stand in contradiction with the doctrine of the impending termination of the present phase of the earth's existence found elsewhere in the Old Testament. As in Genesis vi. 4, עלם, "Time far back beyond the memory of men," so here it designates a future of unmeasured extent: as Rambach has it, *diutissimo tempore, cujus terminus nobis occultus est.*

Ver. 5. The sun here can only be employed as an image of human existence which is straitly confined within the limits of vanity. The natural event cannot, considered in itself, be treated as a subject of complaint, but only as one of joyous wonder and admiration, as is clear from Psalm xix. The mere natural rising and setting of the sun would not form a suitable step in the development of the thought, "vanity of vanities," which is the subject of the writer's comments on to the 11th verse, and which must consequently furnish the test of the correctness of our explanation of all that occurs up to that point. The sun eagerly running through a long course, in order at last to return to the goal from which it started is a true image of human life shut up within the impassable magic-

---

* Quite improperly says Jerome, "quid hac vanius vanitate, quam terram. manere, quæ hominum causa facta est, et ipsum hominem, terræ dominus. in pulverem repente dissolvi."

circle of vanity. The human race seems unable to move a step. A new generation always begins where the old one ended. Notwithstanding all our much vaunted progress, we continue mainly such as we were of old, " burdened with an inheritance of sin, with weakness, with want and death." " That there is motion, cannot be denied : but it is motion in a circle, and consequently leads to no result," (Hitzig.) Following the example of the Chaldee version, of the Septuagint and of the Vulgate Luther connects שואף מקומו ואל אל—" And hasteth to his place that he may there rise again." But this mode of connecting the words is contrary to the accents, according to which שואף must belong to what succeeds : and besides, without any justification from usage, it takes the word שאף in the signification of " to run, to hasten." The usual meaning of שאף is " to snap at, to hanker after, anything ;" in which sense it is employed here also—" And (comes then again) to its place where it longingly arises." שואף corresponds to the expression found in Psalm xix. 6, " He rejoices as a hero to run his course." The first verb furnishes greater definiteness to the second ; Ewald, § 285. A new generation advancing to life with fresh courage, resembles the sun in its longing, its joyousness, its eagerness. אל includes the verb.

Ver. 6. In this verse " is described the vanity of the wind, which is continually moving round and round in a circle, and through its swiftness does not succeed in passing beyond this circle." Here also it is quite plain that the author has no intention of blaming anything in the order and arrangements of nature—a thing which would have been revolting and absurd—but that the wind comes under consideration only as a symbol of human existence revolving constantly in the circle of vanity and unable to transcend its bounds however mighty may be the efforts put forth. The entire verse has reference to the wind, and it is fruitless when the Septuagint, the Syriac, Geier, and others, try to refer the first clause to the sun : " which turns not towards the North." South and North are mentioned in the case of the wind, because East and West were used of the sun. The סביבות of the wind are the turns which it has already made.

Ver. 7. As the water of brooks goes first into the sea and then returns back to the brooks, so is there in human affairs no real result, no progress, no overstepping of the limit of vanity : the old misery manifests itself ever afresh.   Luther recognised the symbolical character of the verse, but did not altogether hit upon a right view of the thought contained in it.   Says he, "we have in these words a subtle comparison : all men's proposals, all their devices, efforts, care, by which they hope to help the matter, rise with the sun, and go down again ; like the water, too, they flow hither and thither ; that is, being mere human thoughts, without God's work and furtherance, they remain just what they were.   Let that man whose thoughts either do not, or have not come to nought, blot out what Solomon says."   That the sea never becomes full is a proof that the streams must return again to the place whence they came.   We must render the words, " to the place from which the streams go out."   Luther's translation is correct, " to the place whence they flow, they flow back again."   The *Construct State* which causes the whole following sentence to be treated as a noun is employed in the same manner in Psalm civ. 8, " unto the place which thou hast founded for them."   As to the way and manner in which the waters return to their source commentators are not agreed.   Luther thinks " the waters run without ceasing into the sea, and then by secret subterraneous passages or channels run from the sea as fountains and brooks filtering through the earth at their place, penetrating and running through mountains and rocks."   It is, however, much simpler to assume that the streams return to their sources through the medium of the clouds.   Compare Genesis ii. 6, " and there went up mists from the earth and watered the whole face of the ground:" Job xxxvi. 27, 28, " For he draws forth the drops of water, they pour down rain from the vapour thereof.   Thence run the clouds, distil much upon men."   In respect of natural processes the Scriptures do not enter upon doubtful hypotheses.   They always confine themselves to that which presents itself to the eye of the general observer, to that which is undeniable.   Some have deemed it possible entirely to evade the consideration of the problem here presented, and they translate, " Whither the streams go, thither go they ever again :" *i.e.*, they pursue incessantly the same course into the sea.   According to this version there would be no reference whatever to the return of the rivers to their sources. In such a case, however, it is impossible to see what purpose is served by the words, "and the sea becomes not full."

Ver. 8. In interpreting the first half of this verse all depends on whether we take דברים in the sense of *things*, in which it is employed in chap. vi. 11, vii. 8, or in that of *words*. The former view is adopted by Luther. He translates, "All men's doing is so full of toil, that no one can utter it."* On this view the words would be more accurately rendered—"All things are so weary, that no one can utter it," that is, they are inexpressibly weary. Usage does not allow of any further meaning being given to יגע than that of "weary." Tediousness or weariness in the things corresponds to *ennui* in the individual person. Nothing goes on with vigour and freshness: spur and whip are everywhere necessary: the world seems to have outlived itself, for ever since the time spoken of in Genesis iii., it has been under the δουλεία τῆς φθορᾶς (Romans viii. 21). From Genesis iii. 17, "cursed be the ground for thy sake, with pain shalt thou eat of it all the days of thy life," we should judge the ground itself to be weary: it no longer hastens to give unto man its strength: all has to be pressed and wrung from it by labour. This interpretation, though in some respects very admirable, has against it the correspondence between דברים and דבר "to speak"—a correspondence which is scarcely to be denied. This would lead to the conclusion that the former word is employed here in the signification "*words*," which is the original one, besides being predominant in this book. Accordingly we should find a parallel to the whole of the first half of the verse in Psalm xl. 5, where it is said in respect of the wonderful works of God, "I will declare and speak of them; they are more than can be numbered." *What* is unutterable, inexpressible, we are not here distinctly informed: but the context leaves us in no doubt on that matter, inasmuch as from verse 2 onwards nothing else is spoken of but human misery. Words fail to describe it, and however many we may employ, the description ever falls far

---

* On this view Rambach gives the sense as follows: Dici non potest quantum laboris et defatigationis rebus et negotiis, humanis omnibus insit. Quidquid dixeris, semper major restabit dicendi materia.

short of the reality.   Ever since the day referred to in Genesis iii. man has been the prey of an indescribable sorrow. The
words, *the eye is not satisfied with seeing, nor the ear with
hearing*, find their commentary in chapter iv. 8, where "his
eye is not satisfied with riches," describes an insatiable desire
for them ; and further in Proverbs xxvii. 20, where the in-
satiability of the eyes of men also stands for desire that con-
not be satisfied ; " Hell and destruction are never full, so the
eyes of man are never satisfied."   That man never finds satisfaction in earthly things, but on the contrary is ever asking
for yet more and more, is a sign of their emptiness. Such
being their nature they can never fill the heart. It is in
this respect that they come under consideration in this place,
and the two halves of the verse agree therefore in the thought
of the vanity of all things earthly.   The first describes it as
unutterable ; the second appeals for proof of the assertion to
their inability to appease and fill the heart of man.   Luther
says, " an exemplification of this may be found in that renowned king and praiseworthy hero, Alexander the Great.
In a very brief space of time (for in all he did not reign more
than twelve years) he subjugated to himself a large portion of
the whole world : and notwithstanding, once upon a time,
when he heard a philosopher arguing that there are more
worlds than one, he sighed deeply, and said, ' Alas ! that I
have not as yet subdued more than one world !' So, if he
had at once gained ten other worlds, his heart would not
have found rest : nay more, it would not have been satisfied
with a thousand, or even with countless worlds." What we
have already fails to please us, and we long for that which
we have not.   Knobel's view of the passage, that " the satisfying of the eye and the filling of the ear describes the coming to a termination with the study and meditation of things,"
is opposed to the parallel place, besides being contrary to the
natural meaning of such modes of speech.   The eye is satisfied
when we have no desire to see more, the ear is filled when
we wish to hear no more.   In the Berleburger Bible it is remarked, " by the entrances of the soul so many thousands of
objects or things are carried into the heart, that man wearies
and distracts himself with them as with an infinite sandhill.
Out of these his heart forms for him innumerable images which

he contemplates and inwardly busies himself with. Thence arise the manifold thoughts and distracted feelings of us miserable men. This is the cause that, through apostacy from the eternal good, from the Creator, our hearts go forth towards a multiplicity of objects, and, instead of desiring and laying hold on God alone, who would have been an eternally satisfying portion, long for and grasp at thousands of created objects, and still never realise contentment. It is indeed impossible that the immortal soul of man should rest in creatures which are vanity. It seeks ever further and desires ever more : it is like a fire which burns on without ceasing, and would fain bring all within its grasp. But now that it is faint, and out of its true element and life, which is God, behold, the soul finds itself deceived, led astray and threatened with ruin by all creatures, finds that it has wasted its time and energies on things without use, and knows not an object to which it may cling."

Ver. 9. Notwithstanding all the fancies and illusions regarding new and glorious things which men bring forward it is now as it was of old. " *That which is done*" is here considered in its results, and is consequently closely connected with *that which is.* *Being* (Seyn) continues ever what it was of old : consequently the results of doing, of action, cannot show any very important difference. Because the old was bad, it is a great evil that there is nothing new under the sun. There is no alternative but to recur ever to the words, " Cursed is the ground for thy sake." Man cannot escape out of the charmed circle into which he was driven by the sentence pronounced in Genesis iii., be his exertions what they may. All progress is but vain show and loose varnish. For example, the old covenant, " thou shalt die," still retains its force, notwithstanding all the progress that has been made in the healing art. Luther remarks, " if we understand these words of the works of God, they are not true : for God works and ever produces something new : it is only men and children of Adam who effect nothing new." This is perfectly well grounded. We have here to do with Negative Philosophy, which searches into the nature of things apart from God. The author's intent is to show what is the matter with earthly and human affairs considered in themselves, to tear up by the roots the countless illusions to which the natural man so readily resigns himself, and by which he frustrates the purpose of the divine judgment pronounced in Genesis iii. The vanity of earthly things can only lead men to God when it is thoroughly felt and understood. For parallels to the words, *there is nothing new under the sun*, reference may be made to Jeremiah xxxi. 22, "behold I create a new thing in the land," and to Isaiah lxv. 17, "behold I create new heavens and a new earth, and the former shall not be remembered nor come into mind," (compare lxvi. 22.) In Matthew xix. 28, the Lord promises the regeneration or the renewal of the world. According to 2 Peter iii. 13, "we look for new heavens and a new earth, wherein dwelleth righteousness." In the Apocalypse, chapter xxi. 1, John sees a "new heaven and a new earth, for the first heaven and the first earth were passed away." He who sits on the throne says there, in verse 5, "behold I make all things new." According to chapter xxi. 2, "the holy city, the new Jerusalem, descends from heaven." At the bottom of all these passages lies the tacit presupposition that "there is nothing new under the sun." The assumption from which they start is that the old earth is a scene of vanity, that all efforts to change it, originating in and depending on its own resources, are utterly fruitless, and that a true alteration cannot be effected from below, but only from above. They comfort us also in the midst of the misery which is our lot, by the assurance that a renewal from above will in fact be accomplished. The new creation will begin at the point where vanity took its rise, even with man : "if any man be in Christ, he is a new creature, old things are passed away, behold all things are become new," (2 Corinthians v. 17.) Thence will the renovation pass to the rest of creation. Nothing new is done under the sun—this should serve to bring down the lofty imaginations which would gather grapes from the thorns of this world, but not to discourage the friends of the kingdom of God, whose true seat is not under the sun, but above it, and whose heavenly protector, by ever creating new things, furnishes materials for new songs, (Psalm xl. 3.)

Ver. 10. Many an undertaking gives promise at its commencement of passing beyond the limits fixed by the old curse-laden world. The world exultingly shouts them welcome. But very soon it becomes evident that in them also a worm is concealed, and they sink down to a level with that which our poor earth has produced in former ages. So was it with the happiness of the days of Solomon, in the background of which there lay decay and ruin, and whose end was such, that men were driven to exclaim, "Lord have mercy," and, "Oh! that thou wouldest rend the heavens and wouldest come down?" It still remains a truth that "here is no true good to be found, and what the world holds in itself must vanish in a moment."

Ver. 11. A fond dream of this world is to possess the immortality of renown. Even this barren consolation is here taken away, and so a conclusion is made, to the development of the thought contained in ver. 3, that man has no profit of all the labour which he taketh under the sun. In accordance with the sentiment of this verse is the hymn by Joh. Pappus, "I have committed my cause to God;"* and another by Andreas Gryphius, of which verses are quoted below.† Contrary to the divergent explanations of these verses, it is to be observed that ראשנים and אהרנים are always "the earlier" and "the later." See Leviticus xxvi. 45; Deuteronomy xix. 14; Psalm lxxix. 8; Isaiah lxi. 4; xli. 4; Ecclesiastes iv. 16. "The earlier," (neuter gender.) is ראישנות in Isaiah xlii. 9. The parallel passages also in chap. ii. 16; ix. 5, serve to put aside every other explanation.

In chap. i. 12,-ii. 26, Koheleth demonstrates the vanity of earthly things, from his own example—from his own personal

---

* " Man trägt eins nach dem Andern hin
Wohl aus den Augen und aus dem Sinn
Die Welt vergisset unser bald
Sey jung oder alt
Auch unserer Ehren mannigfalt."

† " Der Ruhm nach dem wir trachten
Den wir unsterblich achten
Ist nur ein falscher Wahn.
Sobald der Geist gewichen
Und dieser Mund verblichen
Fragt Keiner was man hier gethan."

experience.* He begins in chap. i. 12-18, with Wisdom. This was one of the brilliant possessions of the age of Solomon, as may be seen from 1 Kings x. 8, where the Queen of Sheba says, "Happy are thy men, happy are these thy servants, which stand continually before thee and behold thy wisdom," (compare Matthew xii. 42,) and back to it the after-world looked, with all the more astonished admiration and painful longing, because even the heathen nations, under whose scorn and contempt they sighed, were struck by it with amazement. In the delineation of the glory of Solomon given in 1 Kings x., wisdom occupies the first place : then follows riches. Hitzig's account of the contents and connection of verses 12-18 is as follows : "the speaker tells who he is and how he has come thus to express himself. He has maturely reflected on the works and ways of men, and found that they are feeble and foolish, verses 12-15. Moreover, according to his experience, the wisdom which one may gain is not to be regarded as a good." The subject of the entire section is rather wisdom, and the vanity of earthly things and of human efforts comes under consideration only so far as it conditions the vanity of wisdom. In verse 13, the assertion is made, the thesis is maintained, that "wisdom is not a good but a plague." The following is the proof. Earthly things which are the object of wisdom are vanity, and the more deeply we search, the more distinctly is their vanity seen. Wisdom destroys illusions. The possession of wisdom, therefore, can only bring distress and pain. The wiser a man is, the more unhappy. If the world is nothing and vanity, the wisdom, the science of this world cannot be of much value.

Failing to see that this section has exclusive reference to wisdom, we shall also mistake the entire course of thought. In the following verses, there is a continuation of the proof of the vanity of earthly things from Solomon's own personal experience. Here wisdom is the subject : before, it was the possession and enjoyment of the good things of this world.

Ver. 12. *I Koheleth was King over Israel in Jerusalem.*

---

* Hieronymus : huc usque præfatio generaliter de omnibus disputantis : nunc ad semitipsum redit, et quis fuerit, quomodo experimento universa cognoverit docet.

Ver. 13. *And I gave my heart to seek and search out by wisdom concerning everything that is done under the sun : this is a sore travail which God hath given to the sons of men, that they may exercise themselves therewith.* Ver. 14. *I saw all the works that are done under the sun, and behold, all is vanity and delusive effort.* Ver. 15. *That which is crooked cannot be made straight, and that which is wanting cannot be reckoned.* Ver. 16. *I communed with mine own heart and said, Lo, I have increased and gotten more wisdom than all that were before me in Jerusalem, and my heart saw much wisdom and knowledge.* Ver. 17. *And I gave my heart to know wisdom and the knowledge of madness and folly : I perceived that this also is delusive effort.* Ver. 18. *For in much wisdom is much grief, and he that increaseth knowledge increaseth sorrow.*

Ver. 12. Koheleth refers first of all to his royal position. For the matter in hand this is of no small importance. If the life of earth could offer genuine good it must undoubtedly have been at the command of the king.* Even in regard to wisdom his position has its advantages. He has a wide and extensive view of all that is done under heaven (*ver.* 13). The whole region of human life lies spread out before him. His position is much more favourable than that of the man who philosophizes in a narrow corner. He is still more favoured as regards those regions which are spoken of in chap. ii. 1 ff. Koheleth says—*I was king.* According to Ewald, Elster, and others, the preterite employed here is intended to indicate the historical point of view of the author, for which Solomon's life was so completely a something past and gone, that he involuntarily represents Solomon as speaking of his own life in the preterite. In point of fact, however, the use of the preterite is no argument against Solomon's being the author of the book. Nor, if the composition is assigned to a later period, is it a proof of its fictitious character that the writer in this place forgets himself. The preterite is very frequently employed in descriptions of a past which stretches forward into the present, and therefore is it

---

* Cartwright, "ut nihil subsidii deesset. cujus beneficio, quod assectatus sum, assequerer."

remarked, with perfect justice, in the Berleburger Bible—" I the preacher have been king thus far, and am one still : to him therefore there has been no lack of opportunity of trying experiments and of getting experience." The words, *In Jerusalem,* need not, as has been affirmed, be supposed to refer to another kingship which had not its seat in Jerusalem. They are meant to remind us that Koheleth had gone through the experiences of which he speaks in that very place whose complainings and sighings gave rise to the composition of this work.

Ver. 13. Koheleth informs us that his efforts to search out the nature of things had yielded wretched results. Concerning the relation to each other of the two verbs דרש and תור Hitzig remarks—" That which withdrew itself from the gaze of the דורש, that which lay deeper, that which was secret he sought to *explore.*" But תור is not " search after, spy out," but " try thoroughly, test," (see Deuteronomy i. 33, Numbers x. 33, Ezekiel xx. 6) ; taken strictly it signifies "to follow the trace of things," as opposed to a decision which is arrived at from preconceived opinions. Hitzig says further—" It is not meant that he set himself to collect facts : he did not need to inquire what it is that takes place, but what is the nature of that which takes place." To this view we are directed not only by the word תור, here rightly explained, but further also by the construction with על. Investigations are set on foot in respect of material lying ready to hand. The Vulgate translates בהכמה by *sapienter ;* Luther by " wisely." But this rather dissipates the force of the word. It is wisdom that is the catchword. Nor is it without good reason that the word is pointed with the article. Wisdom is the instrument employed in carrying out the investigation. The object of the investigation is all that is done or happens under the sun. We are not to suppose, however, that it refers predominantly, much less exclusively, to the moral aspects of human action, but rather, as appears from a comparison of ver. 15 with chap. vii. 13, mainly to the results thereof. All that takes place beneath the sun belongs to the sphere which had its origin in the fall of man, is tainted with sin, and is attended by sin's fell train of suffering and punishment. Everywhere the earth shows itself to be a scene of vanity.

" Ah ! how vain, how fleeting, are the days of man ! Like a
stream that begins its flow and never stays in its course, so
hurries our time away. Ah ! how vain, how fleeting are the
joys of men ! As the hours and seasons, as light and darkness, as peace and conflict, so change our pleasures." The
business of searching more deeply into earthly things by
means of wisdom is described as a vexing misfortune which
God has apportioned to the sons of men that they may vex
themselves with it. Following in the steps of the LXX. several commentators explain the words as follow—" that is an
evil business which God has appointed to the children of men,
that they may busy themselves with it." But ענה elsewhere
occurs only in the signification of " to suffer ;" for this reason
therefore the word עִנְיָן, which is never met with out of this
book, and which here stands in the *Stat. constr.*, can only
signify " suffering, vexation." It has the same meaning also
in chap. v. 2, and in all other places. In ver. 18 chagrin
and pain correspond. Hitzig wishes to refer the words—
*This is a sore travail which God hath given to the sons of men
that they may exercise themselves therewith*—to that which
happens, which is done. It is quite clear, however, that they
refer to the search instituted by means of wisdom. The assertion that in this way verses 17 and 18 are anticipated
rests on a mistaken view of the connection between the verses
of this section. The words at the close—*I recognised also
that this is empty effort*—manifestly take up again the theme
of the commencement after proof has been advanced. To our
mind verses 17 and 18 render it impossible to understand by
the " sore travail " any thing but wisdom in search of truth.
The affliction does not consist, as Clericus conceived, merely
in the misuse of the gift, but in the gift itself. More deeply
examined, however, it is a wholesome affliction. That which
is bitter to the mouth is healthy for the heart. That deeper
view of the vanity of earthly things which wisdom affords
drives us nearer to God. Thus we see that wisdom is a
part of the great apparatus by which God humbles fallen
man and prepares the way for his redemption. Wisdom presents other aspects also for consideration besides that which
has here been noted. And even if that which has been here
especially under view is but one side of the truth, it is still

the most important side. Thus much may be regarded as settled—that inasmuch as wisdom yields so melancholy a result, it cannot be the highest good, it cannot be that good which will satisfy the wretched heart of man. Earthly things must be far other than they are, before wisdom can quicken and refresh the soul. Some have thought that the author's reason for calling the efforts put forth in search of wisdom a sore travail was, "that they do not afford distinct information relative to the cause and connection of the processes of human life." This is however a mere guess. Koheleth informs us afterwards why he deems wisdom a sore travail. The only ground assigned by him is, that that which has only the effect of placing in a clearer light the vanity under which men groan, must itself also be vanity: that is, considered simply in itself and apart from the service it renders as a means to another end, wisdom is not a good but a sorrow, is not at all a thing for whose sake Solomon and his age should be envied, for whose loss we should vex ourselves. It is thoroughly true, as has been said, that "a man is foolish who vexes himself about a handful of vanity when God presents him with treasures which ever abide. If thy gains are counted by thousands why trouble thyself about a mite?"

Ver. 14. As part of the proof of his thesis—*this is a sore travail*, the author now asserts the vanity of the object with which wisdom is occupied. Ewald translates—"all the deeds which take place under the sun:" but מעשה does not signify "deed" but "matter of fact." Of course "the ways of men" are referred to, but specially in respect to their consequences, to such facts as those which gave rise to the heathenish saying, "the Gods are envious," and which the Poet had in his eye when he wrote, "He who had shown himself as a Lion, who had wrestled with the Giant, was overcome by a little straw." The words רעות and רעיון are peculiar to Koheleth. The usage of speech in Chaldee from which they are evidently borrowed, decides their meaning. In Ezra v. 17, we find רעות used in the sense of "will:" in Daniel several times in the sense of "thought." The derivation of the words is consequently sought in רעה, "to feed," then "to feed oneself on anything," "to busy oneself with anything;" see Hosea xii. 1, "Ephraim feedeth on the wind, and hunteth

after the East wind;" Isaiah xliv. 20 ; Proverbs xiii. 20 ; xv.
14.   An "empty striving, " (LXX. προαίρεσις πνεύματος,) is a striving without result, such a striving as brings no true genuine
good to realization.

Ver. 15. *That which is crooked cannot be brought into posi-*
tion : חקן does not signify " straight," but " to be in position,"
to " come into position," in Syriac, " to be arranged, to be
ordered ;" LXX. διεστραμμένον οὐ δυνήσεται ἐπικοσμηθῆναι.   From
the parallel passage, chap. vii. 13, it is evident that the writer
speaks of imperfections, not only as seen in human ways,
but also in the arrangement of the world, *i. e.* of those
things in the order of the world which wear an appearance of
imperfection as long as the fall of man is foolishly ignored.
Hitzig gives the meaning therefore correctly as follows,—
" Man cannot alter that which is unjust in the divine arrangement of the world ; he cannot bring it from a state of imperfection to one of perfection."   Knobel thinks that the writer
here " betrays his fatalistic view of the world, according to
which everything pursues so firm and unalterable a course that
no modification whatever thereof is possible."   The question
here however is not one of *opinion*, but of undeniable *facts*.
The world is actually a vale of tears, everywhere are wants,
trouble, fears : and on this rock break all the attempts made
to establish what men deem the best system of things.   For
the rest, the author is not discoursing of the "fixed and unalterable course" of things in particular, but only of the general
character of human affairs and of earthly relations, which must
necessarily, are by God intended to, reduce to despair those
who seek their satisfaction in them :—" man is not to that
end here that he may possess earth."   *That which is wanting*
cannot be reckoned, which is as much as to say that, where
nothing is nothing can be counted, human life consists entirely
of nulls.   In opposition to usage, several translate, " that
which is wanting cannot be supplied."   מנה signifies only " to
reckon, to count."   Luther has several excellent remarks on
this verse of which we must make mention.   " Cicero writing
from his own experience says, " Alas ! how constantly it happens that as sure as anything has been devised and planned
for the best, and with the greatest industry, it turns out so
badly and so strangely !"   God however herein does well, that

He blows away and brings to nought whatever man meditates and undertakes. For as soon as any plan of us men succeeds a little, from that hour we begin to take the honour to ourselves. Forthwith ambition begins to stir within us, and we think to ourselves, this have I done, for this are my country and fellow men indebted to me ; and we grasp at the honour which belongs alone and entirely to God. Wherefore, if God is to continue Lord, and to assert and maintain His first commandment, He must only suffer the lesser part of our thoughts to turn out well, and both in the courts and councils of kings and princes, and in all other affairs, so soon as, and whenever anything has been deliberated and determined, show that the words " if God wills it " still retain their full force. Heathen and ungodly men, who alike fancy that it is enough if they themselves have resolved, must in this wise learn that there has been One absent from their counsels, who has a clear right to a voice therein, and His name is God. Therefore is it the best course and the highest wisdom, to leave and commend all to God, not to plague and worry ourselves too much with our own thoughts, but to follow the wise man who at last, after great experience declared—" Let things go as they go, for do what we may they will go as they go." And how frequently do we see that cunning and prudent rulers, and people who in other respects are exalted and wise, do the greatest mischief, whilst setting themselves with all earnestness, with great restlessness, labour and industry to make all things good. For on earth, under the sun, there never can be established a state of things so good that all will move on evenly, that there will not be still many imperfections, many faults. Wherefore, the best thing of all, is to build and confide heartily on God, to commit the ordering of all to Him, to let Him rule, to pray as the Lord taught us—" thy kingdom come "—and meanwhile patiently to bear and suffer all manner of wrong from the ungodly and wicked, leaving our case in the hands of the great Judge.—When, then, although thou art wise and holy, and pious, and remarkest that many things go wrong, thou hast notwithstanding no power to make all straight that is crooked, do the work with which thou art entrusted, apply thyself with all industry to thy calling : all else that refuses to be rectified, leave to Him who is stronger and wiser than thou, to the good God in Heaven who can rule churches, country, people, princes, house, estate, wife and children better than thou."

Ver. 16. The character of earthly things being such as is described in verses 12 and 15, that wisdom which busies itself with the understanding of their nature, cannot, as the author now shows, have the significance of the highest good, it cannot truly satisfy the soul, but must rather increase its pains. Koheleth says here that in respect of wisdom he surpassed all who came before him in Jerusalem. Gousset, Rambach, and others explain these words to be—"all the great in Jerusalem," of whom there were many in the days of Solomon and David. But it is clear from chap. ii. 7, that kings only are referred to. Jerusalem was the seat of a very ancient monarchy, a noble representative of which meets us even in the time of the Patriarchs. The title borne by these kings, namely, King or Lord of Righteousness, Melchizedek, Adonizedek, leads to the conclusion that they were animated by higher purposes and aims than many around them. Hitzig is of opinion that, "if the author does allude to the old heathen kings, there is something incongruous in it, and in this turn given to the thought, a later writer, one moreover not particularly well versed in history, (!) seems to betray himself, to whose mind was present the series of kings who had reigned since Solomon." But if we attentively examine the passages in the "Books of the Kings," on which the author takes his stand, this comparison with heathen kings will no longer be found incongruous. In 1 Kings iii. 12, the Lord says to Solomon, "Lo! I give thee a wise and an understanding heart, so that there was none like thee before thee, neither after thee shall any arise like unto thee." Here the prerogative of wisdom is ascribed to Solomon, not merely amongst the kings of Israel, as Clericus and others conceived, but amongst kings in general. Examples occurring in heathen countries are also included in the comparison. More distinctly still is the same thing seen from 1 Kings iv. 29, "and God gave Solomon wisdom and understanding, exceeding much, and largeness of heart, even as the sand that is on the sea-shore:" ver. 30, "and Solomon's wisdom excelled all the wisdom of the children of the East country, and all the wisdom of Egypt:" ver. 31,

" and he became wiser than all men: and his fame was in all the nations round about :" ver. 34, " and there came of all people to hear the wisdom of Solomon, from all kings of the earth which had heard of his wisdom." Then again in chap. x. 23-24, "So king Solomon exceeded all the kings of the earth for riches and wisdom ; and all the earth sought the face of Solomon, to hear his wisdom which God had put in his heart." That there was in Solomon's wisdom an element, by virtue of which it might justly be compared with analogous phenomena of the heathen world, is plain even from the visit of the Queen of Sheba, as well as from the sphere within which, as we learn from 1 Kings iv. 33, it moved. His thoughts ran on natural things, on that which was under the sun. Koheleth's comparison of himself with heathen kings in regard to wisdom is an important item in the determination of the true idea of this wisdom : whence also we shall more clearly understand both the depreciatory judgment he pronounces upon it and the presupposition with which he starts, viz., that the people of God were at that time destitute of the wisdom. His intention was thus to comfort them on account of their loss, and to teach them not to set too high a value on the possession. A wisdom in respect of which it may be said that Solomon only had *more* than heathen kings could not be the wisdom which is from above, which had established its seat in the midst of the covenanted people, and the possession of which was inseparable from their existence: it could not be the wisdom which coincides with true piety, which affords true knowledge of God, and which in His light enables us to understand man and earthly things. No ! a wisdom which can bear such a comparison must be earthly, of this world. With this agrees what is said in verse 13 respecting the sphere of this wisdom. Its efforts are only directed to search out and fathom what takes place under heaven : the wisdom which cometh from above strives, above all things, to penetrate into the depths of the Godhead. That the wisdom of Solomon does not coincide with that which is described in James i. 5, that on the contrary it has a common basis with the wisdom of the heathens, being only distinguished therefrom by the illumination which it receives from the light of revelation and of the Spirit of God, might be judged even from 1 Kings iii. 12. When it is in that place said,—"Lo! I give thee a wise and understanding heart, so that there was none like thee before thee, neither after thee shall any arise like unto thee,"—there is certainly no intention of setting Solomon above Moses, in contradiction to Numbers xii. and Deuteronomy xxxiv., nor even above David : the words rather imply that his wisdom was considered as essentially different from that possessed by men of God properly so called, and not to be brought into comparison with it.* In this wisdom, so brilliant and splendid as even to attract the attention of Gentiles, but which, according to what follows, stood on a like level with the possession and enjoyment of this world's goods, Solomon held the first place. The present, so poor in every respect, had no alternative but to look up to him. But that that true wisdom which even children may possess, yet remained, is manifoldly and expressly asserted afterwards (compare chap. vii. 12, 13, 20, 21, x. 14-18).

Ver. 17. Having attained to the highest pinnacle of wisdom, and having by its aid searched into earthly things, Solomon now proceeds to investigate the instrument itself employed in his researches, and arrives here at a humiliating result. The course pursued by Solomon, of inquiring into folly along with wisdom has its ground in the fact that his aim was to determine the worth of wisdom in relation to folly. Besides, as a general truth, contraries explain each other, as Hieronymus says *contrariis contraria intelliguntur :*† for which reason also at the commencement of the Book of Proverbs, wisdom and folly are constantly contrasted with each other.

---

* Seb. Schmidt remarks on this passage : Mosis enim Prophetarum et Apostolorum potior sapientia erat potius illuminatio immediata aut revelatio, quam sapientia cordis. Intelligitur sapientia acuti ingenii, omnia cum studio penetrantis quæ non sunt immediatæ revelationis, sed scrutaminis et judicii, eaque infusa fuit ratione perfectionis, non initii. A natural gift constitutes the basis, an inclination towards speculative inquiries which examines and seeks to penetrate into the nature of things.

† Following the Septuagint, Luther translates : "Wisdom and folly and *prudence.*" But that שִׂכְלוּת in this place is only another mode of writing סִכְלוּת "Folly," is so clearly evident from the parallel passages chap. ii. 12, vii. 25, x. 13, that one cannot conceive how it has been possible for Stier to keep to the translation "prudence."

Ver. 18. According to what has hitherto been advanced, the reason of the pain and discomfort which result from the possession of wisdom must be found in the fact that it lays bare the vanity of earthly things. When wisdom is looked upon as a means to higher ends, this is an advantage. To recognise the true character of earthly things can be wholesome only when we are thereby driven to lay hold on the one real Being, on God, who is an everlasting refuge in the midst of the vanities of earth. It shows, however, that wisdom, considered in itself, in isolation from other and higher things, is but a comfortless sort of good. Luther saw the true reason of the discomfort and pain. His words are, " Great people who have a great understanding, and see further than others, who have had much experience, cannot help frequently being angry with themselves and thinking in great disgust, how wicked and scandalous is the course of things in this world ! But whence does it arise that such persons are so impatient, and become so angry ? The answer is : where there is much understanding and wisdom, there is much discontent ! For such people see and think much, and consequently find in the world all manner of crimes, wickednesses, falseness, unfairness, which others never see nor dream of : and that gives pain. Others who do not see so far, nor think so much, do not take it to heart : therefore also it causes them little trouble or pain. Whosoever, then, desires to be a good Christian and to lead a godly life, let him learn to endure patiently, and commit the ordering of things to God, let him learn to pray heartily the petition taught us by Christ, ' thy will be done ;' otherwise he will only plague himself in vain, make his own life hateful to himself, and lose besides time and everything."‡ We must interpret—

‡ Many commentators have missed the right sense through giving themselves up to mere guesses. So, for example, Hieronymus : Quanto magis quis sapientiam fuerit consequutus, tanto plus indignatur subjacere vitiis et procul esse a virtutibus, quas requirit. (According to verse 13, Wisdom applies itself to the consideration not merely of that which is within, but of all that takes place under heaven). Nisi forte et hoc intelligendum, quod sapiens vir doleat tam in abdito et profundo latere sapientiam, nec ita se præbere mentibus ut lumen visui ; sed per tormenta quædam et intolerabilem laborem, jugi meditatione et studio provenire. Hitzig has " much discontent or chagrin;" namely, during the search for truth which is in many ways wearisome and often fruitless.

Whoso increases knowledge increases sorrow. יוֹסִיף is, as a participial form, without example. In Isaiah xxix. 14, xxxviii. 5, also it is *Fut. Hiphil.*

CHAPTER II.

From wisdom Koheleth turns to the pursuit of mirth, in order to see whether the true good is to be found in it, but here again he finds not what he sought, he finds nothing to still the cravings of his heart (ver. 1 and 2). After this preliminary survey there follows the fuller exposition. Taking the coarsest first, Koheleth tries what wine drinking will do, (ver. 3). Then he seeks pleasure in great works and improvements (verses 4-6), in rich possessions, brilliant connections, and in the manifold enjoyments of love (verses 7-8) at the same time not renouncing wisdom, but keeping it as his companion in all his undertakings, and letting it be their very life and soul, (ver. 9). He follows after mirth with all eagerness, intending thus to obtain a recompense for the great trouble caused him by the procuring of the material of pleasure (ver. 10). On a closer examination, however, this pleasure also evades his grasp, and so all his pains and efforts appear to him vain, (ver. 11). The one thought alone that all that which he has effected by his wisdom will be inherited, to judge from the usual course of things in this world, by an evil successor, mixes gall with the satisfaction with which he regards his creations, (ver. 12). Reflecting on the matter more carefully he sees that wisdom has undoubtedly a considerable advantage over folly (verses 13-14 *a*); but still this advantage is not of such a nature that a man can sincerely rejoice in it and its creations, that he can seek the happiness of his life in it and devote himself with all zeal to the production of such works. Wisdom is unable to protect us against many misfortunes, (verses 14 *b*-15). The same forgetfulness covers the wise man no less than the fool in the future; and how sadly does death, to which the wise man is subject no less than the fool, destroy all joy in wisdom and its creations, (ver. 16-17). And, to recur to that which was anticipatorily mentioned in ver. 12, the thought of a wicked suc-

cessor stifles completely the satisfaction felt in the works
effected at the cost of so much labour and in the wisdom
therein manifested (verses 18-21). Mirth being spoiled by
such considerations, there remain behind only the manifold
pains and disquiet occasioned to man by the production of
that wherein he was to rejoice (verses 22-23). Surely, then
it is better for man to renounce such a chase and hunt, to
live for the present moment, and to take the enjoyments
which offer themselves unsought. And yet such a cheerful
enjoyment of the gifts of God is not in a man's own power:
it comes from God, who must Himself make our hearts capable
of enjoyment, and deliver us from the bonds of avarice (verses
24-26).

The moral of all this is—look not back with painful longings to Solomon and his age, though so brilliant and though
apparently so rich in pleasures. More closely considered its
wealth of mirth was vanity. That unseen source of joy, from
which Solomon actually drew whatever of pleasure he realized,
is still open to you notwithstanding the needy position in
which you find yourselves. Guard then against shutting
yourselves out from it by a base and contemptible covetousness.

Ver. 1. *I said in mine heart, Go to now, I will prove thee
with mirth and look upon good, and behold, this also is vanity.*
Ver. 2. *To laughter I said, Thou art mad; and to mirth,
What doeth it?* Ver. 3. *I sought in mine heart to nourish
my flesh with wine; and my heart prosecuted wisdom, and I
purposed to lay hold on folly, till I might see what is good
for the children of men, what they should do under heaven,
the number of the days of their life.* Ver. 4. *I made me
great works; I builded me houses; I planted me vineyards.*
Ver. 5. *I made me gardens and orchards, and I planted trees
in them of all kind of fruits.* Ver. 6. *I made me pools of
water, to water therewith the wood that bringeth forth trees.*
Ver. 7. *I bought servants and maidens, and servants were
born to me in my house: also I obtained cattle and sheep in
multitude, more than all that were in Jerusalem before me.*
Ver. 8. *I gathered me also silver and gold, and a treasure of
kings and the provinces: I gat me men-singers and women-
singers, and the delights of the children of men, plenty of all*

sorts. Ver. 9. *And I became great, and increased more than all that were before me in Jerusalem, and my wisdom remained to me.* Ver. 10. *And whatsoever mine eyes desired I kept not from them, I withheld not my heart from any joy; for my heart rejoiced in all my labour; and this was my portion of all my labour.* Ver. 11. *And I looked on all the works that my hands had wrought, and on the labour with which I had laboured to produce ; and, behold, all was vanity and empty effort, and is no profit under the sun.* Ver. 12. *And I turned myself to behold wisdom and madness and folly. For what* (will) *the man* (do) *that shall come after the king ? That which they have already done.* Ver. 13. *And I sa:" that wisdom has an excellency over folly, like the excellency of light over darkness.* Ver. 14. *The wise man has his eyes in his head ; but the fool walketh in darkness. But nevertheless I know that one event happeneth to them all.* Ver. 15. *Then said I in my heart, as it happeneth to the fool so also can it happen even to me, and why then have I been so very wise ? And I said in my heart, that this also is vanity.* Ver. 16. *For there is no remembrance of the wise more than of the fool for ever, seeing that in the days to come all is forgotten; and how dieth the wise man with the fool ?* Ver. 17. *And I hated life, for evil appeared to me the history which takes place under the sun ; for all is vanity and empty effort.* Ver. 18. *And I hated all my labour which I had laboured under the sun, because I should leave it to the man that shall be after me.* Ver. 19. *And who knoweth whether he shall be a wise man or a fool ? Yet shall he have rule over all my labour wherein I have laboured, and wherein I have been wise under the sun : this also is vanity.* Ver. 20. *And I turned myself to cause my heart to despair of all the labour wherein I laboured under the sun.* Ver. 21. *For there is a man whose labour is in wisdom and in knowledge and in ability, and yet to a man that hath not laboured therein, must he give it for his portion ; this also is vanity and a great evil.* Ver. 22. *For what hath man of all his labour and of the striving of his heart, wherein he hath laboured under the sun ?* Ver. 23. *For all his days are sorrows, and discontent is his plague ; yea, his heart taketh not rest in the night. This also is vanity.* Ver. 24. *Is it*

not good for man that he eat and drink and make his soul
see good in his labour ?   I saw that this also cometh from
the hand of God. Ver. 25. *For who eateth and who has-*
teneth except me ? Ver. 26. *For to the man that is good before*
Him giveth He wisdom and knowledge and joy ; and to the
sinner He giveth travail to gather and heap up, that he
may give it to him that is good before God : this also is
vanity and empty effort.

Ver. 1-2. In these two verses the new experiment and its
results are described in broad outline : in the third and following verses these summary hints are carried out in detail.
Not only for his wisdom was Solomon renowned, but also for
his possessions and pleasures ; and in this latter respect also
was his age an object of devouring yearnings to the people of
God in their day of tribulation and oppression.   Therefore
does the author introduce Solomon with the confession on
his lips that behind even that glory vanity lay hid.   When
the writer says, " I spake," the " I " is emphatic : " *I* spake."
Some will have it that אני frequently occurs in this book along
with the first person of the verb superfluously even where
no emphasis whatever is intended, as for example in chap. i.
16, ii. 11, 14, 18, iii. 17.   In such cases, however, אני is by no
means pleonastically used.   It calls attention to the importance
of the person who is speaking, who is declaring his experiences.
An address to the soul similar to the one here may be found in
Psalm xvi. 2.   The heart is to be proved, whether perchance
it feels itself contented and fully satisfied by this new object
presented to it.   The *mirth* is that which springs from possessions and pleasures.   The words which follow immediately upon,
and are directly connected with, these, namely, *look upon good,*
(ראה signifying with ב " look upon, to feed oneself upon,") show
that verses 1 and 2 do not relate merely to a life of low and
coarse gratification, but that they have a more comprehensive application.   The *laughter* mentioned in ver. 2 is that
which accompanies common sensual gratification : *mirth* or
joy is not identical with laughter, but has a more comprehensive signification, as is clear from ver. 10.   Extravagant
mirth, the intoxication of the senses, at once shows itself to
be vanity (ver. 3).   But even the joy taken in earthly projects and possessions does not stand the test.   Ver. 11 forms

the comment to the question, " What doeth it ?" of ver. 2.
Geier says : " Why dost thou thus befool men and lead them
basely away from the true good ?" We should involve Koheleth in self-contradiction were we to ascribe to him here
the thought, that all joy is vain and despicable. He rather
takes special pains to urge men to take pleasure in their life,
to live for the present moment, and thankfully to enjoy whatever it offers. That which he here condemns is mirth considered as the highest good, as the end of life, and the too
great eagerness displayed in its pursuit. Luther has seized
exactly the right point of view: " that this is true, experience
tells us. For many a man arranges all his affairs and puts
forth much trouble and labour, that he may ensure to himself quiet and peace in his old age : and yet God orders it
otherwise, and involves him in things which give him his first
true taste of disquietude. Many an one seeks his pleasure in
lust and debauchery, and from that hour onwards his life is
embittered. Therefore, if God does not give us joy and pleasure, but we seek to contrive and create them for ourselves,
nothing comes of it ; and on the contrary, as Solomon says,
all is vanity and vexation of spirit. We can do nothing
better then than willingly to accept and put up with that
which God does to us and for us, and to accustom our heart
to be satisfied and contented with that which God each moment sends us, be it good or evil, sorrow or joy. If a wife is
given thee, regard it as a gift of God, thank Him, and be
cheerful and contented. But if thou settest thyself to go
beyond this, and to add thereto thy human devices, thinking
to secure only gratifications and joys, honeymoons, and merry-
makings, thou wilt make for thyself sadness and sorrow of
heart. For this reason, should we accustom ourselves to resting satisfied with what God does and gives, with what He
wills and intends, and not with what we will and intend.
Solomon's intention, then, is not to induce all the world to
turn hermits and monks, to cast away all joy, mirth, pastime,
all rest, comfort, amusement : what he means to say is, that
thoughts and proposals are nothing when we think by their
help to make to ourselves rest and peace, recreation and good
courage. The truest joy and merriment is that which we do
not expressly seek (for when we plan beforehand a little

hindrance may frustrate the whole), but which God sends us
at the moment." In verses 1 and 2 we have undoubtedly
the germ of the parable in Luke xii. 16-21. This may be
seen from the similarity of the address to the soul which
there occurs ; from the words ἔχεις πολλὰ ἀγαθά there as compared with the expression, "Look upon good," here; from
the word εὐφραίνου compared with, "I will prove thee with
mirth," ἄφρον corresponding to מהלל; and finally from the words
ἃ δὲ ἡτοίμασας τίνι ἔσται (ver. 20) as compared with the 12th
verse of this chapter—"For what will the man do that shall
come after the king?" (compare ver. 19.)

Ver. 3. First of all mirth in its coarsest form, intoxication
of the senses. "I sought in my heart to indulge my flesh
with wine." That חור has the meaning "to prove, to assay,
to try," is certified by Numbers xiii., where the word is repeatedly used of the spies, and by ver. 18, where its force is
given in the paraphrase—"and see the land, what it is, and
the people that dwelleth therein, whether they be strong
or weak, few or many." This sense of the word suits all
the passages in which it occurs, and especially Numbers
xv. 39—"that ye may look upon it and remember all the
commandments of the Lord and do them ; and ye shall
not follow your eyes and your heart *proving :*" that is, ye
shall institute no moral experiments, following the desires
of your own heart and the lusts of your eyes. Such experiments will as certainly be followed by sad and painful results as it is a necessity that God's vengeance should visit
those who turn aside from the way of his commands. The
wise Solomon did not give himself to intoxication of the
senses in the way of a mere voluptuary ; for this latter cannot
help doing what he does, and is a slave of his passions and
desires : but in the manner of an inquirer who, standing on an
eminence above sensual enjoyments wishes to know by personal trial, what can be obtained from them, so as to be able,
in virtue of his own experience, to instruct others how far a
true good is or is not to be found therein. In regard to בשר
משך "to indulge, to cherish the body," consult Gesenius' Thesaurus. The remaining words of the verse carry out further
the hint contained in the phrase "I assayed ;" to the effect
that Solomon did not surrender himself *à corps perdu* to

coarse sensual gratifications, in opposition to what is said of
the duty of kings in Proverbs xxxi. 4-5, "It is not for kings,
O Lemuel, it is not for kings to drink wine, nor for princes
strong drink, lest they drink and forget the law, and pervert
the judgment of any of the afflicted." *And my heart held to
wisdom, i.e.,* it took wisdom along with it into its sensual
enjoyments, retained it by its side, differing thus from mere
voluptuaries, who first bid farewell to wisdom, and then surrender themselves to sensual pleasures. נהג in conjunction
with ב occurs only in the signification "to lead, to convey anything;" see Isaiah xi. 6, and 1 Chronicles xiii. 7, where בעגלה
נהג corresponds to נהג עגלה in 2 Samuel vi. 3. Ewald's explanation, "whilst my heart was satiated with wisdom," is
contrary to usage, as well as to verses 12 ff. Nor is anything contrary to the words, "I will prove thee" of ver 1, or
to those of this verse, "I assayed," according to which it was
a simple experiment that he was concerned with, intended
to be said, which might cast a doubt on Solomon : for Solomon is introduced to notice here, not in his character of an
historical personage, with which the writer has nothing to do ;
but as the ideal of Israelitish wisdom. "And (this took place,
or I did thus, in order) to lay hold on folly," which is the
antithesis to wisdom. He tried whether the true happiness
of life was to be found in sensual enjoyments, in order that,
supposing the contrary to be the case, he might, from his
own experience, know folly to be folly, and learn to abhor it
from the bottom of his heart. "Till I might see what is
good for the children of men, what they shall do the number
of the days of their life." By reason of the shortness of
human existence, which passes very soon irrecoverably away,
it is a thing of all the more importance to come early to
clear ideas in regard to the end of life and the true good.
To live recklessly is the greater folly, seeing that the life of
man does but last some seventy years, or at the best eighty
years. The point of view here taken is the right one also for
all that follows. At the commencement of his experiment,
which begins with wine and ends with women, the writer
says, "and my heart held to wisdom," and corresponding to
these words we find it said at the close, "my wisdom remained with me" (ver. 9). Everything is set before us from

the point of view of an experiment. That coarse sensual enjoyment afforded no satisfactory result; that on the contrary it manifested itself to be folly—about this not a word is wasted. There was the less need to say anything expressly, inasmuch as a general judgment had been pronounced in ver. 2, which left no doubt as to the result of such a trial.

Verses 4-8. I made me great works, I built me houses, planted me vineyards, &c. In 1 John ii. 16 it is said, "all that is in the world, the lust of the flesh, and the lust of the eyes, and the pride of life, is not of the Father but of the world;" on which Bengel remarks, "Concupiscentia carnis dicit ea, quibus pascuntur sensus, qui appellantur fruitivi, gustus et tactus. Concupiscentia oculorum ea quibus tenentur sensus investigativi, oculus s. visus, auditus et olfactus. ἀλαζονεία est arrogans pompa, cum quis nimium sibi aut verbis aut factis assumit—ut homo velit quam plurimus esse in victu, cultu, apparatu supellectile, ædificiis, prædiis, famulitio, clientibus jumentis, muneribus." From the lust of the flesh Solomon now passes to the lust of the eye and to that pride of life which delights in, and understands how to procure for itself, outward splendour. All the modes of activity here enumerated are unable to satisfy the heart, and therefore should we be careful not to pursue them further than is necessary and indispensable—a thing which all those do who seek therein a happiness they can never confer. If we are convinced that a man may possess all these things, and yet be at the same time the most miserable of beings, we shall not occupy ourselves with them further than our rank and position in life demand. That the temple is not included amongst the "houses" is evident, not only from the word לֹו "for himself," "I built houses for myself:" but also from the tone of the entire enumeration, which introduces only such things as had Solomon for their central point. In ver. 7 Solomon is represented as saying—"also I obtained cattle and sheep in multitude, more than all who were in Jerusalem before me." In this some have wrongly supposed that they had discovered "a blunder of the later author," in relation to whom there had been of course many kings in Jerusalem. Amongst the royal predecessors of Solomon in Jerusalem were reckoned not only David and Saul but also the Jebusite kings

up to Melchizedeck. "I gathered me also silver and gold
and a treasure of kings and the provinces." סגלה does not
signify "property in general," but "something of special value
and highly estimated," strictly, "that which men lay by, lay
on one side, treasure :" see *Christology*, iii. p. 635. The
author is speaking here of a treasure of kings and provinces,
in reference to the aforementioned "silver and gold." The
conjunction therewith is the more appropriate, inasmuch as
the gold and silver came from the kings and the provinces.
מלכים stands without article in order to draw attention to the
significance of "a treasure of *kings :*" "*the* provinces" on the
other hand are the definite and well-known ones of Solomon's
kingdom. Corresponding to the kings and provinces here we
find in the allegorical descriptions of Proverbs xxxi. 29, "the
daughters," *i.e.*, the dependent nations, "many daughters bring
wealth." "The kings" are those of the vanquished heathen
countries : compare 1 Kings iv. 21, "And Solomon reigned
over all kingdoms from the river unto the land of the
Philistines, and unto the border of Egypt : they brought presents and served Solomon all the days of his life. Ver. 24.
He had dominion over the whole land beyond the river from
Thipsah and Gaza, over all kings beyond the river." There is
no sufficient reason for reckoning amongst the kings the
officers who, according to chap. iv. 7 ff., were appointed by
Solomon over the twelve provinces into which the original
Israelitish territory was divided, although some amongst
them were the sons-in-law of the king. And quite as little
ground is there for Hitzig's supposition, that by "the provinces" we are to understand those twelve original districts.
The provinces are plainly not to be taken separately from the
kings : the word *gather*, moreover, is not appropriate as
applied to the original territory of the Israelites : and the
twelve tribes did not bring silver and gold, but Solomon drew
from them only the natural productions of the natural districts. The usual explanation of the words is, "a treasure
such as kings have, and such as provinces supply." But there
is no reason for resorting to this more remote view ; besides
that in 1 Chronicles xxix. 3, the word in the *Stat. const.* which
is conjoined with סגלה designates that in which the treasure
consists ; "a treasure of silver and gold." *I gat me men-*

singers and women-singers, and the delights of the children of men, plenty of all sorts. תענוג " caresses " is used only of sexual love. שדה signifies in Arabic, *robur, vehementia.* From the same root is derived the Hebrew word שדי " the almighty." The adjoined plural marks the augmented force of the abstract conception : " multitude and great multitude." According to 1 Kings xi. 3, Solomon had seven hundred princesses to wife, and three hundred concubines. Those who commit the mistake of not finding in the word תענג a reference to Solomon's love of women—a thing which it was quite impossible to pass over in silence in an enumeration of all the things with which he surrounded his own person, and which related peculiarly to himself, have sought in a great variety of ways to import into the words שדה ושדות a reference to Solomon's women. J. D. Michaelis, in justification of his arbitrary explanation, says quite openly, " in this choice of meanings I have not looked so much to philological grounds, as to the consideration that it appears almost incredible that Solomon should have forgotten women in the enumeration of his sensual pleasures." If we understand the words of Solomon's wives, the conjunction of the singular and plural will appear strange " wife and wives." That the wives are here mentioned, because they swelled by their number the splendour of Solomon's court, and set him for whom such things were prepared in a brilliant light, is plain from the verse immediately following, which lays stress on the *greatness* of the king who gathered around himself all these resources.

Ver. 9. And I became great, and greater than all those that were before me in Jerusalem, and my wisdom remained to me: Vulgate, perseveravit mecum. עמד is used also in Chap. viii. 3, in the same meaning of " remain, continue." Inasmuch as wisdom, that noblest of all possessions, remained to the king along with these other possessions, we should with the greater confidence expect him to have a contented and satisfied heart. The words which occur in verse 3, at the beginning of the description—" and my heart prosecuted wisdom"—correspond to those which we find here, " and (אף the emphatic " and" indicates that an important addition is being made) wisdom remained to me." Ewald's explanation is, " served me;" Elster's is, " stood to me," which is as much as to

say "it supported, aided me," in gaining riches and renown.
But עמד with ל cannot have that meaning.

Ver. 10. It cost Solomon labour, yea great labour (ver. 23)
to raise himself to a position where he should be the central
point of all.   For this trouble, however, he felt himself at first
repaid by the joy which he experienced at the thought that
all had been effected by his own wisdom, belonged to him and
contributed to his glory.   But even of this satisfaction he was
speedily deprived.   It only lasted so long as he did not go to
the very bottom of the thing.   When the joy vanished there
remained only the labour behind, and this was felt to be
simple torture so soon as it distinctly showed itself to be
fruitless.—According to verse 11 Solomon looked upon all his
works and on all the labour he had spent on them, and "behold all was vanity."   The expression, " and behold," points
to the unexpectedness and startling nature of the fact.   The
grounds of the general judgment here pronounced are afterwards detailed.   Those who mistake this have recourse to
conjectures.   Thus Hitzig is of opinion that "the work had
afforded him some gratification: but at last he had accomplished all and was unable to devise any further projects.   So
then the work came to an end, and with it naturally the enjoyment which it had afforded."   Similarly Elster, who says:
"the vanity of wearying ourselves in the pursuit of pleasure
consists in this, that when the enjoyment is spent there is
only the feeling of emptiness left behind."   But these are the
thoughts of the commentators themselves, of which there is no
trace in the text.   Besides, the matter in hand would not be
served by any experience that might be ascribed to a hypo-
chondriacal source : plain and palpable reasons are required,
and such are advanced in the succeeding part of the book,
from which the present verse may not be separated.   " And
there is no profit under the sun."   If Solomon, with all his
wisdom and with all the means at his disposal secured no
profit, gained no real good, there surely must be none to be
acquired, (Stier renders "profit," by "nothing abiding;" but
the correctness of the common interpretation is guaranteed by
verse 13 : the Hebrew word only occurs in this book, and it
always signifies "profit, advantage.")   The existence of true
good is by no means denied.   The author treats here only of

such possessions as have their origin under the sun, and which man can acquire by his own efforts. The positive assertion correspondent to the negative one of the text is found in James i. 17—πᾶσα δόσις, ἀγαθή καί πᾶν δώρημα τέλειον ἄνωθέν ἐστι καταβαῖνον ἀπό τοῦ πατρὸς τῶν φώτων

In verse 12 the catchword פָּנִיתִי " I turned myself," used in ver. 11 is again adopted, and for the purpose of indicating that what was there only hinted at will here be fully unfolded. Koheleth turns himself to behold wisdom and madness and folly, i. e. to consider them in their relation to each other, and to estimate their relative worth. Wisdom, which Solomon did not lay aside when he gave his life a new direction, but kept as his companion therein (ver. 9) applying it now to practical, as at an earlier period he had applied it to speculative matters, is here brought forward as the very soul of his undertakings. Consequently, if the inquiry into the relation between wisdom and folly show the result that wisdom is nothing, the works of which wisdom is the soul must also be nothing. At this place Hitzig makes the erroneous remark, that " after having discovered (ver. 11) that his works are nought, he finds out here that the wisdom which he has expended on them is also nought." Wisdom and the works rather constitute one whole, interpenetrating each other :— wisdom is in the works as their animating principle. Koheleth next sets before us that which gave rise to his reflections on the relation between wisdom and folly, and which caused his perplexity as to the value of the former and of the works effected by its means. This was the simple fact that his successor would probably be a man of worthless character, who would disgracefully destroy what he had accomplished by his wisdom and by his great labours. Rehoboam! that is the thought which first presses itself on his mind. Then at verse 13 begins that comprehensive discussion which in verses 18 and 19 comes back again to the circumstance here anticipatorily mentioned. The presumptive folly of his successor ap‧ pears here to constitute the motive to the investigation : in verses 18 and 19, which form a sort of commentary to the somewhat enigmatical words before us, this folly seems to be an important feature in the inquiry itself. By the words‧— " For what is the man ?" we may understand either—" what

is he? what is it with him? or, what will he do?" supplementing the meaning from what follows: "Who will come
after the King," *i. e.* after me, the King, or who will
succeed me in my kingdom? The miserable answer to the
question, "what will my successor do?" is—He will do "what
they have already done." From the fact that folly is the
custom of the world, arises the probability that his successor
also will be foolish, so that Solomon with all his wisdom will
appear to have laboured in vain, and to have spent his strength
for nothing and vanity (Isaiah xlix. 4.) Ewald's explanation,
namely, "what, *i. e.*, of what kind is the man, who will succeed the king, with him, *i. e.*, as compared with him whom
one has made before?" is characterised by great harshness.
The simple word *with* can never stand for *compared with :*
besides, Solomon was not made king by men. The inquiry
into the relation between wisdom and folly, together with the
results of each, to which Koheleth is moved by the thought of
his evil successor which presses itself upon him, leads in the
first instance to the conclusion that wisdom has an unquestion-
able advantage over folly, (verses 13, 14 a.) Wisdom is like
light, which preserves the man that walks in it from many
dangers to which the darkness exposes him: or again, the
wise man is like one who sees, and who can therefore avail
himself of many advantages and avoid many inconveniences.[*]
But still the advantage is not an unmixed, an absolute one :—
"but nevertheless I know that one event happeneth to them
all," (14 b.,) the wise man no less than the fool may break a
leg, and is not less than others exposed to all possible accidents. If this be so, the question naturally arises—" why
have I been then so very wise?" If wisdom with its productions has only a relative value, if it has no power to guard its
possessor against even the very worst that can happen, it follows surely that a man should not occupy himself too deeply
with it, that he should not make it and its creations the real
aim of his life ; it follows also, lastly, that an age in which
wisdom flourishes less strongly, need not on that account grieve

---

[*] Seb. Schmidt.—instituitur comparatio sapientis cum homine, cui oculi non
ex capite eruti sunt, sed sani et salvi adsunt, qui proinde latissime potest cir-
cumspicere, periculosa fugere, ad proficua accedere, et in omnibus provide ac
circumspecte agere.

over much. *And I said in my heart that this also is vanity*
—this, the study of human wisdom, in respect of which the
age of Solomon far surpassed later ages. The meaning found
by Elster in these words, viz., "this arrangement of life itself,
according to which the wise man experiences the same fortune
as the fool, is characterised as vanity," does not suit the connection. Koheleth has no wish to blame the divine government of the world, his aim is to exhibit the vanity of human
efforts and human possessions. The word "for," which follows,
shows that it is wisdom which he considers to be vanity. If
then even this noblest of earthly possessions is vain, how
urgently should we feel ourselves summoned to unite ourselves
the more closely and inwardly to God: compare Proverbs iii.
5,—"Trust in the Lord with all thine heart, and lean not
unto thine own understanding." Luther remarks—"therefore
is it better to commit the supreme government of all things
to the King who has made us. Let every man discharge with
all diligence the duties of his office, let him accomplish whatever God gives him at the present moment to do: if all does
not go on as he expected let him leave it to God. What God
gives let him accept: if God hinders thee in any wise, take
that also for a good. Whatever we can do we are called upon
to do: what we cannot effect we must let alone: the stone
which thou canst not lift thou must needs let lie." The affirmation that "this also is vanity," in proof of which it is
alleged in ver. 15, to be the fact, that wisdom affords no protection against the manifold misfortunes of life, receives a new
and doubly strong confirmation in ver. 16, from the forgetfulness, which in the future covers alike the wise man with his
works, and the fool, and from the necessity by which both
alike are bound to submit to death. If wisdom is incompe-
tent to protect us against any of these troubles it surely should
not be the object of such ardent longings. We ought rather
to leave it and the pursuit thereof to Solomon and his age, and
seek elsewhere the true happiness of life: "Seeing that in the
days to come all is forgotten,"—Vulgate: *futura tempora obli-
vione cuncta pariter operient,*—"and how dieth the wise man
with the fool?" That is the most unworthy and humiliating
thing that can happen to the wise man, to be subjected no less
than the mere fool to the disgraceful necessity of death. The

hatred of life itself, which, as we learn from ver. 17, arises within us when we consider things as they actually are and do not permit ourselves to be deceived by outward show and seeming, is by no means in itself true repentance. A clear proof thereof, is that such feelings are to be found frequently in the heart of the ungodly. They are notwithstanding for the well disposed a powerful motive to return to God. This is however not the precise point of view from which matters are examined here. The aim of all that is advanced is rather to deliver the men of that generation from their devouring yearnings after the glory of the age of Solomon by laying bare its true character before their eyes.

Ver. 18-21. In these verses attention is once more turned to the evil successor who was expected to occupy the throne. The "toil" alluded to in ver. 18 had its roots in that which such an event would bring to pass. "For" (ver. 22,) on the grounds advanced in ver. 21 and previously, inasmuch as I must leave the fruits of my labour to an unworthy successor, since furthermore accidents befal alike the wise man and the fool, since the wise man is no less mortal than the fool, and the remembrance of both alike passes away, the question presses itself on the mind—"what has *man*?" This is as much as to say, "man has nothing." On this view the word כִּי, at the commencement of ver. 23, appears quite appropriate. "Vexation is his torment," (ver. 23,) *i. e.*, he is tormented thereby. From which the practical conclusion is that we ought not to busy ourselves with such distracting and perplexing matters, and that it should be a cause of gladness when our circumstances furnish no occasion and incentive to such a course. In fact it promises too little fruit, nothing is obtained thereby to compensate the expenditure in labour, anxiety and pain.

Ver. 24. Seeing that such is the case with the works men undertake, our wisdom surely is to embark only in such enterprises as are clearly necessary, and in this way to employ the present moment and live for the present moment—a thing which this needy present generation is as able to do as Solomon with all his glory, (ver. 24.) Against taking this ver. as a question—"Is it not good for man?"—it has been objected that in such a case, לֹא would be used instead of אֵין. But the

cognate word אִין is used interrogatively in 1 Samuel xxi. 9.
To simple eating and drinking, the contrast is given in the
wearisome labours some men undergo for the special advantage of their own person, and in order to secure to it the
highest enjoyments life can offer. Labours for the advance-
ment of the kingdom of God belong to an entirely different
region, and form no part whatever of the contrast which is
here mentioned. The words—"let his soul see good" recommend joy in *conjunction with*, as distinguished from joy *at*
our labours. Verses 2 and 3 stand in the way of an epicu-
rean misinterpretation of what is here said in regard to eating
and drinking. No one who has been at all penetrated by the
deep earnestness of the book can for a moment entertain the
thought of such a profane interpretation. The last words of
the ver., namely—"I saw that this also comes from the hand
of God"—draw attention to the consideration that even such
eating and drinking, such cheerful enjoyment of the gifts of
God, are not in the power of men by themselves, but must
come from above, like every other good gift—*that is in fact
also a gift of God.* How far this is so ver. 26 teaches us.
The foe of such joy, avarice, which was one of the principal
diseases of that age,—this foe can only be overcome by God.
God alone can free the soul from his bonds, ver. 25. From
his own experience Koheleth can say that he has richly enjoyed
this gift of God. Between the enjoyment mentioned in ver.
10, and that referred to here, there is this difference, that the
latter may be the portion of the man who has but small means.
That חוּשׁ is used here in its usual, and alone clearly ascertained
signification, "to hasten," is evident from Habakkuk i. 8,
where it occurs in conjunction with "eating," and with the
same meaning as here. In Psalm cxix. 60, "delay" forms the
contrast to "haste." The next following words are a commentary on this verse. The avaricious man does not hasten to eat,
for his eye is looking into the uncertain future, but he delays
therein and stores up his pleasures against another day. מִי
הֵרִין are nowhere else used in the Old Testament in the sense
in which they are employed here; frequently however in the
Talmud and in the writings of the Rabbis. Hitzig translates
—"and who can delight himself except from him?"—and
remarks, "Following the Septuagint, the Syriac, Jerome and

Ewald we read מִמֶּנּוּ. In this form (מִמֶּנִּי) the words are plainly more suitable as a basis for the first part of ver. 24 : whilst the reading מִמֶּנּוּ corresponds admirably to the second half of the same verse." But according to the authenticated reading the words suit the whole verse : "for who has by God's gift." Independently, however, of the unwarranted alteration of the reading, it is against that explanation that חוּשׁ can only mean "to hasten," and not "to delight oneself," or as others would have it "to drink ;" and further that such an expression as "eat from God," can scarcely be employed. The reason of the double future which is here used, is that the matter is still going forward.

Ver. 26. In this verse Koheleth refers back his own individual experience to a general ground. *For to the man who is good before Him giveth He wisdom and knowledge*, that his heart may not cling to the dead mammon, *and*, precisely in this way he receives also, *joy*, in that he enjoys what God has assigned him. To the sinner, on the contrary, God in his righteous judgment *giveth travail to gather and heap up !* That also is vanity and empty effort, even this gathering together; and the circumstances of the time rendered it peculiarly necessary to lay stress on the folly of such a course : the less God bestowed, the more avaricious was it deemed necessary to become. Hitzig thinks it is "the struggle to find happiness in sensual enjoyment enjoined in ver. 24." But that is too farfetched, is moreover wrong and in contradiction with the fundamental idea of the book. A discreet and solid enjoyment of that which God confers is everywhere earnestly recommended. Here we very plainly see that the refrain, "this also is vanity, &c.," by no means involves a complaint against God, but is a cry of warning to men who in the perversity of their hearts seek happiness where God has not willed that it be sought.

CHAPTER III.

In regard to the position and circumstances of the children of Israel to which this book owes its origin and character, the following data may be derived from the chapter now coming

under notice. Israel was *ecclesia pressa :* it was in a state
of persecution, (ver. 15.) It was being purified in the furnace
of affliction (ver. 18.) Wickedness triumphed over righteousness : on Israel lay the yoke of heathen dominion, (ver. 16,
17.) It was for the chosen people a period of death, of the
rooting up of what was planted, of complaint, of silence and
so forth, (ver. 1-8.) In such circumstances they harassed
themselves fruitlessly by their own toilsome and anxious
undertakings, (ver. 9-18.) In view of such a situation the
author proceeds further in his design of conferring weapons of
defence against the attacks of despair. In chapters i. and ii.
he developed the thought, that on earth, the scene of vanity,
men may not seek true happiness, that times which seem most
fortunate and happy are not so different from wretched ones
as a superficial examination might lead us to think, and finally,
that all earthly happiness is but glittering misery. In the
present chapter, Koheleth seeks to comfort his suffering fellow countrymen by directing their thoughts to the all-ruling
providence of God. The theme of his discourse is the words
of Jeremiah x. 23,—"I know, O Lord, that the way of man
is not in himself : it is not in man that walketh to direct his
steps. He labours to impress upon them the truth, that all
prosperity and misfortune comes from God alone," and admonishes them to humble themselves beneath his mighty hand,
that in his own good time he may exalt them. Everything
has its season, and there is a time ordained by God, when every
desire of the faithful shall be satisfied. Here then our duty
is not to be careful and murmuring, and to harass ourselves,
but to surrender and submit ourselves to, and patiently wait
on God, (ver. 1-8.) "Nothing comes of being early and late
at all my works : my care is in vain," (ver. 9, 10.) What
God intends to do man cannot know, and consequently
cannot conveniently order his doings : man is not set to work,
but simply to wait, and meanwhile to take whatever good
falls to his lot unsought, (ver. 11.) Instead therefore of being
anxious and overworking ourselves, we should rather live for
the present moment, cheerfully enjoy the pleasures it puts in
our way, and at the same time do good, so that we may not
hinder the grace of God, (ver. 12.) In conjunction with this,
it is to be remarked, that the capacity of cheerful enjoyment

in life is a gift of God, who alone is able to deliver the heart from cares, (ver. 13.) Our disquietudes and griefs, and self-inflicted pains cannot alter the eternal counsels of God, (ver. 14.) Everything comes just as God foreordained it, and that is a consoling reflection for the persecuted, inasmuch as in his own good time the Lord must again undertake their cause, (ver. 15.) When wickedness has risen to power and rule on the earth, we may cherish the hope that there will be a revelation of God's judgments, (ver. 16-17.) But when God delays his judgments, it is in order that men may be purified and humbled, seeing that in such times of suffering, experience forces on them the conviction that they are as helpless as the beasts of the field, (ver. 18.) Man, who so readily puffs himself up is in one respect on a level with the cattle, in that, no less than they, he is exposed to all kinds of accidents, and must die and return to the dust, (ver. 19-20.) The difference between them, namely, that the spirit of man goes upwards to God, whilst the breath of the beast perishes with the body is one of a very subtle nature, and hard to be discerned in presence of that outward resemblance in their fates which first presses itself on the attention, (ver. 21.) To give once more the summary of the whole argument—seeing the utter uncertainty of the future, man should not trouble himself about it, —"why should I then harass myself and think about that which is to come?"—but enjoy the present, (ver. 22.)

Ver. 1. *To everything there is a season, and a time to every desire under the heaven : Ver. 2. A time to bear and a time to die ; a time to plant and a time to pluck up that which is planted : Ver. 3. A time to kill and a time to heal ; a time to break down and a time to build up. Ver. 4. A time to weep and a time to laugh ; a time to mourn and a time to dance. Ver. 5. A time to cast away stones and a time to gather stones together : a time to embrace and a time to refrain from embracing. Ver. 6 A time to seek and a time to lose ; a time to keep and a time to cast away. Ver. 7. A time to rend and a time to sew ; a time to keep silence and a time to speak : Ver. 8. A time to love and a time to hate ; a time of war and a time of peace. Ver. 9. What profit hath he that produceth in that wherein he laboureth ? Ver. 10. I have seen the travail which God hath given to the sons of men to be exercised in it.* Ver. 11. *He maketh every-thing beautiful in his time, eternity also he hath set in their heart, so that no man can find out the work that God maketh, from the beginning to the end.* Ver. 12. *I know that there is no good in them, but that one rejoice and do good in his life.* Ver. 13. *And also every man that eats and drinks, and sees good in all his labour, that is a gift of God.* Ver. 14. *I know that whatsoever God doeth it shall be for ever: nothing can be put to it and nothing can be taken from it: and God doeth it that they should fear before Him.* Ver. 15. *That which hath been is now; and that which is to be hath already been, and God seeketh the persecuted.* Ver. 16. *And further saw I under the sun; the place of judgment, wickedness is there; the place of righteousness, the wicked is there.* Ver. 17. *I said in mine heart, God shall judge the righteous and the wicked, for there is a time there for every desire and about every work.* Ver. 18. *I said in mine heart, because of the children of men that God may purify them, and in order that they may see that in themselves they are beasts.* Ver. 19. *For accident are the children of men, and accident are the beasts, and one accident befalls them, as the one dies so dieth also the other; yea, they have all one breath, so that man hath no pre-eminence above the beast, for all is vanity.* Ver. 20. *All go unto one place, all are of the dust, and all turn to dust again.* Ver. 21. *Who knoweth the spirit of the children of men, that goeth upward, and the breath of the beast that goeth downward to the earth?* Ver. 22. *And I saw that nothing is better than that a man should rejoice in his own works, for that is his doing, for who shall bring him to see what shall take place after him?*

Ver. 1. To everything there is a season: not one that is based on a blind fate, for that would be but a miserable con-solation, but one that is ordered by a God who is compas-sionate, gracious, long-suffering, of great love and faithfulness, who even in his anger never forgets mercy, who has thoughts of peace towards his people languishing in misery, and who, though he chastises them, never gives them over to the power of death. If things go ill all we have to do is to wait patiently for the hour of redemption, and at the end the people of God must receive that which is best for their por-

tion. Parallel with this are the words of Psalm lxxv. 3,
"For I shall take a set time, then shall I judge uprightly."
This set time is that which God has appointed for the accomplishment of the counsels he has decreed. Compare also
Psalm cii. 14, "Thou shalt arise and have mercy upon Zion,
for the time to favour her, yea the set time is come." To this
time appointed by God we ought to direct our eye in the
midst of our afflictions. This point of time will arrive when
God's visitations of His Church have reached their final termination (Isaiah x. 12). These visitations also have their
season, and whoso knows this, whoso recognizes that in afflictions God's hand lies upon him, cannot surely fail to experience joy and consolation. On this passage are based the
words of John vii. 30, "They sought to take him ; but no
man laid hands on him, because his hour was not yet come."
Gesenius' explanation : "Everything lasts but for a time,
nothing is permanent," is quite incorrect. Ver. 14 is sufficient
to show this. The idea is rather this, that in misfortune we
must learn to wait, inasmuch as man has no power to alter
the times and seasons, and can take to himself nothing which
is not given him from above. "Accept cheerfully, docile
child, what it pleases God to send, and though the winds blow
and are so tempestuous as to threaten everything with destruction around thee, be comforted, for that which befalls thee is
according to the will of God." Those also completely miss
the right meaning of the words who suppose that they contain a direction to men to do whatever they have to do at
the right time.* *And a time for every desire under the*

---

* In opposition to this view, says Rambach—"ex quibus omnibus apparet,
non hic voluisse Salomonem vitæ regulas, de tempestivitate in actionibus omnibus observandas præscribere ut tamen multi censuerunt: si quidem ea hic
enarrantur quæ non dependent ab hominis arbitrio et voluntate, ut nasci, mori,
perdere, etc., unde hic præcepto de canta temporis observantia nullus locus
relinquitur." J. D. Michaelis says : "Unless the proposition, so variously
illustrated in verses 1-8, is to be explained as if it had no connection with what
precedes and follows, and were thrown out at random, it is impossible that it
should be a prescription to do everything at the right time: it must rather be
intended to teach that everything happens and comes at a time definitely appointed, be it prosperity or misfortune. The sense is clear from the following
ninth verse, where Solomon draws from the proposition the conclusion—"What
profit hath he that worketh in that wherein he laboured?" Since God determines everything, a man's happiness will not depend on his own work, but how

heaven. It is usually assumed that חפץ is employed here in the sense of " thing, affair." Elsewhere, however, חפץ is always used to designate "favour, good pleasure." In this book also, as is universally allowed, it occurs several times in this sense (see chap. xii. 1-10, chap. v. 3) ; as also in the contemporaneously written book of Malachi (see chap. i. 10). Consequently if at all practicable this meaning must be retained here, as well as in ver. 17, and chap. v. 7, viii. 6 ; here especially, because if we accept the signification " business," we shall have a mere tautology, for there is no difference whatever between עת and זמן. This clearly ascertained meaning suits the connection also perfectly : חפץ denotes the desire which believers have to see the kingdom of God established. They thought it ought to come immediately, but they will be compelled to wait for the time which has been fixed in the counsels of God. Our wish is not fulfilled when we will, but when God wills. It is enough that it will one day be satisfied. The application of the words, " Every desire," is, of course, limited and defined by the character of the persons to whom the singer speaks. In reality he refers to the wishes of the people of God which longs for the coming of His kingdom. This limitation is absolutely necessary. Applied to the world, both the declaration here and Paul Gerhard's paraphrase of it, given below, would be utterly false.† Luther's remarks on this place are as follows—"This then is to be understood, that everything has its time and every human purpose its brief season : *i. e.,* there is a certain fixed hour for everything. As when kingdoms, lands, and principalities are to arise there is an hour for them ; if they are to fall there is also an hour for that ; for war and tumults there is a season : for peace

he stands with God. At all events, I am not fortunate enough to be able to find any connection between an admonition to do everything at the right time, and the words of the above-mentioned ninth verse."

† " Kommt's nicht heute wie man will
Sey man nur ein wenig still
Ist doch morgen auch ein Tag
Da die Wohlfahrt kommen mag.

Gottes zeit hält ihren Schritt
Wenn die kommt, kommt unsre Bitt,
Und die Freude reichlich mit."

also and quietude there is a season ; and when the time for
these things is come, no wit of man can hinder or prevent it.
There was a set time for the Roman Empire and all great
kingdoms to grow, and no thought of man rendered any help
therein.   Again, when the hour struck which was to see
them decline and fall, no propping and supporting was of any
use.   All this is, therefore, directed against the free will of
man, and against all human purposes and fancies, but especially against the notion that it is in our power to determine
seasons, and hours, and persons, and measures, and place; that
we can settle how the affairs of this world shall go, how its
great potentates shall rise and fall, how joy and sadness,
building up and pulling down, war and peace, shall succeed
and take the place of each other, how they shall begin and end :
it is to impress on us the fact that ere the hour arrives it is
wasted effort for men to think, and their proposals are useless and vain : in fine, we are taught that nothing comes to
pass before the hour fixed for it by God.   His doctrine the
writer confirms by examples from all branches of human experience, and says, "Building has its time and breaking down
has its time," and so forth, from which he judges that all the
counsels, the thoughts, the devices, and the efforts of men are
but as shadows and mock-fighting, unless the thing is already
determined on in Heaven.   Kings, princes, and lords may
take counsel and agree together upon all as they shall think
fit, but whenever the hour strikes for any event whatever, it
takes place and other matters remain standing and hinder
each other ; and although it seems as if the well planned
scheme must now be executed, nothing comes of it, and
nothing can come of it till the predetermined hour has struck,
even if all men on earth were to put forth the most violent
efforts.   God will not suffer the hands of his great clock to
be pointed by the kings and princes and lords of the
earth : He will Himself point them : nor may we take upon
ourselves to inform Him what hour has struck : 'tis He who
will tell us.   Wherefore also Christ said, "mine hour is not
yet come."   And how many stern counsels, nay, how did all
the efforts of the Pharisees and chief men of the Jews remain
fruitless until that hour arrived.   Wherefore also Christ spake
further, "A woman when she is in travail hath sorrow be-

:ause her hour is come." Thus hath the Lord fixed a season
for everything, for being rich and poor, for living and dying.
and for every other phase of human experience. In reference to the words, "and a time to every desire under the
Heaven," Luther remarks: "The Hebrew word Chephetz
signifies that with which one is occupied, that which is the
object of desire, love, purpose. Thus in Psalm i. it is said,
'those who have the desire and determination to keep God's
law.' The writer includes under the term Chephetz everything which men would fain possess, to which their heart in-
clines, after which their yearnings go forth; and he intends
to say here, because thereof they worry and afflict themselves,
every man in his season: princes and lords vex themselves
for great glory, power, reputation, and renown, and so forth;
others for honour, possessions, luxury, and good days, and so
forth. But their thoughts and cares will prove in vain, unless they hit upon the appointed hour: and even though
they may be the very persons who are destined to receive all
these things, still their haste and anticipatory labours are useless until God's gracious season arrives—then all is speedily
effected. Therefore does it behove each of us in our several
positions to do the work and discharge the office entrusted to
him, to commend all his ways to God, to use cheerfully that
which God bestows on him at the present moment, and to
leave the arrangement of the future to His Divine Wisdom.
Whoso is of the mind to act otherwise, and determines *in
despectum Dei* to rush on before the appointed hour, will
reap nothing but misfortune and sorrow of heart for his pains,
and, let him rage and murmur as long as he will, God heeds
him not." To these excellent remarks of Luther's we have
only one exception to take, namely, that, as is the case also
with Melancthon, too little stress is laid on the special reference to the people and kingdom of God. The general thought
here expressed is further discussed in the succeeding seven
verses, each of which touches upon two pairs of subjects.
That the discussion contained in these verses has respect to
the entire Church of God, and not merely to the experiences
of individual believers, though of course bearing an analogous
application to them, is evident at once from the words of
ver. 2, "a time to bear," and of ver. 3, "a time to kill and a

time to heal." Such modes of activity can only be predicated,
and therefore suggest the thought, of a great whole ; and besides, the highly important words in Deuteronomy xxxii. 39.
" See now that I even I am he, and there is no God with me :
I kill and I make alive, I wound and I heal : neither is there
any that can deliver out of my hand," render it easy to conceive that by this great whole is meant the people of God.
That national events are alluded to is implied also in the
words, " Cast away stones, and gather stones together." Further, a guide to the just understanding of the whole is furnished by the concluding verse, the 8th, " A time for war
and a time for peace." The parallel passages moreover involve this reference to the nation ; a view which, according to
the testimony of Jerome, is exceedingly ancient.*

Ver. 2. There is a time to bear and a time to die. The
mistake with respect to the national reference of this passage
led to the adoption of the meaning—" to be born," Vulgate,
nascendi. The infinitive of ילד occurs no fewer than twenty-
four times, and always in the signification of " to bear," never
in that of " to be born." An example of this is Genesis xxv.
24—" and her days were full ללדת to bear," not, " to be born :"
another is found in Isaiah xxvi. 17, " Like as a woman with
child that draweth near the time of her delivery." עת לדת
is " time of bearing, of delivery," in Genesis xxxviii. 27, in
Job xxxix. 2 : Compare also Luke i. 17 ; τῇ δὲ Ἐλισάβετ ἐπλήσθη
ὁ χρόνος τοῦ τεκεῖν αὐτήν. In fact no instance whatever can be
adduced in which the Active Infinitive stands for the Passive.
In Proverbs xii. 7, to which Gesenius appeals, הפך signifies
" they destroy," in xv. 22, הפר signifies " they bring to nought."
The people of God personified as a woman is not unfrequently
said to " travail and bear," when in times of prosperity it grows
and waxes strong, and the number of its members becomes
greater. Thus for example in Isaiah liv. 1, " Sing, O barren,
thou that didst not bear ; break forth into singing and cry
aloud, thou that didst not travail with child, for more are the

---

* Hebræi omne hoc quod de contrarietate temporum scriptum est, usque ad
illum locum in quo ait: tempus belli et tempus pacis, super Israel intelligunt.
Explaining their meaning Jerome says—Tempus fuit generandi et plantandi
Israelem, tempus moriendi et ducendi in captivitatem. Tempus occidendi eos in
Ægypto et tempus de Ægypto liberandi.

children of the desolate than the children of the married wife,
saith the Lord." See also Isaiah lxvi. 7, "Before she travailed,
she brought forth, before her pain came she was delivered of
a manchild :" verse 8, "for as soon as Zion travailed, she
brought forth her sons." If our explanation of the words is
correct, the reference to them which John xvi. 21 unmistake-
ably bears, becomes perfectly clear. There the hour approaches
for the woman who is to bear, and she is the image of the
Church. In the main this is for her a time of gladness. The
momentary pain which forms necessarily a point of transition
therein, is a feature added by the Saviour.—In contradistinc-
tion to *bearing* stands *dying.* Both however are in like manner under the superintendence of holy love. Both come from
our faithful heavenly Father, who has thoughts of peace towards His people, who chastises them even unto death, but
never gives them over into the hands of death. A very
extensive use is made of death in the Old Testament as the
symbol of the severe afflictions of the people of God. "My
God and mine Holy One," cries Israel in Habakkuk i. 1 2,
"let us not die." In Psalm lxxxv. 7, it is said—"Wilt thou
not revive us again, and shall not thy people rejoice in thee ?"
—In Psalm lxxi. 20, "Thou which hast shewed me great and
sore troubles shalt return and quicken us again :"—In Hosea
vi. 2, "After two days he will revive us : in the third day he
will raise us up, that we may live before him." We find the most
detailed employment of death to describe the degeneracy of the
Church and of resurrection to express its restoration in Ezekiel
xxxvii. The chief passage however is Deuteronomy xxxii. 39,
"I kill and I make alive." Compare besides Psalm xlviii. 15,
lxviii. 21, lxxx. 19. Israel was in a state of death when the
author wrote. If it recognised God's hand working in this
death it must prove an easy matter for it to rise to the hope
of that life which the same God had promised in His word,
and which stands ever at the termination of God's dealings
with His people. Moreover death, although in itself bitter,
becomes sweet to the man who is thoroughly penetrated by
the conviction that he is in God's hands, and is drinking from
God's cup. Luther says—"To believers and Christians all
this is very consolatory ; for they know that no tyrant's
sword can kill or destroy them, and that before their hour

comes no creature whatever can harm them. Hence they do not
trouble and worry themselves much about death, but when it
comes they die unto the will of God as he pleases, like lambs
and young children."—*A time to plant and a time to pluck
up that which is planted.* In this respect also the people of
God experience change according to the holy purposes of their
Lord, who sends them at one time the undeserved grace of
prosperity, and at another time, as punishment merited by
their ingratitude, he inflicts upon them the loss of everything
When these troubles befal us we must not murmur nor despair
but humble ourselves under the strong hand, repent and hope
Even to feel the angry hand of God upon us is a sweet comfort. Compare Psalm xliv. 3, where, in regard to the period
under Joshua so rich in signs of grace, it is said : " Thou hast
with thy hand driven out the heathen and planted them ;"
also Psalm lxxx. 9, "thou broughtest a vine out of Egypt:
thou didst cast out the heathen and didst plant it." Compare
further also what is written in Psalm lxxx. 13, 14, in reference to the plucking up of what was planted, which was
effected by the power of this world, into whose hands degenerate Israel had been given over for punishment : " Why
hast thou then broken down her walls so that all they which
pass by the way do pluck her ? The boar out of the wood
doth waste it, and the wild beast of the field doth devour
it."

Ver. 3. A time to kill and a time to heal. Here also again
the principal passage is Deuteronomy xxxii. 39: " I kill and
I make alive ; I wound and I heal." On it are based both
the present words and those of Hosea vi. 1 : " Up and let us
return to the Lord ; for he hath torn and he will heal ; he
smites and he will bind us up." To the הרג of this place corresponds there the " tearing and smiting." הרג " to murder "
is predicated of God in relation to His people in Psalm lxxviii.
31, 34: "When he slew them, then they sought him and they
returned and inquired after him," (compare Jeremiah xii. 3,
vii. 34, xix. 6.) The state of the people must have been
desperately bad, if God, who in his treatment of them is
gracious and merciful, long-suffering, and of great kindness,
finds himself compelled to resort to such terrible means. Still,
destruction is never the end of the ways of God with His

people. Only as a passage to life, does he ordain death. In regard to the "healing" compare besides Exodus xv. 26, where the Lord describes himself as Israel's physician, (compare Isaiah vi. 10.)—*A time to break down and a time to build up.* פרץ signifies not "to destroy," but "to pull down." It is used especially of pulling down protecting walls and hedges. Compare Isaiah v. 5, where the Lord says in reference to the vineyard of Israel : "Break down its hedges and he will tread it down ;"—Psalm lxxxix. 4, "Thou tearest down all its hedges," (compare lxxx. 13.) In chap. x. 4 the phrase is found in completeness. Nehemiah speaks in chap. ii. 13 of his book, of the walls of Jerusalem which were broken down, פרוצים, and of its gates which were burned by fire, in consequence of the destruction by the Chaldeans : further in 2 Kings xiv. 13, it is said, "and he brake down of the wall of Jerusalem four hundred cubits" (compare besides Nehemiah iv. 1). This tearing down and building up may take place, in an outward manner, as it did at the time of the occupation of Jerusalem by the Chaldeans, and after the return from the captivity, or it may take place *spiritually*, through the entrance of the Church on times of great degeneracy, and the restoration and elevation thereof to prosperity. Thus in Jeremiah xlii. 10, where we read—"if ye will settle again in this land, then will I build you and not pull you down, and I will plant you and not pluck you up,"—*persons* are the object of the building up and pulling down, which terms must therefore be understood figuratively, as Michaelis takes them, *longævitate, liberis, opibus omnibusque bonis vos aucturus.* The same thing is true also of Jeremiah xxiv. 6, "and I bring them again to this land ; and I will build them and I will not pull them down ; and I will plant them and not pluck them up :" and of chap. xxxi. 4, "Again I will build thee and thou shalt be built, O virgin of Israel." The second clause of Psalm li. 18—"do good in thy good pleasure unto Sion, build thou the walls of Jerusalem," is explained by the first :—God builds the walls of Zion in that he furthers its well-being. The mere fact that it was composed by David forbids us taking the external view. In a material sense, the walls of Jerusalem were not destroyed in the days of David. In the same way are we to understand Psalm cii. 14, 15 : "thou shalt arise

and have mercy upon Zion, for the time to favour her, yea the
set time is come.   For thy servants take pleasure in her stones,
and they grieve over its dust."   Under the image of a building
in ruins is brought before us the Church of God in its reduced
condition.   Consequently the time for pulling down is always
present when God abandons his Church to inimical powers.
Such a time of pulling down, for example, was that of the
dominion of Rationalism.   But the men whose hearts bleed
during such a period should never forget that above and behind the destructive forces stands the Lord, and that in the
long run his counsels, and his alone, shall be accomplished.
After a manner very similar to that of this book are the diverse
modes of God's action contrasted in Jeremiah i. 10.   The prophet was commissioned on God's behalf to "destroy, to throw
down, to build, and to plant."   In Jeremiah xviii. 7-9, it is
said in regard to Israel—"suddenly I shall speak concerning
a nation, and concerning a kingdom, to pluck up and to pull
down, and to destroy it : if that nation against whom I have
pronounced, turn from their evil, I will repent of the evil that
I thought to do unto them.   And suddenly I shall speak concerning a nation and concerning a kingdom, to build and to
plant."   The people of God has this privilege, however, that
God always pulls down and destroys as a means and preparation for building, and that to this latter as a final aim the
divine purposes are directed.*   Hence in the kingdom of God
it is possible to be joyous and contented, even when, for the
moment, the season of pulling down is present.   Up to this
point commencement was made with the redemptive and beneficent aspect of human and divine activity : here it forms the
conclusion.   That the author intentionally makes it form the
commencement and the close of the whole, is unmistakeable.
It began with "bearing," and it ends with "peace."   If then
beginning is good, and end is good, we may reasonably be less
anxious and careful about that which meanwhile befals us, and
may look with a calm and cheerful mind on the changes now
taking place around us.

---

* Jerome: "Non possumus ædificare bona nisi prius destruxerimus mala.
Idcirco sic Jeremiæ verbum a deo datum est, ut ante eradicaret et suffoderet et
perderet; et postea ædificaret atque plantaret."

Ver. 4. A time to weep and a time to laugh. There are
seasons when those who belong to the kingdom of God must
weep, because the Lord hides his face from the house of Israel,
(Isaiah viii. 17,) and there are also times when they can rejoice.
Joy always comes last. For this reason the weeping of the
children of God is quite different from that of the world. It
always has a background of hope. Theirs is not the anguish
of despair ; it is a sadness which takes comfort. Our Lord
alludes to this passage when He says in Luke vi. 21, μακάριοι
οἱ κλαίοντες νῦν ὅτι γελάσετε. In close connection also with this
passage stands John xvi. 20 : ἀμὴν ἀμὴν λέγω ὑμῖν ὅτι κλαύσετε
καί θρηνήσετε ὑμεῖς, ὁ δὲ κόσμος χαρήσετε, ὑμεῖς δὲ λυπηθήσεσθε, ἀλλ' ἡ
λύπη ὑμῶν εἰς χαρὰν γενήσεται. When it is the time for weeping
it is useless to try and force ourselves to laughter, as is the
fashion of the world, which seeks to forget and gild over its
misery until at last it falls a victim to despair. Our course
should be that which is enjoined on us in 1 Peter v. 6, ταπει-
νώθητε οὖν ὑπὸ τὴν κραταιὰν χεῖρα τοῦ θεοῦ ἵνα ὑμᾶς ὑψώση ἐν καιρῷ :
Bengel—*in tempore opportuno*, when the season for laughter
has arrived. This season however we may not endeavour to anticipate : our moods of feelings should go hand in hand with the
various phases of divine providence : we should act in short
like the children of Israel, who once in the days of their captivity hung their harps on the willows and refused to sing the
songs of Zion. *A time to mourn and a time to dance.* On
these words it is remarked in the Berleburger Bible—" If any
man at another time is visited by still severer misfortunes, then
weeping will not suffice, but wailing must be added thereto,
that is, a great and public mourning must take place in that
we wring our hands above our heads and express our lamen-
tation in the gestures and attitude of sorrow."

*Ver. 5. A time to cast away stones and a time to gather
stones together.* What the Lord says in Mark xiii. 2, βλέπεις
ταύτας τὰς μεγάλας οἰκοδομάς ; οὐ μὴ ἀφεθῇ λίθος ἐπὶ λίθῳ ὃς οὐ μὴ
καταλυθῇ, holds good of the Church in all its periods of degeneracy. When the Church ceases to be the true house of God,
the time for the scattering of its stones is not far off. With
the scattering, however, the gathering always goes hand in
hand. At the time when the old Temple of Jerusalem was
destroyed, there rose up in its stead the glorious edifice of the

temple of the Christian Church. Previously God scattered
stones by the hands of the Chaldeans : through his servant
Cyrus he gathered them together.—*A time to embrace, and a
time to refrain from embracing.*   There is a season when the
Lord embraces his people, and a season when he does ñot permit them the enjoyment of his love, but repels them from his
presence.   When He treats us in the latter way we should
revolve in our hearts the words of Psalm xlii. : "Why art
thou cast down, O my soul ?   And why art thou disquieted
within me ? hope thou in God ; " and we should beg and pray
and acknowledge and express our sins until He becomes once
more gracious.   The expression "embrace" takes its rise in
the "Song of Solomon," chap. ii. 6, where the bride, which is
Zion, says—"His left hand is under my head, and his right
hand doth embrace me."   That elsewhere also in Solomon's
writings this transference of embracing to spiritual relations
occurs, as for example in Proverbs iv. 8 ; v. 20, I have shown
in my Commentary on that passage.   The name Habakkuk
is probably derived from the "Song of Solomon."   It signifies
"hearty embrace," and is used to describe the tender relation
of love in which Israel and the Prophet, who is the nation's
representative, stand to the Lord : as in fact Isaiah styles the
Lord in chap v., דודי and ידידי.   As to substance, Jeremiah xiii.
offers a parallel : for there, in consideration of the close and
living relation which subsists between them, Israel appears
under the image of a girdle which the Lord lays around Him
and which He puts off in the time of His anger, only howevei
to put it on again, when the season of wrath has passed away

Ver. 6. *A time to seek and a time to lose.*   At one period
the Lord interests Himself tenderly in His people : at anothei
He lets them go to ruin, yet in such a manner, that in the
midst of wrath He remembers mercy.   "To seek " is generally
predicated of believers who seek the Lord : but God also is
said to "seek" when His retributive righteousness comes into
play (Joshua xxii. 23), and when in love He shows compassion : "God seeks the persecuted" (ver. 15).   With the word
לאבד Jarchi compares Leviticus xxvi. 38, "; and ye shall perish
among the heathen, and the land of your enemies shall eat
you up." *A time to keep and a time to cast away.*   Now,
the Lord protects and preserves His people as a precious jewel:

then He casts it from Him as a despicable and hateful thing. Usually God's casting away signifies banishment from His presence. Thus in 2 Kings xiii. 23, it is written in respect of the ten tribes, "and the Lord was gracious unto them, and had compassion on them, and had respect unto them because of his covenant with Abraham, Isaac, and Jacob, and would not destroy them, and *cast them not from his presence.*" Michaelis: *ut postea factum est* (xvii. 18-20), also in Jeremiah vii. 15, where the Lord says to Judah, "and *I cast you from my presence,* as I cast out all your brethren, the whole tribe of Ephraim." In Psalm lxxi. 9, also, where Israel, now growing old, cries, "*cast me not off* in the time of old age ; forsake me not when my strength faileth :" and in Psalm cii. 11, as here, the word הִשְׁלִיךְ is employed alone. Deuteronomy xxix. 27, furnishes an example of the use of the verb in regard to God, who in his anger casts out his people into a strange land.

Ver. 7. *A time to rend, and a time to sew.* There is a time when the people of God must mourn, and again a time when they can rejoice. קָרַע is used with special reference to the rending of the clothes, which in Israel was a sign of mourning. When it is said in Genesis xxxvii. 34, "and Jacob rent his clothes, and put sackcloth upon his loins, and mourned for his son many days," we recognize in Jacob a type of the people of God and of the Church in all ages, a prophecy in the form of a fact which is being fulfilled ever afresh. Where there is the like cause, there is the like result. Was it necessary that the ancestor should be visited with severe afflictions on account of his sinfulness, for the same reason must his descendants also suffer, and to preserve their heart from exalting itself God ordains that through much tribulation they shall enter his kingdom, that times of refreshing from His presence shall alternate with times of sorrow, and His unchangeable love disguises itself in many ways and frequently appears under forms fitted to awaken terror. In Joshua vii. 6 we read, "and Joshua rent his clothes, he and the elders of Israel:" and in 2 Samuel xiii. 31, "and the king arose and rent his clothes and lay on the earth; and all his servants stood by with their clothes rent." *A time to keep silence and a time to speak.* There are times when silence must be observed, as Jacob was compelled to keep silence when he heard how Sichem had defiled Dinah his daughter, until his sons arrived (Genesis xxxiv. 5) : and then again come times when we may speak and stand up boldly in the presence of the enemies of God's people, as when the Lord spake to Paul in the vision by night, when the Jews of Corinth tried to force him to silence—" Be not afraid, but speak, and hold not thy peace," (Acts xviii. 9.)   When the hour appointed by God arrives, the words of Psalm cxxvii. 5, "they shall not be ashamed when they speak with their enemies in the gate," come fully true.   Till then we must cover our faces and keep silence.   But it is notwithstanding a blessed silence, for it is attended by the conviction that a time to speak will inevitably come again.

Ver. 8. A time to love and a time to hate.   There is a time when the Lord causes the world to incline in love towards His people : and again a time when He gives them over to the world's hatred.   In respect to the latter, and in connection with the period of Israel's residence in Egypt, it is said in Psalm cv. 25, "He turned their heart to hate his people, to deal subtilly with his servants."   In regard to the former compare Exodus xi. 3, where the Lord is represented as having given the people such favour in the sight of the Egyptians, that they offered them gifts ; also Psalm cvi. 46, where concerning the Asiatic oppressors of the nation, it is declared that "he made them to be pitied also of all those that carried them captives," (compare 1 Kings viii. 50) ; further, Daniel i. 9, "and God brought Daniel into favour and tender love with the prince of the Eunuchs ;" and lastly, 2 Kings xxv. 27, according to which the Lord moved the heart of Evilmerodach to compassion towards Jehoiachin. The time at which this book was written might in the main be characterised as one of "hating," as the faithful were compelled to acknowledge by the painful experience of every day : but the word of God was pledged that a "time of love" should arrive, such as had never previously been witnessed, and in the hope of this, they found it easier to accept temporary hatred from the same kind hand, that would one day bestow upon them love.   The era was before the door, of which Isaiah prophesied when he wrote, " and kings shall

be thy nursing fathers and their queens thy nursing mothers,"
(chap. xlix. 23), and "thou shalt also suck the milk of the
Gentiles, and shalt suck the breast of kings" (chap. lx. 16),
and thus saith the Lord ; behold I will extend peace to her
like a river, and the glory of the Gentiles like an overflowing
stream ; then shall ye suck, ye shall be borne upon her sides,
and be dandled upon her knees." Though Zion was still
" deserted and hated " (Isaiah lx.15), it had no need to be very
much concerned on that account. Here also we may apply
the saying, " At the end comes the best." *A time of war
and a time of peace.* The sweet name of peace, which is an
object of such deep affection to the heart of the struggling
Church, forms the conclusion to the whole. " Peace, peace, to
him that is afar off, and to him that is near, saith the Lord."
(Isaiah lvii. 19.)

*Ver. 9. What profit hath he that produceth in that wherein
he laboureth ?* The conclusion which follows from the preceding reflections is here drawn. Inasmuch as there is a time
for everything, it follows that " all our toils, early and late,
are for nought, all our care is in vain." The Berleburger
Bible remarks, " for he can neither pass beyond nor alter the
fixed limits set by divine providence, so as, for example, to be
joyful when the hour for mourning is come." All care and
labour, all our exhausting efforts apart from God, (Cartwright,
*deo non aspirante, a quo rerum omnium effectio suspensa
tenetur,*) are pronounced fruitless. In this, however, are not
included the " doing good," (ver. 12,) and " unwearied scatter
ing of seed," (chap. xi. 6,) with which we must go forward
because of God's command, on whose will it depends whether
it prove a blessing or not : much less is there any reference
to the prayers of believers, which in fact are as strongly called
for and enjoined, as our own anxieties and labours are forbidden and excluded, by the word " there is a time for everything." Nay, it is even possible that prayer, if earnest, may
alter the aspect of the times. If there is really a time for
everything, then surely when things press us down as a leaden
weight, we should lift up heart and hands to Him who can
change the times and seasons.* Luther renders the words—

* "Wenn wir in höchsten Nöthen seyn
Und wissen nicht wo aus noch ein,

"what can a man do more, let him work as he will?" and remarks on them—"it is just this, that till the hour arrives all our thought and labour are lost. Notwithstanding we must all work, each man in his office, and use diligence, for God commands this. If we hit the right moment, then the business succeeds: if we do not, nothing comes of it, and no device of man can be of the least use."

Ver. 10. *I have seen the travail which God hath given to the sons of men to be exercised in it.* The travail does not perhaps consist so much in the occupation of contemplating and inquiring into the government of the world, as, according to ver. 9, in the useless anxieties and exhaustive labours to which men subject themselves in that they desire, and yet are unable to effect anything, because everything comes to pass as it has been fixed and predetermined by God. On this Luther observes: "they who wish to anticipate God's appointed hour, weary themselves in vain, and reap only anxiety and trouble of heart." The faith which looks upward to God and leaves all to Him, which says: "why should I then distress myself? Heart, why art thou cast down? Why dost thou trouble and pain thyself? Trust in God thy Lord who made all things!" delivers us from this torment. But in this life even faith is liable to become weary and to change, and no sooner does the believer begin to be negligent therein, than he receives his share of the travail to which all the children of men are condemned, in a word, he begins to exhaust himself with cares and toils. And in truth, it is good for him to have his share thereof. The travail is a wholesome discipline. By such means the children of men are constrained to humble themselves, and to feel their own insufficiency. Care and toil begin, when faith

> Und finden weder Hülf noch Rath
> Ob wir gleich sorgen früh und spat:
> So ist das unser Trost allein
> Dass wir Zusammen insgemein
> Dich aurufen O treuer Gott
> Um Rettung aus der Angst und Noth."

Compare also the remarks of Cartwright—"Non equidem ut abjecto laborandi studio desidiæ et ignaviæ se dedat: sed ne ita consilio et labori confidat, ut Dei opem et benedictionem precibus impetrandam neglectui habeat. Qui ut tempora et temporum momenta in sua manu et potestate comprehensa habet ita illa precibus suorum flexus, eorundem commodo dispensat."

and prayer cease : but out of care and toil we rise again to faith and prayer. When the heart is emphatically broken by the sore travail to which God subjects the children of men, it obeys the injunction—"O troubled soul, betake thyself to God."

Ver. 11. *He maketh everything beautiful in his time, eternity also he hath set in their heart, so that no man can find out the work that God maketh from the beginning to the end.* The principal thought of the verse is contained in the last words : "man cannot find out the work of God from beginning to end ;" which some interpret to mean—"man cannot perfectly comprehend God's doings ;" but which may be more appropriately explained—"To man the knowledge of the future is altogether denied ;"—as Luther has it—"neither beginning nor end." Inasmuch as, apart from revelations concerning the future which God communicates to his servants the prophets (Amos iii. 7), man, as such, is and will remain destitute of this knowledge, to the end that he may learn to humble himself before God, it is impossible for him to order his doings with judgment, and he is consequently directed in all cases to trust not in himself but in God. The following remarks are found in the Berleburger Bible : "The conclusion which Solomon wishes to draw is, that no man can so order and arrange his affairs for the future as that he shall be thoroughly happy in this world, but must leave them to time and destiny ; and should he seek by his own energies to secure to himself the object of his desires, his efforts will be useless, and at the end there will be still no other course open to him than to commend himself and his affairs to the fatherly care of God." A twofold subsidiary thought precedes this main idea of the passage. The first is—"He maketh everything beautiful in his time." That God's rule is one with a fixed aim and method is here expressly mentioned, in order to remove as far away as possible the notion of an almighty arbitrary ruler—a notion which might easily take its rise in the fact that the method of divine government is so concealed from our eyes that we cannot tell beforehand what He will do. According to the accents יפה is connected with בעתו. J. D. Michaelis remarks—"The words 'beautiful in his time,' according to the accentuation, are closely connected together. And, in view of that which goes before, what other

meaning can be attached to them, than the following?—
among the things mentioned in verses 2-8, there are, it is true,
many that are unpleasant and evil, but at the time when God
sends them they are not only good but even right beautiful."
These things which in and for themselves are evil, must consequently occur in such a connection that they shall further
the good purposes of God. Only at the fit season are they
beautiful, and then they form an indispensable link in the
chain of this world's events. Accordingly, that is not a bad
saying of Raschi, that "at a good season to reward good works
is beautiful: and at an evil season to punish evil works is
also beautiful." The second accessory thought is contained in
the words—"Eternity also hath he set in their heart." In the
verse considered as an organic whole this thought occupies the
following position :—God makes everything beautiful in his
time, but man is unable to see it notwithstanding that God
hath set eternity in his heart. מבלי is to be taken in its usual
signification of "without" (which occurs moreover oftener than
the Lexicons allow), "without that not finds,"* which is as
much as to say, with this exception or with the exception,
that not finds* how such knowledge of the future doings of
God seems notwithstanding to follow from the fact that in
the heart of man, and specially in the heart of his own people,
He hath set eternity ; for apparently this latter gift stands to
the former in the relation of the particular to the general. If
God's nature is accessible to man, surely, one would think,
God's doings will not remain hidden from him, especially as
they follow a fixed plan. The commentary to the words, "and
he set eternity in their heart," (Rambach: *notitiam dei aeterni*),
is furnished by Psalm xc. 1-5, where the fleeting character of
our earthly life is contrasted with the eternity of God: compare especially ver. 2—"Before the mountains were brought
forth, or ever thou hadst formed the earth and the world, even
from everlasting to everlasting thou art God." And then we
must compare also Romans i. 20—τὰ ἀόρατα αὐτοῦ ἀπὸ κτίσεως
κόσμου τοῖς ποιήμασι νοούμενα καθορᾶται ἥτε ἀίδιος αὐτοῦ δύναμις καὶ
θειότης. According to the Apostle's words, man has an intel-
lectual intuition of God's eternal power and Godhead, or as it
is here expressed, of the eternity which is manifested and

---

* I have rendered the German literally *ohne dass nicht findet.*—TR.

developed in the words of creation. So far as man springs from God, his eternity is inseparably bound up with that of God (chap. xii. 7). It is man's highest privilege to discern something eternal behind the transitory objects of the present world, and to be able to cling closely to this eternal substance. And inasmuch as this eternity of God is set in his heart, it would appear reasonable to expect that the knowledge of the doings of God in time should be attainable by him. But at this point man stumbles all at once upon bars and bolts, and finds that God has reserved something for himself alone. Many interpreters explain עלם by "world;" others by "philosophy," or by "worldly mind." But usage is against this. עולם is never used in the entire Old Testament in any other sense than of "unmeasured time," and of "eternity:" and in this book above all is it employed in the signification "eternity," (see chap. i. 4, ii. 16, iii. 14, ix. 6, xii. 5; "long time," chap. i. 10). There is also the additional objection that this explanation of the term gives no appropriate sense. The words, "except that, &c." would then be unsuitable. For the setting of the world in the heart of man, does not render it in any way probable that he will be able to command a knowledge of the ways of God : it may easily, however, and with justice, be regarded as something exceptional, and so to speak abnormal, that man, in whom there dwells the knowledge of the divine nature, should be refused the knowledge of the divine works.—In reference to the main idea of the verse, Luther observes, "Man cannot hit upon the work, which God does; that is, no man can know beforehand the hour which is ordained above ; and however much he may plague himself, he can never know when it will begin or come to an end.—It behoves us therefore to say, O Lord, to thee belongs the supreme direction, in thine hand it rests entirely, to order and settle everything in the future : under thy control is my life and my death ; as I need my life, so long thou givest it and not a moment longer. And inasmuch as in respect of them, no care and thought is of any use, I will act thus in regard to other gifts, using them as they come ; care and anxiety I will cast to the winds, and commit the rest to thee."

Ver. 12. *I know that there is no good in them, but that one rejoice and do good in his life.* Seeing that man is not the lord of his own destiny, it follows that his best course is to let God act and arrange, and, in place of caring for the future, to enjoy the present, instead of labouring and scheming with a mind ever restless and ever looking for results, to do quietly what is given him to do.* The Hebrew words which we have rendered "in (or with) them," that is "men," (בני אדם of ver. 10), are rendered by several commentators, most recently by Stier—"therein, *in illis rebus omnibus.*" But that the former is the correct explanation is evident from chap. ii. 24, באדם אין טוב, and from chap. viii. 15, "it is not good" לאדם, where for the ב, in this passage, ל is employed. Joy forms the contrast to restless care and useless worry : compare Matthew vi. 34 : μὴ οὖν μεριμνήσετε εἰς τὴν αὔριον. ἡ γὰρ αὔριον μεριμνήσει τά ἑαυτῆς. ἀρκετὸν τῇ ἡμέρᾳ ἡ κακία αὐτῆς· Luther observes : "this is all the better understood from what goes before : he means to say, that because so many hindrances and mishaps in their business befal even those who are industrious and who wish to act well and truly, and because there is so much misfortune in the world, there is nothing better than cheerfully to use what God puts into our hands at the present moment, and not vex and distress ourselves with questions and cares about the future." Not to be careful, but to dare to trust in the Almighty, and consequently to be able to rejoice, is a precious privilege bestowed by God on the children of men (Psalm xxxvi. 8), of which they should take care not to rob themselves by their own wickedness. Doing good should go hand in hand with a cheerful and thankful enjoyment of the blessings which the moment brings, in order that thus we may run in the way commanded by God, may preserve a good conscience, which is the necessary condition of all joy, and not shut but rather open the entrance for God's goodness and grace. To the "do good" of this verse, corresponds the "fear God and keep his commands" of chap. xii. 13. Following Luther's example, several adopt the explanation, "Do good, act kindly, to thyself." Usage however decides against this view : and, in opposition to usage, such supposed parallel pas-

---

* Rambach remarks : "Cum itaque tanta sit rerum humanarum vanitas, tanta hominis circa eas impotentia, ut hactenus ostensum, inde ego certum exploratumque habeo, etc."

sages as chap. ii. 24, iii. 22, v. 17, 18, are adduced to no purpose. Compare Psalm xxxiv. 15 : "cease from evil and do
good : seek peace and pursue it ;" Psalm xxxvii. 3, "Trust in
the Lord and do good ;" and Isaiah xxxviii. 3, where Heze-
kiah says—" I have done that which is good in thine eyes."

*Ver. 13. And every man that eats and drinks and sees good
in all his labour, that is a gift of God.* The word ￼ refers to
the whole sentence. Not only is it a gift of God that any
man's sufferings are averted, but also that, despite suffering,
whether present or threatened, he should be cheerful. It is
in the power of God alone alike to bring us happiness and to
quiet the heart and free it from cares. Our heart is as little
in our own power as is our destiny.* The capability of en-
joying divine blessings is called in chap. ii. 24-26, a gift of
God, because the heart of the natural man is in bondage to
avarice : here the same thing is affirmed on the ground that
it is bound by care with such bonds as human strength can
never loosen. After the words just quoted Luther remarks
further: "but that is just the art to be acquired : that we
are able to do it at all is the gift of God. I myself, says
Solomon, can teach and tell this to others, but I can give it
neither to myself nor to others : the heart capable of doing
this, God alone can bestow. Solomon thus teaches us, firstly,
what we shall do, and secondly, where we are to get the ability
to be thus minded and thus to act : that is, he teaches us,
that we with our own thoughts, anxieties and cares, can make
nothing better or other than it is : our part is to pray with
all earnestness, and call upon God that He may deliver us from
sadness and useless cares, and give us a calm and believing
heart."

*Ver. 14. I know that whatsoever God doeth it shall be for
ever : nothing can be put to it and nothing can be taken from
it ; and God doeth it that they should fear before Him.* No
one can frustrate his plans : no one can hinder their fulfilment. Wherefore, " it behoves thee to trust the Lord, if it
shall go well with thee. With care, dejection and self-inflicted

---

* Cartwright says: "Quod non ita intelligi velim, acsi suo aut merito aut
arbitrio hoc illis obveniret; quando quidem quisquis est, qui edendo et bibendo
ex labore suo commode vivit, illud ipsum (quantulumcunque hominibus videatur) dei est gratuitum bonum.

pains thou canst gain nought from God ;—he must be sought unto." Compare Isaiah xlvi. 10, where God says—" my counsel shall stand fast, and all my will, will I accomplish :" Psalm xxxiii. 11, " The counsel of the Lord standeth for ever, the thoughts of His heart to all generations :" and further, Psalm cxxvii,—" it is in vain for you to rise up early, to sit up late, to eat the bread of sorrow ; thus giveth He it to His beloved in sleep." In face of the eternal decrees of God, it is to no purpose that we resolve to carry any undertaking through : our part is to cast ourselves as a child into our Father's arms, and entreat Him to have pity on us. Of God's counsels, however, it is not true to say with the poet, that, " Bound by the brazen laws of eternity, men accomplish the cycles of their existence." God's counsels are undoubtedly unalterable from without ; no creature, let him commence as he will, can effect an encroachment upon them : but they do not stand above God himself as a foreign power, as a kind of fate ; so that it is not our prayers, but our own workings that are useless. " And God doeth it that they should fear before Him." Driven by sheer necessity, and feeling their absolute weakness, they cry out, in the words of Psalm cxxiii. 1-2, " unto thee lift I up mine eyes, O thou that dwellest in the heavens Behold as the eyes of servants look unto the hand of their masters, and as the eyes of a maiden unto the hand of her mistress, so our eyes look unto the Lord God until that he have mercy upon us." Luther's remarks on this subject are : " But why does God afflict men with such countless, varied, and great cares of government, of household, of trade, of business, compelling them to run and race, and ride and drive, and travel by land and water, and often to risk their lives, whilst He has kept in His own hands the right moment when any thing shall take place, and all the rest is in vain ? The answer is : in order that men may fear Him, that they might keep his first commandment, that He may remain Lord and God, and that all may recognise Him to be God : further, that we may all learn thorough and hearty obedience and humility, and begin nothing trusting to our own wisdom, thoughts, abilities; as St Paul admonishes the Romans in chap. ix. 16, saying,— " it is not in him that willeth, nor in him that runneth, but in God, who sheweth mercy." Whoever believeth that the aforementioned things are not in his own power, will not undertake anything on his own responsibility, will not worry and vex himself too much, but let God rule in all things : what God gives, he uses, what God withholds he dispenses with ; if God takes aught away he endures it patiently. In this way God maintains fully His own divine honour, and at the same time restrains us from arrogance, inasmuch as no man then can say—I am king, prince, lord, manager, governor, learned or otherwise, but must always confess that God also is Lord. That is the true fear of God, that is the highest, holiest and most suitable service of God, the service to which Solomon, David, and all the prophets earnestly summon men, namely to believe and be certain that God sees all our doings, and works all in all, (Ephesians i. 11.)

Ver. 15. *That which hath been is now and that which is to be hath already been, and God seeketh the persecuted.* The commentary to these words is furnished by the parallel passages : Psalm cxxxix. 16: " Thine eyes did see me when I was yet imperfect, and in thy book were they all written, the days which should yet be, and none of them was there ;" on which I have remarked in my *Commentary to the Book of Psalms,* " if our whole existence from beginning to end is pre-ordained by God, how is it possible that anything should ever befal us, with which His hand was not concerned, which He did not see, and which in His own good time He did not help on ? A further illustrative passage is Job xiv. 5, " His days are determined, the number of his months with thee." What was (or became) is already, existed already in the divine counsels before it was openly manifested, and hence we learn, that God's decrees decide everything, that in all the circumstances and ways of life we should look up to God, and that we may not look to our fellowmen, who are the companions of our weakness, and who, however much they may puff themselves, and however great pretensions they may make, are, in truth, but instruments in the hand of providence. The word *is* refers us to the *timeless,* the eternal nature of that which God pre-ordains,—which timeless element is able to represent itself in the form of the present. Knobel's explanation, " it is already, *i. e.,* it is now," is inadmissible, for the simple reason that כבר cannot possibly mean "already." The third memoer of the sentence, "and God seeks the persecuted," falls into harmony with the other two, so soon as it is peiceived that the reference they contain to the divine preordination is intended as a consolation : " Nothing can happen to us which He has not sent, and which will not conduce to our blessedness." Of the accuracy of the translation given of the third clause of the sentence there can be no doubt.* Just in the same way is seeking ascribed in ver. 6 to God, who takes compassion on his forlorn and wretched children. In the only place where it occurs besides here, namely, in Lamentations v. 5, the Niphal form of רדף has the signification " be persecuted." The people of God there give utterance to the complaint נרדפנו, " we are persecuted," and the Niphal form in itself would scarcely allow of being otherwise interpreted. This explanation is further confirmed by verses 16-17, where we find exactly the same thought. To those verses this 15th verse forms a link of transition. Following the Vulgate (*Deus instaurat quod abiit*) most modern interpreters assume that נרדף signifies " the past," and that the idea is, " the phenomena and events of life keep repeating themselves in a fixed circle." This idea, however, would do violence to the whole connection, and besides, that נרדף cannot signify " the past," is as certain as that רדף means " to persecute " and nothing else. Following the correct view, the Berleburger Bible remarks : " Therefore thou shouldst not so take offence thereat as to allow thyself on its account to be drawn away from the highest good. For God will not leave unpunished the injustice and the violence which are done to those that fear Him." We have in this passage the Old Testament basis for the words of our Lord in Matthew v. 10. : μακάριοι οἱ δεδιωγμένοι ἕνεκεν δικαιοσύνης ὅτι αὐτῶν ἐστιν ἡ βασιλεία τῶν οὐρανῶν.

Verses 16-17. These two verses comfort the people of God whilst groaning beneath the unrighteous oppression of worldly

---

* It may be found even in the Septuagint, which has rightly conveyed the meaning of this verse, so often misunderstood by more recent interpreters : τὸ γενόμενον ἤδη εστὶ καὶ ὅσα τοῦ γίνεσθαι ἤδη γέγονε, καὶ ὁ θεὸς ζητήσει τὸν διωκόμενον : the same may be said also of the Syriac and of the Targum, Deus requiret obscurum et pauperem de manibus improbi, qui persecutus fuerit eum.

powers by pointing them to the divine judgments which are shortly to be executed. Ver. 16. *And further saw I under the sun.* In the previous ver. allusion is made to the overthrow of the people of God and the triumph of the world : here to the misapplication of authority to purposes of tyranny and oppression. *The place of judgment, wickedness is there :* the seat of judgment is the place whence, by divine appointment and legal sanction, justice should be administered, for Rulers and Judges govern and give sentence in God's stead (2 Chronicles xix. 6-7). שמה signifies always " thither," never " there:" wickedness moves thitherwards, takes possession of the place. The wickedness is that of the heathen authorities. Parallel to this is Psalm xciv. 20, where, in view of the deluge of Chaldeans which overwhelmed the people of God, they ask— " Is the throne of iniquity in fellowship with thee, which frameth misery by a law ?"—misery, which is the result of violence and wickedness. In Psalm cxxv., which like the present book was composed during the time of the Persian dominion, it is said (verses 2-3): " The mountains are round about Jerusalem, and the Lord is round about his people from henceforth even for ever. For the sceptre of wickedness shall not rest on the lot of the righteous, lest the righteous put forth their hands to iniquity." From beneath the yoke of their heathen oppressors will the people of God once again rise to the glorious liberty of children. *The place of righteousness, the wicked is there.* In Daniel iv. 27, Daniel says to Nebuchadnezzar—" break off thy sins by righteousness, and thine iniquities by showing mercy to the poor." *The righteous and the wicked God will judge,* (ver. 17). Here the righteous man is Israel : the wicked is the Heathen : and the ungodly in Israel as being degenerate are left unnoticed. By destiny, and at the core, Israel is the nation of the upright, Numbers xxiii. 10. In Habakkuk i. 13, it is written in reference to the Chaldean catastrophe : " wherefore lookest thou upon them that deal treacherously, and holdest thy tongue when the wicked devoureth him that is more righteous than he ?" *i. e.,* him that stands opposed to the evil one, as being righteous. On this passage compare Delitzsch, who considers the merely relative view of righteousness untenable. The judgment of the wicked may be looked for with the greater confidence, when they are found occupying the seat of law and justice, thence practising wickedness, and misusing their authority for injustice.   The tribunal of justice is of God (Deuteronomy i. 17); whoever appears there appears before God (Exodus xxi. 6, xxii. 7-8.)   For this reason it is impossible that God should leave unpunished the misuse of authority : a thought which is further carried out in Psalm lxxxii.   Our duty is to wait patiently for this judgment of God's.   The more shamelessly and wantonly their heathen rulers abuse their authority, the more certain may we be that it will come, and the more cheerfully may we wait.   In 2 Thessalonians i. 5, Paul describes the persecutions and oppressions of believers as an ἔνδειγμα τῆς δικαίας κρίσεως τοῦ θεοῦ, " a notice, a proof, that God will shortly in*erpose."—*For there is a time there for every desire and about every work*, with God, Psalm lviii. 12 : " and man says, Verily, the righteous has a reward : verily, God judgeth on the earth."   Koheleth points as it were with lifted finger away from the earth, the seat of unrighteousness, to heaven.   " There " is employed in the same way in Genesis xi., ix. 24.

Ver. 18. The introductory words, " I said in mine heart," set this verse on the same footing as ver. 17, and show that the question raised in ver. 16, is here examined from another point of view.   The problem is this—How is the singular fact of the prosperity of wickedness to be explained and justified ?   The first answer is given in ver. 17, and the consideration is brought forward, that this prosperity is only temporal, and that by God's judgments the disturbed order will in due time be established.   But this by itself is not fully satisfactory.   There is the further and more difficult task of showing why the righteous, why God's own people, are visited with temporal misfortune.   This is done here.   The cross of the righteous is disguised mercy.   It serves to purify them : specially does it help to purge them altogether from pride, and to lead them to humility.   *Because of the children of men*, do these things happen : for their sake does wickedness sit in the seat of judgment, and the wicked one in the place of righteousness. Koheleth speaks of the " children of men " in general, but has specially in view the children of Israel.   We find a case exactly similar to this in Psalm xxxvi. 7-8.   This designation is chosen because it expresses human *baseness*, the consciousness of which, according to the close of the verse, is intended to be awakened by the cross. Knobel's explanation is as follows— "I thought in my mind on the relation of the children of men." But עַל דִּבְרַת occurs in this book as well as in the Chaldee portion of the Book Daniel, only in the sense of "Because of, on account of;" and then further the accents are decisive against this view.* The general and vague expression —" for the sake of the children of men," is more precisely defined to mean—" in order to purify them;" and then amongst the evils from which they are to be purged, special mention is made of *pride.* בָּרַר signifies properly "to separate," (Ezekiel xx. 38,) and then "to purify." It occurs in a sense precisely correspondent to that of this passage in Daniel xi. 35—" and some of them of understanding shall fall to try them, and to purge and to make them white for the time of the end." בָּרַר stands there between צָרַף and לָבֵן "to make white, to make clear." The "time of the end," is the period when these visitations of God shall terminate. That such an end must of necessity come, is here taken for granted, in agreement with ver. 17. The process of purification is only a temporary one. בָּרַר is employed also in Daniel xii. 10, "many shall be purified and made white and tried:"—Ch. B. Michaelis—*per tyranni- cas illas afflictiones ex divina sapientia et directione a vitiis suis purgabuntur et a maculis albabuntur et velut metalla excoquentur multi, scil. intelligentes quod sequitur.* Hitzig is disposed to give בָּרַר here the meaning of "try," but entirely without grounds that will bear investigation, and contrary to the remarkable agreement between this verse and the parallel passage in Daniel. בּוּר in chap. ix. 1, is not to be brought into comparison. It is rather a cognate of the word בָּאַר. *And in order that they may see that in themselves they are beasts.* That is the result to be gained by the purification. Substan- tially parallel is Job xxxvi. 8, 9, where it is said concerning the sufferings of the righteous—" and if they be bound in fet- ters and be holden in cords of affliction; then he showeth them their works, and their transgression that they have

---

* Rambach: qui cum consequentibus connectunt habent accentus faventes, secundum quos verba priora: dixi in corde meo, per majorem interstinctionem u seqq. separata, *signum* dicti, reliqua vero dictum ipsum continent.

become proud." Among the stains from which we are to be cleansed by means of the cross, pride is the worst. לראות is not so much "that he may see," as "that they may see," being convinced by facts, by stern and terrible realities. Here it is not as in Psalm lxxii. 22, the *behaviour* of beasts that is referred to, but their fate, that which happens to them, just as in Habakkuk i. 14, where the community of the Lord complains —"thou makest men like the fishes of the sea, like the beasts, that have no ruler over them." Catastrophes in which men are treated as beasts, are well fitted to teach them their nothingness. Through the fall man received the disposition and feelings of an animal. In righteous retribution, therefore, and to cure him of the pride which occasioned his fall, the fate of mere animals befals him, and he is subjected to death like the beasts. But not content even with this, God allows catastrophes to befal His people from time to time, which bring men into still closer relation to the beasts. המה stands for the *verb. subst.* "are." להם, "in themselves," apart from God's protecting care, and when He does not extend to them his helping hand; which is as much as to say, that they themselves are as powerless to aid and protect themselves, as are the unreasoning beasts. When they see this, a thing which their pride causes them constantly to forget again, they turn to God saying—"Asshur shall not save us: we will not ride on horses; neither will we say any more to the work of our hands, our God! for in thee the fatherless find mercy. Then comes forth the divine answer: "I will heal their backsliding, I will love them freely," (ver. 5 ff.) For, as he goes on in verse 19 to say, such is actually the state of the case: as a part of mere nature, in contrast to God, and apart from the bond uniting him with his creator, from that which becomes his through the life in God, who by breathing into him His Spirit raised him above the beasts of the field, (see Gen. ii. 7,) —man, godless man, is in truth no better than the cattle. מקרה being in the *stat. absol.* can only be translated—"for haphazard are the children of men, and haphazard are the cattle," which is as much as to say that the children of men are no less haphazard than the cattle. Men themselves are designated *chance*, because they stand under the dominion of chance, of casualty. Chance or haphazard is opposed to the free determination of one's own fate. Their lot is irresistibly determined and fixed *from without.* מקרה, "occurrence," from קרה "to occur," in 1 Samuel vi. 9, is set in contrast or opposition to that which arises out of the determined decree of the God of Israel : in the present passage, on the contrary, it forms the contrast to that which is the effect of the free self-determination of man. It is used in a similar manner in 1 Samuel xx. 26, (viz. of pollution in accordance with Deuteron. xxiii. 11 ;) and in a strikingly similar way in Ruth ii. 3, where, in regard to the most important event in the life of Ruth, which must certainly be looked upon as under the special leading of God, it is said—"and there happened to her an occurrence," that is, it happened accidentally. In that place also מקרה designates "haphazard, chance" in one particular aspect thereof. Similar also is Luke x. 31 : κατὰ συγκυρίαν δὲ ἱερεύς, and so forth. "Accident," there, is put in contrast to the intention or purpose of the priest himself. The words—"and one accident or chance befalleth them," *i. e.,* they are both under the rule of the same chance, serve to explain the somewhat obscure expression—"they *are* chance." Hitzig observes: "the author means, and, as we learn from what follows immediately after, can only mean, the same final fate, namely, death." But the relation of this to what follows is rather that of the general to the particular. The general is, that men, no less than the cattle, are subjected to a foreign power ; the special or particular is, that they must die. מקרה is employed of fates in general in chap. ii. 15 also ; there is nothing to justify limitation of its application. *And one breath have they all.* רוח signifies here "the breath of life," as in chap. viii. 8, and in Psalm civ. 29, where we read, "thou gatherest together their breath, they depart and return to their dust." See also Genesis vii. 21, 22. "And all flesh died that moves upon the earth, both fowl and cattle and wild beasts,——and all men. All, in whose nostrils was the breath of the Spirit of life, died." The flood, that type of all other judgments, was a sublime confirmation of the indisputable truth here expressed. Then were the "heroes," "the men of name," compelled to experience that everything on earth has the same breath. "No pre-eminence has man above the beast," that is, of course, in those aspects which have already been brought under notice. That Ko-

heleth had not the remotest intention of setting man in general
on a level with the brute creation is evident, both from ver.
11, where he makes man's exalted pre-eminence to consist in
the eternity which God hath put in his heart, and further,
from the entire relation in which Koheleth stood to the faith
of Israel, of which faith, the likeness of man to God was so
important an element.   Luther says—" Why are we then
proud and arrogant, we, who are no more certain of the hour
of our death than the beasts or the cattle ?"—The foundation
of *verse* 20 is Gen. iii. 19, " In the sweat of thy face shalt thou
eat thy bread, till thou return unto the ground ; for out of it
wast thou taken ; for dust thou art and unto dust shalt thou
return."   That is a truth which man is led ever afresh by his
pride to forget.   *All go unto one place:* in Job xxx. 23,
Sheol is designated " the assembly house for all living," *i. e.*
for all living *men*.   Of that however the writer is not speaking here, but, as Hitzig remarks, " of the place whither the
body comes (all was formed from the dust, and all returns to
the dust).   Beasts (Genesis ii. 19, i. 24) as well as men
(Genesis ii. 7) are originally born of dust, and return to the
dust. (Psalm civ. 29, Genesis iii. 19, Psalm cxlvi. 4).   This
holds good of the body in both spheres."—Ver. 21. In this
verse Koheleth goes on further to say, that man has notwithstanding a great and glorious superiority over the beasts, in
that, when his body crumbles to dust, the spirit returns to
God who gave it (xii. 7); whereas the soul of the beast perishes with the body.   This pre-eminence is, however, hard to be
perceived ; it is concealed beneath that which we have in common with the beasts ; and the fact, that his pre-eminence is
thus hidden, ought in itself to be sufficient to lead man to
humility and extinguish in him all proud thoughts.   *Who
knoweth the spirit of the children of men that goeth upward ?*
Precisely as in Psalm xc. 11 (compare Isaiah liii. 1), the
words מי יודע direct attention to the difficulty of discerning
this superiority, which does not lie on the surface : whereas,
on the contrary, the resemblance man bears to the beasts
forces itself on our notice.   העלה is the participle with the
article, which here, on account of the guttural that follows, is
pointed with Kametz, instead of with Patach and a following
Dagesh, as in the corresponding word היורדת.   The participle

with the article is often employed for the *verb finit.* with a relative : as for example "the ascending one," instead of, "he who ascends," (see Ewald, § 335). In regard to the word הוא Ewald's remarks, § 314, hold good : he says—"the most delicate manner of giving prominence to a person is by means of the pronoun הוא, αὐτός, Latin *ipse;* a person is thus specially referred back to, and distinguished from others. As הוא adds only a freer kind of accessory distinction, it stands without article after the particular noun." This consideration does away altogether with the objection urged by J. D. Michaelis, that : "According to the grammar, another ה would be required before הוא, in case it should be said that הוא is added by way of emphasis, and that the translation may run as follows, quis novit spiritum hominis ascendentem *illum ?*" Compare, for example, Numbers xviii. 23 ; הלוי הוא, "he, the Levite." The foundation of the characteristic of man here brought into prominence is contained in Genesis ii. 7—"He breathed into his nostrils the breath of life." If the spirit of man is a breath from God, it cannot perish with the body, but, when the dust returns to the dust, must return to Him who gave it. That which belongs to the earth is given back to the earth ; and so that which belongs to heaven must be rendered back to heaven. *And the breath of the beast, that goeth downward to the earth.* This is in itself easy to be known. The sense however here is the following—" Who knows both,—the immortal soul of man, and the perishable soul of the beast, in their difference from each other ?" The Septuagint, Chaldee, and Syriac, take the ה in העלה and in הירדת to be interrogative, rendering the words—" Who knows whether the spirit of the children of men goeth upward, and whether the breath of the beast goeth downward ?" and this interpretation, the rationalistic exegesis has adopted. From the point of view offered by this translation Knobel remarks—" Koheleth shews an acquaintance with the dogma of the immortality of the soul, but he throws doubt on it, in order not to invalidate the view expressed in verses 19, 20. Had he believed in a going upward of the soul to God, he would have contradicted himself." But the contradiction here affirmed exists only in appearance. Verses 19 and 20 speak only of the physical, bodily nature of man. The fact that as to his body man is under the same necessity of dying as the beasts, should suffice to humble him, and to make clear the folly of arrogance.   Against this view of ה as used interrogatively the following reasons may be urged: I. According to the points ה can only be the article, and cannot be the interrogative particle, (compare Ewald, § 104): and this ground, by itself, is sufficient.   That the present pointing, which rests on the authority of tradition, is incompatible with the interrogative view, is frankly conceded by Ewald: "In chap. iii. 21," says he, "the Masorah has twice changed the interrogative הַ into the article—manifestly, because it deemed the question objectionable."   If the vowels of the Old Testament were really the work of narrow minds, whose judgment was guided only by what the exegesis seemed *to them* to require, the vocalization would present a very different appearance.   II. This interrogative view, wrung from the text by the alteration, involves the author in a glaring contradiction with himself.   That which he is here said to call in question and deny, he distinctly avows his belief of in chap. xii. 7.   It is the more difficult to allow the existence of such a glaring contradiction, as elsewhere the writer is always self-consistent, never following the suggestions of the moment, but everywhere setting before his readers fixed and clearly defined teachings.   The words of chap. ix. 10 also,—"the Sheol whither thou goest,"—are decisive against the supposition that Koheleth sets the soul of man on an equality with that of the beast which goeth downward to the earth, that is, which perishes along with the body.   III. The interrogative view, further, involves the author in a contradiction with the original records of the Jewish religion, the possibility of which no one will allow who has entered into the spirit of the book, and the presence of which would make the admission of the book into the Canon an insoluble problem.   To co-ordinate the soul of man and the soul of the beast is manifestly to contradict the Thorah, which was the standard of all thinking in Israel ; "In the Pentateuch man is exalted to a very high position.   He is created last of all and is set at the head of creation.   Everything else exists for his sake.   According to Genesis i. 26, 27, he is created in the image of God, namely, so that the whole divine glory shines forth from him in a reduced measure.   According to Genesis ii. 7, two elements are

united in man, an earthly and a divine, which latter no other
creature shares with him.—We have here the anthropological
basis of the doctrine of the immortality of the soul. As in
the earthly element of man's nature, there lies not only the
possibility, but even, so far as it is not penetrated. pervaded
and glorified by the spirit, the necessity of death : so in the
fact that man shares the divine image, participates in the life
which comes from God, there is involved the possibility, yea,
the necessity, not only of immortality in general, but of an
immortality of blessedness or misery, of eternal life or damnation. The soul which bears the divine image, is, as such, removed not only from the sphere of the perishable, but also
from the ranks of those creatures which merely exist or vege-
tate." Beitr. 3 s. 570. Throughout the entire Old Testament this all-important distinction between the soul of man
and the soul of the beast is firmly maintained ; so that this
passage would occupy quite an isolated position. Everywhere,
at all events, we find the doctrine of the Sheol.

Ver. 22. Here the practical conclusion is drawn not only from
ver. 21, but from the whole chapter. Such a close was the
more necessary because verses 19-21 are pretty far removed
from the main thought,—so far removed indeed that they
might form a parenthesis. Man, this is the thought, is not
master of the future : therefore he must rejoice in the present.
The same practical conclusion had been already drawn in
ver. 12. To that our attention is here again directed. *And
I saw that nothing is better* (מֵ טוֹב "better," chap. iv. 3,
1 Samuel i. 8), *than that a man should rejoice in his own
works,* in the works themselves, and in that which is produced and effected by their means, so that he has his portion from them (chap. v. 18). *For who shall bring him to
see what shall take place after him ?* "After him," that is,
not after his death, but after the condition in which he now
finds himself. Jerome says : Pro eo quod nos posuimus : ut
videat id quod futurum est post ipsum, apertius interpretatus
est Symmachus dicens : ut videat ea quæ futura sunt post
hæc. In the parallel passage, chap. vi. 12, it is said, "What
will happen after him *under the sun.*" According to this,
those general events are referred to, which exercise a decisive
influence on his fate. It is not, therefore, permissible to ex-

plain the words to mean—"what will become of him,"—as those are compelled to do who suppose that a conclusion is being drawn from the verse immediately preceding. This supposition is based moreover on a false interpretation of ver. 21, where immortality is not denied but affirmed (Knobel: "one must enjoy before death in order not to go away empty.") If ver. 21 has been rightly explained, this present verse would not form at all a suitable conclusion from it alone. Man knows not what God will do to him (ver. 11). Therefore is it foolish to give ourselves up to wearisome exertions in pursuit of happiness, to distress ourselves with cares (verses 9, 10); and quite as foolish is it to enter upon many distracting schemes and occupations, to hunt after the πλούτου ἀδη᾽ ότης (1 Timothy vi. 17), to gather together and to heap up for ι.im on whom it shall please God to bestow it (chap. ii. 26); wise, on the contrary, is it, to rejoice in the present.

CHAPTER IV.

The link of connection between the different parts of this chapter is the common reference to the misery under whose yoke the people lay groaning.

According to verses 1-3 the earth is not a place where righteousness dwells, but a scene of injustice and violence. This was a knowledge at which the Church of God arrived with peculiar ease, and which was impressed on it with peculiar force, at the time when it was itself under the tyrannical rule of worldly power. The chapter now under notice suggests that the book was composed during that period. Some have, in this connection also, spoken of the "bitterness of Koheleth's view of the world," and have found in these verses the "expression of the complaints of a bitter and desperate spirit." But this is quite incorrect. Koheleth does not *complain:* he considers ("I saw all the oppressed"), and simply sets before us, *facts.* To know and present these in their naked truth is a privilege of the wisdom which dwells in the midst of the people of God; whilst on the contrary the world is compelled in many cases to close its eye against them and to surrender itself to illusions, unless it be prepared to become the prey of despair. The wretched state of things here depicted could only justify complaints against God if there had been no fall, if man were still in the condition in which he was when he came forth from the creative hand of God. Since the day spoken of in Genesis iii. the best world is that of which it has been said, "The world is but a vale of tears, and everywhere need, trouble, fears." Such a state of things, however, can only breed despair in the minds of those who have fixed their eyes on the earth, and who, by their own guilty conduct, have sealed up the fountains of consolation, to which the writer directed attention in chap. iii., and to which he will again point in the following chapters. From these fountains our misfortunes and troubles should drive us to draw.

Ver. 1. *And I returned and considered all the oppressed that are made under the sun, and behold there the tears of the oppressed, and they have not a comforter, and, in the hand of their oppressors, power, and they have no comforter.* Ver. 2. *And I praised the dead which are already dead more than the living which are yet alive.* Ver. 3. *And more than both, him that hath not yet been, that hath not seen the evil work that is done under the sun.*

Ver. 1. That שׁוּב is not to be taken in the sense of "to turn oneself," but in that of "to return," is clear from the parallel passage, Zechariah v. 1, "And I *returned* and lifted up mine eyes and behold a flying roll:" as compared with Zech. iv. 1 : "and the angel that talked with me *came again* (returned) and waked me, as a man that is wakened out of his sleep." It might be supposed that the words—"I returned and saw," —indicate that the present subject had been already brought under consideration ; (compare chap. iii. 16 f.) The words however rather imply that the author's meditations are taking a new turn, as is clear not only from Zechariah v. 1, but also from the parallel passage, chap. ix. 11, where the phrase— "I returned and saw,"—manifestly introduces a new thought. In ver. 7 also, the expression—"I returned and saw,"—indicates that the meditation which had been interrupted is taken up again, and is turned to a new subject. שׁבתּי points out in general, that a train of thought is taken up again after a pause during which it had been dropped : Vulgate, "verti me ad alia." And then the fresh subject is described. *All oppressed who are made.* That the author, in referring to the oppressed, had especially in view the people of Israel which was trodden under the foot of the powers of this world, is clear from chap. iii., but especially from Jeremiah l. 33,—"thus saith the Lord of Hosts, the children of Israel and the children of Juda are *oppressed* together, and all that took them captives held them fast and would not let them go." עשׁוקים never signifies "oppression," always "oppressed." The עשׁוקים of Amos iii. 9, stand to the עֹשְׁקוֹת of chap. iv. 1, evidently in the relation of *patiens* to *agens.* The עשׁקים of the former passage are the דלים and the אביונים of the latter. Job xxxv. 9 is to be explained— "by reason of the multitude of the oppressed they cry:" that is complaint is raised that there are on earth so many who are unrighteously oppressed. There is the more reason for retaining this meaning in this clause, as the word is undeniably employed in a like sense immediately afterwards in the course of the same verse. נעשׂים suits this meaning very well. The oppressed are *made* such by their oppressors.

Ver. 2. On this verse Luther remarks—"when one attentively regards the innumerable sorrows of the heart, miseries, great evils and troubles on earth, and the awful wickedness there is in the world which is the devil's kingdom, one must surely be of the mind that it were better to be dead than to see so much wretchedness." The thought expressed in this verse occurs also frequently under Christianity, notwithstanding the abundant sources of consolation opened to us by its doctrines and promises. There are seasons in the life of nations, and of individuals when this thought presses itself on the mind with peculiar force. It has full truth, though of course of a one-sided character. In view of the severe sufferings to which our life is exposed, it can scarcely appear, considered in reference to that which is usually described as the happiness of life, to be a desirable good. In this aspect of the matter the dead are more to be envied than the living. In other aspects, however, life appears as a high and noble possession. And even in the general human aspect that saying holds true, "a living dog is better than a dead lion," (chap. ix. 4,) and that other one,— "Light is sweet, and a pleasant thing is it for the eyes to see the sun," (chap. xi. 7.) On the believer, moreover, as he walks

in the darkness of this earthly life, there shines a bright light,
(Job. xxxv. 10,) so that he can say—"my flesh and my heart
may fail, but God is the rock of my heart and my portion for
ever," (Psalm lxxii. 26 :) he takes delight in fearing God and
keeping His commands, (chap. xii. 13 ;) he is able, with a
heart that rests and is satisfied in God, to enjoy the blessings
which the present never fails to offer even when public affairs
are in the most wretched condition ; he hopes in the retributive righteousness of God which will bring the perversions
and wickedness of the world to an end, (chap. iii. 16 ;) and,
finally, in the momentary perversion of justice he recognises a
wholesome means of divine chastisement, (chap. iii. 18.) שבה
is the *infin. absol.* which with an emphatic brevity, appropriate
to the excitement here felt, is employed for the *verb finit.*
(compare chap. ix. 11 ; Ewald 351c.) It is not the Particip.
in Piel with rejected מ,—an aphaeresis which scarcely occurs
in the Piel form,—for קשבה in Nehemiah i. 6-11, is an adjective, feminine of קַשֵׁב, and there is no ground for regarding
מהר in Zephaniah i. 14, as a participle, since it is often used as
an infinitive with the signification "hastily." That כבר does
not mean "long ago," but "already," and serves to define
the preterite more strictly, is very clear in this passage. It
forms the contrast to עדנה, contracted from עד הנה, "still."

Ver. 3. With increased force of expression the author here
says that it is better not to have been born at all than to
live. Parallel with this is the passage (chap. iii.) where Job,
who had no peace nor repose, and who was disturbed ever
afresh, wishes for himself the lot of "an hidden untimely
birth," and curses the day of his birth, or where in verse 20
of the same chapter he asks—"Wherefore is light given to
him that is in miser, and life to the bitter in soul ?" So
also when Jeremiah in chap. xx. curses the day of his birth,
and in ver. 18 complains, " Wherefore came I forth out of the
womb to see labour and sorrow, that my days should be consumed with shame ?" In regard to such expressions, however,
we must remark that so far as they occur in Scripture they
contain only one side of the truth. In proof of which the
same Jeremiah, in a passage immediately preceding the one
just quoted, says : " Sing unto the Lord, praise ye the Lord,
for he delivers the soul of the needy from the hand of the

evil doers." Such a feeling of human misery is not only
natural, but is intended by God who brings us into circumstances which call it forth. By thoroughly disgusting us
with the world, and by making us realize its absolute vanity,
God means to draw us to himself. Only in this way can
Jahveh, the true and absolute Being, become to us what he
really is. Through much tribulation must our hold on earthly
things be loosened and ourselves enter into the kingdom of
God.

CHAPTER IV. 4-6.

The emptiness of earthly happiness betrays itself clearly
in the fact that it is accompanied by envy (ver. 4): "when
any man has good fortune and good days, then envy is sure
to rave and rage." We must not, however, suffer this sad
experience to mislead us into inactivity (ver. 5). Still, in
view of such a fact, we shall do well not to mix ourselves up
too much with distracting affairs, and, on the contrary, rejoicing when they are not forced upon us, (like Israel at that
time), be content with a humble lot in life (ver. 6).

*Ver. 4. And I considered all travail and all skill of work.
that this is the envy of a man from his neighbour : this also is
vanity and empty effort. Ver. 5. The fool foldeth his hands
together and eateth his own flesh. Ver. 6. Better is one hand
full of rest, than both fists full of travail and empty effort.*

Ver. 4. The word כשרון, which occurs only in Koheleth, is
rendered by the LXX. here and in chap. ii. 21 by ἀνδρεία, virtus.
Derived from כשר, " rectus fuit," it is used partly of " skill,
ability in action," and partly of the " fortunate results "
thereof. In the latter signification, namely, " advantage,
gain," it occurs in chap. v. 10 ; in the former we find it used
in chap. ii. 21, in conjunction with wisdom and knowledge :
" a man whose work is in wisdom and knowledge and Kish-
ron (כשרון). There follow after, the words : " and to a man
who has not laboured therein must he give it." According to
the contrast here drawn כשרון must refer to the labour, the
activity itself, and not to the result. The matter of complaint is that the skill developed in labour has no higher pre-

rogative. כשרון is employed in the sense of "skill, ability,"
here also.—*That this is the envy of a man from his neighbour :*—the end of the whole matter is that a man is envied
by his neighbour ; Vulgate, " eum patere invidiæ proximi."
Following the example of the Decalogue מרעהו draws attention to the baseness of the fact that the friend, of God and
right, grudges him the successful results of his skilful labour.
It is of course better to be envied than pitied, but still envy
with all the hostile and pernicious acts flowing therefrom, and
which frequently bring about the ruin of their object, is a
great evil, and it is no small consolation for a man who, like
Israel at the time, finds himself in an unenviable position, to
know that he is not exposed to this torment. Several interpreters think that here all distinctions are traced back to the
principle of rivalry. That would be an incorrect thought :
whereas it is a demonstrated truth that " men envy the happy."
In Isaiah xi. 13, קנאת אפרים is the jealousy felt by Ephraim
of Judah, who was preferred : in chap. ix. 6, of this book,
envy is conjoined with hatred. The verb also is frequently
used to denote envy or jealousy of advantages. It is hard
that a man's zeal should be interpreted by his neighbour to
be an envious desire to surpass, to outstrip him. Then further, the connection with verses 5, 6 is decisive against this
view. " Vanity and empty effort " are not usually predicated
of labours which are morally worthless, but of such as bring
no advantage (compare chap. ii. 17). Ver. 5. In order to
avoid envy we may not throw ourselves into the arms of inactivity. The only effect of that would be to ruin ourselves.
To lay or fold the hands together is a gesture of laziness. To
devour one's own flesh is to work one's own ruin (compare
Isaiah xlix. 26). The principal passage is Proverbs vi. 9-11 :
" How long wilt thou lie, O sluggard ? When wilt thou
arise out of sleep ? A little sleep, a little slumber, a little
folding of the hands to sleep. So shall thy poverty come as
one that travelleth, and thy want as an armed man."

Ver. 6. Men are warned, however, by the bitter experience
mentioned in ver. 4, to do well, and not to go beyond that
which is strictly necessary. Taught by such an experience
they will be satisfied with a humble and limited lot. עמל and
רעות רוח point back to ver. 4. " Both fists full of, etc," is as

much as " both fists *full of good*," which more carefully looked
into, is after all only travail and empty effort. Israel then
had the hand full of rest : the heathen power, both fists full
of travail. To make Israel content with its lot by laying bare
the vanity of that which it was destitute of, but which the
world possessed, is the usually misunderstood main drift of
verses 4-6.

CHAPTER IV. 7-12.

How little the life of a man depends on many possessions,
the author shows in a picturesque description of the example
of a rich man who has so completely isolated himself by his
selfishness and avarice, that he stands alone and deserted,
without enjoyment and without protection in life.

The author repeatedly recurs to the subject of avarice and
earnestly combats it. We may conclude therefore that it was
one of the principal diseases of the time. It comes before us
as such, also, in the other literary monuments of that period.
" Ye run every man to his own house," says Haggai in chap. i.
9. Malachi complains in chap. i. that the worst offerings are
presented to the Lord, and in chap. iii. 7-12, of dishonesty in
the bringing of tithes and offerings. Nehemiah, also, according to chap. v., was compelled to resort to stringent measures
against the usurous practices then in vogue. The temptation
to avarice lay in the unsatisfactory nature of the general circumstances, which exposed men to the danger of centering all
their interest in their own private affairs : but then also
further in the distress of the times, and in the exactions of the
heathen authorities by which they were misled into clinging
the more tenaciously to that which they already possessed.

The description has however two sides. It is directed not
only against avarice, but also at the same time against envy
of the riches of the world, of their heathen tyrants. One
ought not to vex oneself about " a handful of vanity ;" one
should not allow oneself to be beguiled into discontent with
the leadings of divine providence, into murmurings against
God, for such a cause. The aim both of the preceding and
following observations is to lead Israel to a just estimate of

that which the heathen possessed, and which they themselves lacked ; and taking both together, we may say that the passage has a predominant reference to that side of the description last mentioned. Ver. 1-3 exhibits the misery of the covenant people : ver. 4-16 opens up points of view from which their condition appears in a more favourable light.

Ver. 7. *And I returned and saw vanity under the sun.* Ver. 8. *There is one and not a second, he hath neither son nor brother, and there is no end of all his labour, his eyes also are not satisfied with riches, and for whom do I weary myself and bereave my soul of good ? This also is vanity and a sore plague.* Ver. 9. *Better the two than the one, because they have a good reward in their labour.* Ver. 10. *For if they fall the one will lift up his fellow, and woe to him, the one, who falleth and hath not a second to help him up.* Ver. 11. *Again, if two lie together, then they have heat : but how can one be warm alone ?* Ver. 12. *And if he prevail against him, the one, two shall withstand him, and a threefold cord is not quickly broken.*

Ver. 7. The words—" I returned and saw vanity,"—indicate that a new species of vanity is now brought under consideration.—How far the possession of earthly wealth is from being in itself a good, the author shows in ver. 8 ff, by sketching before us in a picturesque manner a scene from life which illustrates this truth in a most palpable manner. It is an entire mistake to assume, as Rambach and others do, that the author's controversy is with celibacy, or with the "fuga vitæ sociæ." Luther's remarks are substantially accurate ; " Greedy bellies are to be found yet, who hunt after money and property night and day and still do not want it." Ver. 9. *There is one and not a second, he hath neither son nor brother.* The *second* here mentioned is different from the son and from the brother. According to what follows there is one whom he might have, but has not through his own guilt. He has isolated himself by his own selfish avarice, has driven all companions away, and stands alone in the world. The words, " he hath neither son nor brother," are meant to bring clearly to light, on the one hand, the folly of blind passion—he stands alone in the world, has no one to care for, and consequently has no apparent reason for his avarice—and on the other hand

the wretchedness of his position. He ought the more eagerly
to seek to make to himself friends, seeing that he has no rela-
tives of his own.

Ver. 9. The *two* in this verse form a contrast to the one
without second in ver. 8.   Wherein the reward consists is detailed in ver. 10 ff.   They afford each other protection and
help, and mutually render life agreeable.   The isolated man
on the contrary must work in vain, since he is destitute of
enjoyment in life, and without protection in danger.

Ver. 10. When they fall, that is, either the one or the
other.   אִי, "woe," occurs only here and in chap. x. 16 ; the
cognate word הִי in Ezekiel ii. 10 : Elsewhere אוֹי and הוֹי are
employed.

Ver. 11. Several commentators fancy that they find here a
reference to the wife : but inappropriately.   A wife the rich
miser might have, and be a prey to the feeling of desertion
which invariably accompanies an avaricious and selfish disposition.   It is sure to have its revenge.   Lovelessness always
finds its echo.

Ver. 12. The subject alluded to here is the enemy which
must be supplied from the tone and circumstances of what is
said, (Ewald § 294 b.)   תָּקַף always means "to prevail against,
to overpower," never "to attack :"   compare the adjective תַּקִּיף
"powerful" in chap. vi. 10.   "Him, the one," is as much as
to say, him, in his isolation, or because of his isolation.   The
image of a "threefold cord,"—in making a firm, strong cord,
three threads were usually used,—is the more appropriate
here, as the number *two* in general only represents plurality.
The author must not be considered as arguing from the point
of view of mere prudence.   The moral abominableness of isol-
ating selfishness and heartless mammon worship are brought
clearly to light by the unhappy positions in which they
set men.

CHAPTER IV., 13-16.

In the preceding part of the chapter, the writer has laid
bare the vanity of possessions ; now he proceeds to show
the vanity of rulers, in order to console his fellow country-

men in bondage, who could not forget their own loss of dominion.

Ver. 10. *Better is a youth, poor and wise, than an old and foolish king, who knoweth no more to be admonished.* Ver. 14. *For out of prison he cometh to reign, whereas impoverished is he that was born in the kingdom.* Ver. 15. *I saw all the living which walk under the sun, with the youth that stands in his stead.* Ver. 16. *There is no end to all the people, to all whom he precedes. Nevertheless those who came after him shall not rejoice in him. For this also is vanity and empty effort.*

" Ah ! how vain and fleeting are the honours of men ! To-day we are compelled courteously to kiss the hand of the man whom to-morrow we tread under our feet in the grave." An illustration of these words is given here in the portrait drawn of the old king who is displaced by another ; and then in that of the upstart who is first extolled and courted, and at last loses the favour which exalted him to the throne. At his ascension, millions of voices cried, " Long live the King ;" words which contain the " Pereat" of him who is deposed. But the scales are again turned. He becomes in the end as unpopular as his predecessor. " This rounded earth can afford no rest, for what it at one moment raises up, at the next it casts down." Because of the loss of such vanity we ought not to fall into inconsolable sadness. Every attempt at an historical exposition of this section is useless. That which appears to imply such a reference, is but minute and special portraiture, and not otherwise to be judged : it is like the picture given from life in ver. 8, where the general thought is not barely advanced, but clothed with flesh and blood.

Ver. 13. " *Better* is a youth," not in a moral point of view, but because, notwithstanding his temporarily low position, he gains the kingdom which the other loses, and so is better off, So also מובים in ver. 9, טוב in ver. 3.

Ver. 14. The first half of ver. 14, gives the reason of the expression " better :"—" For out of prison he cometh to reign,"—namely, " that youth." That הסורים is a contraction of האסרית, (Ewald § 86 b.) is plain from Judges xvi. 21 : " and he, (Samson) groaned בבית אסירים (ver. 25 :) also Genesis xxxix. 20, where בית הסהר is explained by—" the place where the king's prisoners were bound." The author appears to have borrowed this feature, that the youth rises to power out of prison, from the history of Joseph ; only, however, this one feature, for as to the other circumstances there is no resemblance. *Whereas impoverished is he that was born in his kingdom.* The abasement of the governing king is the condition of the rise of the youth. This sentence thus assigns the motive for that which is advanced in the preceding one. The catchword is לְמַלֵּךְ. The Hebrew word rendered "whereas, although" means literally " also :" it is used however in the sense given. See Proverbs xiv. 20, Ewald § 362 b. *Born in his kingdom :* i. e., one who came to the possession of the kingdom, of his dignity as ruler, by birth : like the kings of the Philistines, who being hereditary, bore the title Abimelech, that is, king's father, and might therefore quite as well have been styled king's sons. רָשׁ is not a participle, but the preterite from רוּשׁ, and contains an allusion to Psalm xxxiv. 11 : " lions are impoverished and suffer hunger." It is evident from the whole connection that in רָשׁ the old king is to be taken as the subject. Symmachus rightly expresses this : ὁ δὲ καίπερ βασιλεὺς γεννηθεὶς ἠπορήθη.

Ver. 15. This verse, according to which " all the living which walk under the sun" fall to the share of the upstart, shows that the circumstances on which the description is founded, are not those of any petty state, but of the great universal monarchies of Asia, which took particular pleasure in identifying themselves with the entire orbis terrarum. Compare Daniel iv., where the tree, which signifies the kingdom of Nebuchadnezzar, stands " in the midst of the earth," and spreads itself out " to the end of all the earth," " all flesh" was nourished from it, and where Daniel in giving to Nebuchadnezzar the explanation of the vision says—" thy dominion reacheth to the end of the earth."

Ver. 16. *All whom he precedes*, that is, all who do homage to him as their monarch (Micah ii. 13). The word נֶם here corresponds to נֶם in ver. 14, and directs attention to an addition of a singular kind, which falls quite as much to the lot of the second king as the first. Whether the change is brought about by the fault of the king, who was not able to bear his good fortune, and failed to display the wisdom in his *conduct as actual ruler*, which he showed in the *attainment* of power ; or whether by the changeableness of the people we are not told, and simply because it did not lie within the aim of the author to speak of the causes, but only of the fact, of the change itself. Luther observes : "and so we find in histories that at first many rejoiced and hoped in Nero, and looked for a fine able ruler in him. The first five years of his reign were hopeful and were commended : but afterwards he was tyrannical, and that in the most aggravating way. So likewise of Heliogabalus and Commodus were good hopes entertained, that they would turn out praiseworthy princes and rulers : but the hope failed. The one, Heliogabalus, was a vile wretch, who gave himself up to all manner of profligacy and debauchery, and was a thorough beast. The other ought to have been styled, not Commodus but Incommodus, that is, a curse to the land." "This also is vanity," to wit worldly greatness. The practical conclusion for Israel is— "Why vexest thou thyself about a handful of vanity, when God bestows on thee unchanging treasures ? If the pound is thine surely thou mayst let the farthing go."

CHAPTER V. 1-6.

The author whose task it was, now in the way of consolation and then in the way of admonition, to lay before the people of God, groaning under the yoke of the Persians, that which might be for the health of their soul, here passes over to an entirely new theme. He proceeds to bring to light the evils which at that time were to be found in connection with the public worship of God. If his admonitions went to the heart their effect would be contentment with the divine arrangements. True self-knowledge throws light on the otherwise dark ways of God. When one learns to murmur against one's own sin, one ceases to murmur against God. A superficial piety sought to put God off with sacrifices, instead of walking in the way of His commands: prayer in many cases degenerated into mere chatter : vows were lightly taken, but when it came to the fulfilment they hung back. There was lacking a true and hearty fear of God : and that was the root and spring of all these evils. This section shows that the book belongs to a time when the very hearts, which at an earlier period had openly renounced God, and given in their adherence to heathenism, were devoted to a *dead orthodoxy*. Such a time began shortly after the return from the exile, as soon as the first mighty stirrings of the hearts had relaxed, as soon as the first enthusiasm had vanished. How strongly disposed the people were in the time of Nehemiah to withdraw themselves from the services due to God may be seen in Nehemiah xiii. 10-20.

Ver. 1. *Keep thy foot when thou goest to the house of God, and be ready to hear, which is better than that fools should give sacrifice, for they consider not that they do evil.* Ver. 2. *Be not rash with thy mouth, and let not thine heart be hasty to utter a word before God, for God is in heaven and thou upon earth ; therefore let thy words be few.* Ver. 3. *For the dream comes through the multitude of annoyance, and the voice of fools through the multitude of words.* Ver. 4. *When thou vowest a vow unto God defer not to pay it, for fools are not pleasing : what thou vowest, pay.* Ver. 5. *It is better that thou shouldest not vow, than that thou shouldst vow and not pay.* Ver. 6. *Suffer not thy mouth to cause thy flesh to sin, and say not before the angel, for it is an error. Why should God be angry at thy voice and destroy the work of thine hands ?* Ver. 7. *For where many dreams are, there are vanities and (even so where) many words : for fear God.*

Ver. 1. The words, " Keep thy feet," show us that the going to the house of God is a serious matter, which had better be omitted if not done in a right spirit. Jerome says : " Non enim ingredi domum dei, sed sine offensione ingredi laudis est." The essential thing is of course to preserve the heart, but the posture of the heart is represented and revealed in the manner of going. The author speaks of feet, perhaps, because through them he had often discerned the state of the heart. The Kri : רַגְלְךָ, " thy foot," probably owes its origin to a comparison of Proverbs i. 15, iv. 26, 27. Psalm cxix. 101, where the plural is employed, might just as well have been made the subject of comparison. כַּאֲשֶׁר " so as " is stronger than the simple " when." קָרוֹב never occurs as an *Infin. absol. ;*

always only as an adjective. As such James took it in this
place : see the Epistle chap. i. 19 : ἔστω πᾶς ἄνθρωπος ταχὺς εἰς
τὸ ἀκοῦσαι βραδὺς εἰς τὸ λαλῆσαι :—the latter is an allusion to
chap. v. 1. If the word "hear" be referred to the public
worship of God, we must look to the reading of the law conjoined with the singing of Psalms : (compare my work, *On
the Day of the Lord* :) and then this passage would furnish a
proof that, at the time of the author, it was customary to
read from the law, and probably to connect therewith exposi-
tions and applications. Taking this view the Berleburger
Bible remarks : "We must not be satisfied merely with hearing : else it is merely that ; and this is not all that is intended. External is external : and the true aim of the external rites of worship is to conduct to the internal." But
that the matter to be heard is much rather the voice of the
Lord, and that consequently "hearing" has substantially the
same force as "obeying," is clear from 1 Samuel xv. 22, where
Samuel says to Saul, "hath the Lord delight in burnt offerings and sacrifices, as in hearing the voice of the Lord ? Behold, to hear (obey) is better than a good sacrifice, and to
hearken better than the fat of rams." In Jeremiah vii. 33,
also, to hear the voice of the Lord is set in opposition to
soulless sacrifices. God, says the prophet, did not command his people concerning soulless sacrifices, but said
to them : " Hear (obey) my voice, and I will be your
God, and ye shall be my people." Parallel also is the passage, Hosea vi. 6, "for I have pleasure in love, and not
in sacrifices ; and in knowledge of the Lord more than
in burnt offerings : see also Proverbs xxi. 3 : "to do justice and judgment is more acceptable to the Lord than sacrifice," with which compare ver. 27 : "the sacrifice of the
wicked is abomination." What the voice of the Lord calls for
are love, righteousness, justice ; whereas soulless sacrifices are
not claimed by him : to bring them therefore instead of love
and the like is the contrary of obedience. The voice of the
Lord is known in the first instance from the "roll," *i. e.,* "the
volume of the book," (Psalm xl. 8), "the law of Moses,"
which Malachi, the contemporary of Koheleth admonishes
(chap. iii. 22) the lovers of ceremonies to remember. At the
same time, however, the voice of the Lord makes itself heard

also in the hearts of the faithful : compare Psalm lxxxv. 9,
and the words—"thou hast digged through my ears"—of
Psalm xl. 6. By a rather harsh construction, "before that,
that fools should give sacrifice," stands for "which is better
than that fools should give sacrifice." That זבח signifies here, as
always, "slain sacrifices," (not sacrifices in general), which are
particularly selected from the whole number of sacrifices, is
evident from a comparison of 1 Samuel xv. 22, Hosea vi. 6,
Psalm xl. 7, where "slain sacrifices" are mentioned along
with "burnt sacrifices." Not of "sacrifices" in general does
Koheleth here speak, but of the sacrifices of *fools*, which were
not an outward form expressing the worship which is in spirit
and truth, but the contrary thereof, namely, an invention
whose purpose was to appease God and to silence the conscience. Several commentators explain—"for they know
not, in order that they," or, "so that they do evil," appealing
to the fact that ידע is frequently used without specification of
the object, which must either be supplied from the context,
or be taken in the most general possible way (Isaiah xliv.
5, 6, 9, 18, xlv. 20, xvi. 10, Psalm lxxiii. 22). But that the
words must rather be explained—" they know not that they
do evil," (Ewald, § 280*d*), is clear from that saying of our
Lord's which refers back to this passage, πάτερ ἄφες αὐτοῖς· οὐ
γὰρ οἴδασι τί ποιοῦσι (Luke xxiii. 34. Without knowing it they
do evil, so that their manner of procedure is to be carefully
shunned and avoided.

Ver. 2. From the same want of living fear of God which
was at the root of the offering of soulless sacrifices, arose also
the use of many words in prayer, and the lightness and frivolity in making vows. The expression—"let thy words be
few," as compared with that of ver. 7, "many words," shows
that vows are here included. Piel from בהל, in the sense of
"to haste," occurs also in chap. vii. 9. The explanation of
על is, that the mouth forms, as it were, the foundation of the
hasting (Psalm xv. 3). Whoever properly takes to heart that
God is in heaven and we upon earth, will be sparing in his
words, will say nothing which has not the fullest inward
truth, which does not come from the deepest depths of the
heart ; will be circumspect in his vows, vowing nothing which
he cannot, or does not intend to pay. The most grievous

violation of the reverence we owe to God, the most guilty
disregard of the fact that God is in heaven, and we on earth,
that He is the rich and we the poor, that He is the Almighty
and we the powerless, is not to pray at all, to remain entirely
dumb towards Him in whose hand are the souls of all living.
The admonition, "let thy words be few," is not meant to set
limits to the glow and fire of devotion.   It is directed not
against the inwardly devout, but against the *superficially religious*, who fancy that in the multitude of their words they
have an equivalent for the devotion they lack.   That the saying of our Lord's against the Pharisees who made long prayers
by way of pretext (Mark xii. 40): προσευχόμενοι δὲ μὴ βαττο-
λογήσητε, etc. (Matthew vi. 7, 8), contains a reference to this
passage is the less to be called in question, seeing that that
type of a short and good prayer which He gave his disciples
immediately afterwards, begins with the words—" Our Father,
which art in *Heaven*."   In the Berleburger Bible it is remarked: "What a wide application may be made of these
words both to teaching and preaching, to prayer and to our
ordinary life!   How many sermons, hours long, would be
expunged by this censorship, although never so skilfully
arranged and put together according to the preaching-art.
And if all sermons and other discourses concerning divine
things were purged, as in truth they ought to be, from all
useless, unedifying, fruitless, offensive and wrong words, how
few would the censorship leave standing.—The Saviour took
note of this advice, and therefore prescribed a short form of
prayer, at the very commencement of which the petitioner is
moved to remember the majesty of God who is in Heaven,
though the majesty is tempered by the kind and lovely name
of Father."

Ver. 3. Between the two clauses of this verse there is no
internal connexion, except in so far as one wretched thing is
compared with another.   The main point is simply the relation of cause and effect.   The voice of fools is the result of
many words so far as by their means it is *recognised or known*.
If we draw out the sum total of many words, the result is,
the voice of the fool.   In regard to ענין which is not "business" but "annoyance," compare what is said on chap. i. 13.

In Job vii. 14 also mention is made of the terrible dreams to which sufferers are exposed.

Ver. 4, 5. These verses have special respect to vows, and refer back to Deuteronomy xxiii. 22, 23 : " When thou vowest a vow to the Lord thy God, thou shalt not slack to pay it : for the Lord thy God will surely require it of thee, and it will be sin in thee. But if thou forbearest to vow, it is no sin in thee." That the divine names are employed not at random but according to definite principles is quite clear in this place. In this quotation, which otherwise is almost literal, the simple לאלהים stands instead of the words " Jehova thy God," of the original passage. The Berleburger Bible says : " Many persons when they are in need or desire aught from God precipitate themselves into certain vows, and promise more than they have afterwards any desire to fulfil when avarice comes in and incites them not to perform that to which they have solemnly engaged themselves. In the hour of need many promise to God golden mountains—how thankful they will be, how they will improve themselves if they should only become again free and healthy. But alas ! how soon does the deceitful heart forget all that when it is out of the strait."

Ver. 6. According to several the meaning of the words, " Suffer not thy mouth to cause thy flesh to sin," is that " vows lightly taken excite the carnal mind to stronger opposition." But in the Old Testament בשר never signifies the fleshly mind. Only one passage, namely Genesis vi. 3, contains an approximation to this signification. In James iii. 6, where we read of the tongue, ἡ σπιλοῦσα ὅλον τό σῶμα, and the dependence of which from the passage under consideration can the less be denied as the succeeding words καί φλογίζουσα τὸν τροχὸν τῆς γενέσεως refer back to chap. xii. 6, and thence receive their assured explanation, בשר is rendered by σῶμα, and not by σάρξ. Σῶμα is not employed there in opposition to soul, but to designate the body as endued with a soul ;—in short, it is a designation of the whole person from the bodily side, because, in the first instance, the tongue is a member of the body. So also here בשר signifies the entire personality. In several passages the soul appears as an appurtenance of the בשר ; see Leviticus xvii. 11, Job xii. 10. Cartwright's remarks here are quite to the point : " Cave ne ore tuo, unico

eoque perexiguo membro, reatum tibi cum corpore tum animo
accersas." הַהִטִיא here is not " to lead into sin," as in Exodus
xxii. 33, but, " to set into the position of a sinner," " to bring
guilt on any one," as in Deuteronomy xx. 4, and Jeremiah
xxxii. 35.   God, who will not be mocked (Galatians vi. 7),
will punish the whole person for the misuse of the tongue in
vowing that which one does not afterwards perform.——*And
say not before the angel :* (do thine office, atone for me, bring
the sacrifice usual in such cases), *for it is an error.* מַלְאָךְ is
" a messenger in general," then specially "messenger of God,"
"angel."   The priestly order is described as the angel, in order
to indicate its high dignity, and the heavy responsibility
attaching to frivolous conduct towards it.   It supplies God's
place (2 Corinthians v. 20).   The Septuagint and the Syriac
have rendered—"before God."   We may not explain the
words—"before the *messenger*,"—for it is uncertain whose is
the messenger.   In the term *angel* is implied the sending from
God.   There is here a remarkable coincidence with Malachi.
In chap. ii. 7, 8, (and except there nowhere else in the Old
Testament), the priestly order is brought forward as the messenger of the Lord—"for the priest's lips should keep knowledge, and they should seek the law from his mouth, for he is
the angel of the Lord of Hosts."   The words—"for it is an
error"—point back to Numbers xv. 27-31.   There a distinction is drawn between sins which are committed בִּשְׁגָגָה and
בְּיָד רָמָה, *sins of weakness,* which still cleave even to such as
believe and as are consequently right-minded, and *wilful sins*
—a distinction which forms the basis of the New Testament
doctrine concerning the sin against the Holy Ghost (compare
Hebrews x. 26-28).   The *former* can be atoned by sacrifices :
(compare Numbers xv. 28 : "And the priest shall make an
atonement for the soul that sinneth ignorantly") : the *latter*
are on the contrary punished with destruction.   One should
not be too quick with one's proposal to the priest to offer a
sacrifice, fancying that in this way the whole matter is de-
spatched.   It may very easily happen that the supposed over-
sight has a more serious character.   In such a case the sacrifice is presented in vain, and the sin remains and involves the
soul in God's judgments.   It is no light thing to make a mock
as it were of the Lord of Heaven and Earth by vowing to Him

what we have no serious intention of performing. We meet in Malachi with the same religious superficiality which fancies that the good God will not be so particular, that he will surely be easily satisfied, especially at a time when He Himself bestows so little upon men. We read in chap. i. 8, "When ye offer the blind for sacrifice, it is not evil : and if ye offer the lame and sick, it is not evil :—bring it now unto thy Governor, if he will be pleased with thee !" On the ground of such facts Malachi in ver. 6 brings against the people the charge of contempt of the name of God.— *Why should God be angry at thy voice and destroy the work of thy hands ?* On this the Berleburger Bible observes : " Vows were made for the most part of the fruits of the earth and of cattle ; and when they were not performed the offenders were punished by a special curse on that which was vowed."

Ver. 7. *For where many dreams are, there are vanities and many words*, with them is it even so. *For fear God.* כי refers to the exhortation, indirectly contained in what precedes, to avoid many words in our intercourse with God. Whoever fears God truly will speak nothing before Him that does not come from the very centre of his heart, will vow nothing which he is not resolved inviolably to perform.

CHAPTER V. 8-9.

The point of departure of these verses is the heathenish tyranny under which the people of God sighed. But this should not be permitted to lead us astray : we should rather direct our eyes to the heavenly King who in His own appointed time will bring everything again into order.

Ver. 8. *If thou seest the oppression of the poor and violent perverting of judgment and justice in the province, marvel not at the purpose, for one who is high watches over the high, and a highest over them.* Ver. 9. *And the advantage of the earth is in all : a king to the cultivated field.*

Ver. 8. גזל is employed with the genitive of that which is robbed in Ezekiel xviii. 18. The robbery is committed on judgment and justice. So certainly as the Lord hath spoken in view of the unrighteous oppression of his people by the heathens, " I hate unrighteous robbery," (Isaiah lxi. 8,) so certain is it that he cannot behold such conduct unmoved. מדינה, which properly means "jurisdiction," is the *terminus technicus* for the provinces of the Asiatic World-Empires, and is used especially of the provinces of the Persian Empire. The word occurs only in the post-exile Authors, (Books of Kings, The Lamentations, Ezekiel, Daniel, Esther, Ezra, Nehemiah,) amongst which, the use of the term shows that Koheleth must be reckoned. The province can only be the Jewish one, מדינתא יהוד (Ezra v. 8,) which comes before us just in the same manner as *the* Province in Ezra v. 8 ; Nehemiah i. 3 ; vii. 6 ; xi. 3. To the exhortation "not to marvel," at the strange *quid pro quo* by which we may easily be led to wrong conclusions regarding God and His Kingdom, correspond the words— ἀγαπητοὶ μὴ ξενίζεσθε τῇ ἐν ὑμῖν πυρώσει, ὡς ξένου ὑμῖν συμβαίνοντος in 1 Peter iv. 12. חפץ (compare on chap. iii. 1,) may be referred either to the divine pleasure, or to the *tel est mon plaisir* of the authorities who usually introduced their edicts with the words—"it is seemly before me," "it is good before the king," (Daniel iii. 22 ; vi. 2 ; iv. 22 ; Ezra v. 17.) The antidote to surprise is that One who is high watches over the high, one too who is able to cope with all the high, seeing that He is the Highest of All. The sense is quite mistaken by those who find here the empty consolation that—"sooner or later the higher prefect or the king will hear of it, and will interfere with his punishment." The saying here holds true that " one crow does not peck out the other's eyes." A real parallel may be found in Psalm lxxxii., the theme of which is—"God judges amongst the gods." נבהים is used precisely in the same way as עליונים, "the Most High," in Daniel vii. 18-22, and as בוראים "the Creator," in chap. xii. 1, of this same book. For remarks on plural designations of God, which are independent of Elohim, and which owe their rise to the same source, namely, to the intention of indicating the fulness of powers in God, see my "*Beiträge*," 2 P., 256, 59, 60, 309, 19. A similar plural relating to the same subject occurs also in Psalm lviii. 12,—"Verily God judges, שפטים, on the earth." The suffix in עליהם has relation to the plurality which lies in the second נבה. As to thought there is a perfect agreement between this passage and Psalm xcvii. 9,—" For thou, Lord, art Most High over all the earth." Luther says : "This book consequently teaches thee to let thine heart have rest and peace, and not to trouble and worry thyself over much when things go wrongly, but to accustom thyself to be able to say, when the devil brings malice, injustice, violence, and burdens on the poor, 'Such is the way of the world, but God will judge and avenge it.' And again, when thou seest things going well, learn to say, 'God be praised, who, after all. so rules, that we do not merely suffer evil and injustice, but receive also much good.' Moreover, let every man, according to his rank, and God's command, do his work with the best industry : other things let him commend to God ; let him be patient and wait for Him who is able to find out and judge the ungodly and unjust. He who cannot lift a great stone, let him leave it lying and lift what he can. Wherefore, when thou seest that ⁚ings, princes and lords misuse their power, that judges and advocates take bribes and allow causes to sink or swim as they being wise and sensible thou wilt think within thyself,— ' ᾽ ' will sometime bring about a better state.'"

Ver. 9. "The tilled field" of this verse denotes the earth, so far as it is cultivated and inhabited, the תבל the *οἰκουμένη*. In Genesis ii. 5 also " the field," is the broad and wide plain, the plain of the earth. The King is the Heavenly one, who has the will and the power to put an end to the oppressions of the earth at the right time, the " Father of the orphan and the Judge of the widow," and the Saviour to whom all *personæ miserabiles* look up and after whom their hearts cry out. In regard to matter, Psalm xlvii. 8, " King of the whole earth is God," is a parallel passage. בכל may mean either " in all that, in all gloomy events and conditions" presented by the earth, or, on the whole, "in general," like לכל in 1 Chronicles vii. 5. Both come substantially to the same thing. For even on the latter view, בכל calls attention to the fact, that in such and all similar circumstances God is " the sure stronghold of persecuted souls." Several different renderings have been given, which originate in the incapacity properly to enter into the spirit of the poetical expression—" the cultivated field ;" for example, Luther renders " and besides that, is the King in the whole land to cultivate the field," with the explanation that, he defends and protects his subjects against wrong, burdens and violence :—Ewald, "with all that a king is set over the country," with the explanation, "and since with all that it remains an advantage for the country to have a king, that is, a well ordered government," or as Elster expresses it, "the worst government is better than unbridled anarchy." Stier even translates—"and the profit of the earth is everywhere; he who cultivates his field is a king." Against all these interpretations the consideration is decisive, that the Niphal of עבד occurs only in the signification "to be cultivated." Knobel's ingenuous observation, that, "Strictly taken, the sentence does not belong to this connection," is exactly applicable to all these explanations. The faulty Kri הוא for היא arose simply from exegetical perplexities.

CHAPTER V. 10-20.

In verses 8 and 9, Koheleth comforted the poor who lay groaning under the oppressions and exactions of the heathen authorities, by directing their minds to the heavenly Ruler and Judge; and thus he put into their mouth and heart such words as, "to thee lift I up mine eyes, O thou that sittest in the heavens," and, "we raise our heart and hands towards the day of redemption." In these verses now before us, he seeks to raise them up to the right point of view for the consideration and estimate of those earthly possessions at whose loss they were so grieved: "What is the wealth of this life? It is but a handful of sand, and uneasiness for the heart." His first purpose is to counteract the pain felt because of their loss. At the same time, however, he has the further aim of opposing avarice, which, in times of distress, so easily lays hold on men's hearts. Avarice and envy have the same root, namely, the false estimate of earthly possessions. The intention of the author to warn his fellow-countrymen against avarice is pretty plainly shown in ver. 17-19.

Ver. 10. *He that loveth silver shall not be satisfied with riches: and he that loveth riches hath no gain. This also is vanity.* Ver. 11. *When goods increase, they are increased that eat them, and what good is there to the owners thereof, saving the beholding of them with their eyes?* Ver. 12. *Sweet is the sleep of the labouring man, whether he eats little*

*or much: and the abundance of the rich will not suffer him to
sleep.* Ver. 13. *There is a sore evil which I have seen under the
sun,—riches kept by the owner thereof to his hurt.* Ver. 14.
*But those riches perish by a sore evil, and he begetteth a son and
there is nothing in his hand.* Ver. 15. *As he came forth of
his mother's womb, naked does he go away again as he came,
and he takes nothing, notwithstanding his labour, which he
might carry away with him in his hand.* Ver. 16. *And
this also is a sore evil, that in all points as he came so shall
he go, and what profit hath he, that he hath laboured for the
wind.* Ver. 17. *All his days also he eateth in darkness and
hath much discontent, and then his sickness and wrath.*
Ver. 18. *Behold what I have seen : that it is good and comely
to eat and to drink, and to see good in all his labour wherewith he laboureth under the sun the number of the days of
his life, which God gave him, for that is his portion.* Ver.
19. *Also to whatever man God giveth riches and possessions,
and giveth him power to eat thereof and to rejoice in his labour, this is a gift of God.* Ver. 20. *For he thinks not much
of the days of his life because God hears him through the joy
of his heart.*

Ver. 10. The rich man is the heathen. This is especially
clear in verse 6 where the same subject is treated. But it is
also evident from a comparison with verse 7, where the poor
man is the Israelite. The connection with verse 7 and 8 is
quite plain. *There* the minds of those who lie groaning under
the oppressions of the heathen are directed to the impending
judgment of God. *Here* the author exhibits to them the true
significance of riches, and thus teaches them to regard in a
different manner their own losses, and the heathen gains.
Hitzig remarks, " this section consoles the poor man, or him
who is poor in the way described in verse 7 ; the friend of
money, (ver. 9,) is one who from covetousness oppresses the poor,
(ver. 7.) In James ii. 1-13, and v. 1-6, also is the rich man
the heathen.[*] " He is foolish who vexes himself about a
handful of vanity :"—this is proved in the first class, by the

---

[*] Bengel remarks on James ii. 7: loquitur apostolus maxime de divitibus
ethnicis, cf. 1 Peter iv. 14 ; ii. 12. Inter Judæos enim non erant multi divites,
certe Hieros.

fact that riches do not satisfy the heart,—a fact which must be patent to every one who has noticed how the rich man is ever craving for more.   In the second clause of the verse it is affirmed that riches afford no profit at all, that they are unfruitful.   To the words here, "He that loveth silver shall not be satisfied with riches," Jerome adduces the parallel dictum from Horace, "semper avarus eget." Luther compares chap. i. 8, "the eye is not satisfied with seeing, nor the ear filled with hearing :" and remarks—"Alexander the Great had not enough in his many kingdoms, not even in a whole world. It is just so in other things also.   The man who has learning, wisdom, honour, property, strength, beauty, health, and so forth, is notwithstanding not satisfied therewith.   Thus the wretched poverty-stricken life of the covetous man is a good mirror for the rest of us.   For as the greedy bellies and penny kissers have money and yet dare not use a farthing of it cheerfully, but are constantly looking further for money which they have not, so is our conduct in regard to all other gifts.   What is a poor, troubled, uneasy heart and mind, which is always looking for that which it does not yet possess but avaricious : therefore is it vanity and vexation ?   Are not on the contrary those happy people who content themselves with God's present mercies, with moderate means of life, and leave God to care for the future ?"   *And whoso loveth riches hath no gain :* Vulgate : fructum non capiet ex eis.   In regard to מי אהב, which corresponds to the simple אהב previously employed, see Ewald, § 331 b.   המון never signifies directly riches, but always, noise, bustle.   In Psalm xxxvii. 16, the noise of the wicked stands for their wealth, which surrounds them who scrape together, who employ cunning and force, with noise, bustle and disquiet : and so here riches are represented as tumult, noise.   We are thus taught that they have much inconvenience from this wealth of nothing.   Why there is no profit is further shown subsequently when the author seeks by a vivid and picturesque representation to impress their hearts with the fact that life does not consist in the multitude of our possessions.   Also this is vanity ; like so much besides on this poor earth which offers so many fictitious possessions.

Ver. 11. *When goods increase they are increased that eat them.*   Eaters come from all sides, for the rich are always

subject to claims proportionate to their wealth.   Luther says :
" this is a weighty and glorious saying.   An avaricious man
is never contented ;   he is always scraping and collecting.
And for whom does he gather ?   For, whatever he may fancy,
it is as the proverb says,—' A niggard will have his spender.'
So warns the Scripture, and such is the lesson of experience
from the beginning of the world, that all hoarded-up treasures,
especially such as are due to injustice, find their distributors
and devourers either during the life, or after the death of the
avaricious collectors, who themselves get nothing but the toil
and labour.   King Solomon was also a rich king.   Who made
use of his great possessions?   His royal household.   Who
uses, who eats and drinks up the wealth of princes ?   All
manner of attendants, troopers, servants, waiters, officials and
innumerable other fellows who do not in the least deserve it.
Whoso then gathers riches, gathers devourers.   Therefore, why
plague thyself to collect much and to increase thy treasure ?
However many possessions thou hast thou canst not do more
than fill thy belly and clothe thy poor body.   If God gives
thee riches use thy share as thou usest thy share of water,
and let the rest flow on : and if thou doest it not, thy gathering will still be in vain."   The plural בעלים is used for the
abstract " lordship."

Ver. 12. *Sweet is the sleep of the labouring man,* of him
who is compelled to act according to the instruction given in
Exodus xx. 9, " six days shalt thou labour," and to eat his
bread in the sweat of his brow, as was the lot of Israel at that
time. *And the abundance of the rich will not suffer him to
sleep :* Jerome says, " incocto cibo in stomachi angustiis æs-
tuante."   According to the general usage of Scripture, a " rich
man" is not always one who has much wealth, but also one
who acts contrary to the admonition of the Psalmist in Psalm
lxii. 11, and whose heart cleaves to riches.   In Mark x. 23-
25, the " rich man," and the man who *trusts* to his riches,
seem to be used interchangeably.   He to whom riches are a
secondary matter, who does not set his heart upon them, will
not be so designated.   Amongst the heathen it was one and
the same thing to have possessions externally, and to be
internally possessed by riches, to be worshippers of mammon.
For they were destitute of that saving liberating power which

springs from a connection with the living God : Mammon
must necessarily be their God, because they did not know the
true God, or rather, were not known of him.

Ver. 13. *A sore evil :* properly, a painful evil, חֹלָה = נַחְלָה,
Nahum iii. 19 : Jeremiah xiv. 17: compare in my Christology
the remarks on Isaiah liii. 10. *Riches kept by the owner
thereof to his hurt,* inasmuch as he loses them, (ver. 14,) and
becomes so much more unhappy than if he had never possessed
them.   This is true of individuals : this holds good also of
entire peoples.   How miserable were the Egyptians after they
were cast down from the height of their power and wealth.
So also the Persians, whom the writer immediately refers to in
this place.   The fact that "riches attract murderers and moreover often lead to eternal damnation," does not here come into
consideration.   The author himself gives an explanation of
the words—"to his hurt or misfortune,"—in the 13th verse,
and beyond that we may not attempt to go.   In this way all
random guessing is prevented.

Ver. 14. *By a sore evil ;* (compare i. 13, iv. 8).

Ver. 15. And, the author proceeds to say in this verse,
apart from such catastrophes, death puts an end utterly to
the possession of wealth.   In death the rich and the poor
are alike.   What ceases with death cannot make us truly
happy, even while we have it.*   That that which is here
spoken of is something common to men as men, to men in
general, is evident from the fundamental passage in Job i. 21,
and the parallel passage, 1 Timothy vi. 7, where the vanity
of riches and the advisableness of contentedness are grounded
on the fact that, as we brought nothing with us into the world,
so we can take nothing with us out of it.   *Notwithstanding
his labour :* which consequently he has employed in vain
and for nought.

Ver. 16. The thought contained in ver. 15 is here repeated
with emphasis, in order to point out its weight and to set
the folly of envy in its true light.   *This also,* no less than
the *sore evil* of ver. 13.   There it was the πλούτου ἀδηλότης

---

* Seb. Schmidt, "Novum hoc est pro fugienda avaritia argumentnm, sumtum
ab eo, quod opum possessor, licet morte etiam naturali moriatur, et divitias suas
usque ad finem vitæ retinuerit, nihil tamen eorum, quæ habet, secum auferre
possit, sed nudus abire cogatur."

(1 Timothy vi. 17), the vicissitudes to which riches are exposed (Matthew vi. 19, 20) : here it is death that puts an end to all possessions.

Ver. 17. And what must a man not endure for the sake of such an empty and vain good. *He eateth in darkness,* even though he may be seated in a well lighted hall. For he has no light in his heart : there all is gloom and sadness. In 1 Timothy vi. 10, it is said of those who seek to become rich, ἑαυτοὺς περιέπειραν ὀδύναις πολλαῖς, "they pierce themselves through with many sorrows." Whoso is visited by such pains, for him external lights are kindled in vain. Analogous is the frequent employment in the Old Testament of the darkenings of the sun and moon as an image of hard and gloomy tim s : see Jeremiah iv. 23, Amos viii. 9-10, Micah iii. 6, and chap. xii. 2, of this book. The sun shines truly only for the happy. אכל is used in its strict and proper meaning, as is evident from ver. 18. Luther remarks : "To eat in darkness is nothing else than to pass one's life in sadness and melancholy. Avaricious and uneasy people always find something which does not please them, which causes them to murmur and scold. For they are full of cares, griefs, and anxieties : they can neither eat nor drink cheerfully : they are always meeting with something that frets and annoys them." כעם is the third preterite. *And then his sickness and wrath.* The origin of the sickness is clear from the preceding כעם and the following קצף: he becomes sick with vexation and wrath at those who touch the mammon on which his heart is fixed. Cartwright says—"nihil ut illi ex omni labore et fatigatione emolumenti supersit, non magis quam si leves quasdam et nullius ponderis glumas s. pulverem coacervasset, quem ventus uno flatu subito dispelleret."

Ver. 18. That after אני we must mentally set a colon : "Behold, what I have seen : that it is, etc." is evident from the separating accent at the word אני and from the pointing אָנִי and not אֲנִי. We may take either טוב or יפה as an adverb, or even explain—"that it is good, comely." *To eat, to drink, to see good* (chap. ii. 24) forms the contrast to scraping avarice. To the securing of that which the writer has recognised as good there needs no heaping up of treasures. The words—"the number of the days of his life," are meant to remind us that the shorter man's life is, so much the more ought we to be on our guard against seeking happiness where it is not to be found.

Ver. 19. *Also :* that is, to say further this also, Ewald, 352 b. *God gives him power,* in that He frees him by His Spirit from the bonds of avarice. This takes place, however, only in connection with the divinely appointed means, only within the bounds of God's heritage. The heathen *must* serve mammon ; they are sold under his dominion, and for this reason their riches are not to be counted as good fortune. השליט always signifies " to make to rule," (Psalm cxix. 133 ; Daniel ii. 38-48). The object of the rule is either *one's own heart,* which the natural man, separated from God, has not in his own power : or *riches,* which without this action of God that makes free, are not a good, but a torment. The Berleburger Bible remarks : "made him Lord over it, that is, along with possessions has bestowed on him also a free and generous soul, so that he may not be a slave of mammon, but understand how to use it freely and rightly." In the clause, "that is a gift of God," the emphasis does not lie on אלהים but on מתת, as is clear from the word כי at the commencement of ver. 19—"it is a noble gift, for." The divine causality was prominently brought forward previously.

Ver. 20. *He thinks not much of the days of his life,* that is, they pass smoothly on. 1 Kings viii. 35, and 2 Chronicles vi. 26, furnish a sufficient warrant for the meaning " answer " given to the Hiph. of ענה. All other meanings are incapable of proof. Berleburger Bible : " To the pure all things are pure (Titus i. 15), and so a pure man may undoubtedly use riches with purity ; and it will, therefore, chiefly depend on each one's own heart, on how it stands before God. But if any person is unable to remain just as contented and calm, when house and home are burnt down, or when some other damage is done to his property, he proves himself to be not yet truly composed and satisfied : *that is the test thereof.*"

CHAPTER VI.

The discussion of the theme—" the vanity of riches "—
is here continued, with the intent, in the first instance, of
repressing the envy felt at the advantage enjoyed by the
heathen world in this respect, and then in order to undermine
the prevailing covetousness which proceeded from the same
root as envy, namely, the false estimate of earthly possessions.

Ver. 1. *There is an evil which I have seen under the sun,
and heavily does it weigh upon man.* Ver. 2. *A man to
whom God giveth riches, wealth and honour, so that he
wanteth nothing for his soul of all that he desireth, and God
giveth him not power to eat thereof, for a stranger will eat
it, that is vanity and an evil disease.* Ver. 3. *If a man
beget a hundred, and live many years, so that the days of
his life be many, and his soul be not filled with good, and
also that he have no grave: so, say I: an untimely birth
is better than he.* Ver. 4. *For in vanity came it in, and it
departeth in darkness, and with darkness is its name covered.*
Ver. 5. *Moreover it saw not the sun, and knew it not: this
hath more rest than that.* Ver. 6. *And if one should live a
thousand years twice, and should not see good: do not all
go to one place?* Ver. 7. *All the labour of man is for his
mouth, and yet the soul is not satisfied.* Ver. 8. *For what
advantage hath the wise over the fool? What, the miserable
that knoweth to walk before the living?* Ver. 9. *Better is the
sight of the eyes than the wandering of the soul: this also
is vanity and empty effort.* Ver. 10. *What he is: long ago
was his name named, and it is known that he is man and
cannot contend with Him that is mightier than he.* Ver. 11.
*For there are many things that increase vanity, what profit
hath man?* Ver. 12. *For who knoweth what is good for
man in life, for the number of the days of his vain life,
which he spendeth as a shadow: for who can tell a man
what shall be after him under the sun?*

Ver. 1. רבה may refer either to *frequency* (Septuagint, Vulgate, "frequens;" Luther; "and it is common amongst men,")

or to *size*. In favour of the latter view are decisive the principal passage, Genesis vi. 5, and the parallel passages, chap. ii. 21 ; viii. 6, where רעה רבה signifies "a *great* evil." That which on a superficial examination appears as a great *good*, turns out, on more careful inquiry to be a great *evil*. The author's commencing at once with such a description of the riches of worldly-minded men must have produced a great effect and given envy a severe blow.

Ver. 2. The rich man is the Persian (chap. x. 20). One ought not to envy him his riches. He does not dare to enjoy his wealth, and the enemy will soon take it away from him. How is it possible that that should be a matter for envy which more closely viewed is but a vain show? There were of course rich spendthrifts among the Persians also. But the example of the covetous rich man served as a proof that riches in themselves are not an enviable good. *Riches and wealth and honour*, are put together in this way also in 2 Chronicles i. 11. *God gives him not power*, that is, he delivers him not from the bonds of avarice by which he is held bound ; (compare chap. v. 18). *The stranger* is the successor of the Persian in the dominion of the world. נכרי is quite generally used of such as belong to another nation and society (Deuteronomy xvii. 15), and that it is to be taken in this sense here is evident from the correspondence that exists between the words, "a stranger will eat it," of this verse, and those of the 3d verse, "also he will have no grave." References cautiously made to the impending catastrophe of the Persian empire may be found also elsewhere : see chap. xi. 1-3 ; ix. 18. The expression, "evil disease," which has much the same force as "an evil is like a disease," is taken from Deuteronomy xxviii. 59.

Ver. 3. *Hundred*, namely, sons. The phrase—"the days of the years," is constantly used, especially in the Pentateuch, to designate the time of one's life (Genesis xxv. 7 ; xlvii. 8, 9. Psalm xc. 10). The words, "his soul is not filled with good," correspond to the words, "God giveth him not power to eat thereof," of ver. 2 : and "he has no grave," to the words, "a stranger will eat it." קבורה elsewhere signifies always "Grave," and therefore we must give it this meaning in the only passage, namely Jeremiah xxii. 19, where the meaning "Burial" seems to be required. The grave of the ass is the flaying ground. The preposition is omitted there, because the relation is quite clear in itself. Allusion is here made to a catastrophe like that depicted in Psalm lxxix. 3, " their blood have they shed like water, and there was none to bury them." Compare parallel passages, such as Jeremiah viii. 2, where of the godless it is declared, " they shall not be gathered, nor be buried : dung shall they be on the field," ix. 21, xxv. 33 ; Isaiah xiv. 19, 20, and what is written of Jezebel in 2 Kings ix. Seb. Schmidt and Rambach explain incorrectly, " ex turpi tenacitate non audeat aliquid honestæ sepulturæ destinare." Better than the lot of such a rich man,—a life without enjoyment, and then not even a grave,—is the lot of an untimely birth, which, though it has enjoyed no good, has experienced also no suffering.

Ver. 4, 5. On these verses it is remarked in the Berleburger Bible, " the meaner and worse the condition of an untimely birth is made, so much the greater must also appear the misery of a covetous man." The last words of verse 5, " this has rest above that," give the ground of the judgment that " an untimely birth is better than he," (ver. 3). Rest, *freedom from suffering*, it is in regard to which an untimely birth has the advantage over such an unfortunate rich man, who ought in fairness to be an object of *pity*, instead of being one of *envy*.

Ver. 6. *And if one a thousand years* (which measure the lives of the first fathers of the human race nearly reached) *should live twice over*, (Jerome, " et non ut Adam prope mille sed duobus millibus vixerit annis") is he then to be counted happy ? *Do not all go to one place?* Can he perhaps fetch up in Sheol, where all arrive in a like state of poverty, (οὐδὲν γὰρ εἰσηνέγκαμεν εἰς τὸν κόσμον, δῆλον ὅτι οὐδὲ ἐξενεγκεῖν τι δυνάμεθα, 1 Timothy vi. 7) that which he has lost on earth ?

Ver. 7. *All the labour of man is for his mouth*, (falsely explained by Luther—" on every man is labour imposed in his measure"), which is easy to fill, and in the rich man is not larger than in the poor. The Berleburger Bible says : " Can they carry more than one garment on the body ? Can they eat more than till they are filled ?" The rational conclusion to be drawn from the fact presented in these words, is that which is given us in 1 Timothy vi. 8,—ἔχοντες δὲ διατροφὰς καὶ σκεπάσματα, τούτοις ἀρχεσθησόμεθα. But that still, notwithstanding its limited capacity of enjoyment, the soul of man is not satisfied, is very strange, and is a strong proof how greatly the human race has been under the dominion of sin and folly which produce ἐπιθυμίας πολλὰς ἀνοήτους καὶ βλαβερὰς (1 Timothy vi. 9), ever since the day spoken of in Genesis iii.*

Ver. 8. In this verse are advanced the grounds of the proposition laid down with such generality in ver. 7, "that the soul of man is not satisfied." So deep laid is that hereditary disease of the human race, avarice, that not even the covenant people, not even the congregation of the chosen, is free from it. Wisdom is invariably represented in this book as the prerogative of Israel, folly as belonging to the heathen. The *wise man* ought in all fairness to be free from such a disease. But in reality it is otherwise. Even in the midst of the covenanted people must the Lord preach: "Take heed that ye be not covetous, for a man's life consisteth not in the abundance of the things which he possesseth." To a Timothy even, St. Paul felt it necessary to write: σὺ δὲ, ὦ ἄνθρωπε τοῦ Θεοῦ, ταῦτα φεῦγε (1 Timothy vi. 11). In the old Testament the members of the kingdom of God are frequently styled "poor and wretched." For them many sources of pain open themselves up, which the world does not know: in all the sufferings which befal them they confess a visitation of their sins, and receive them as a token of God's wrath: they do not try to distract their minds nor give themselves up to illusions, they do not gild over their misery but take up their cross willingly: and finally they are hated by the world because God has chosen them out of the world. That these miserable ones

---

* The meaning of the verse was accurately given by Cartwright: "Quod ob rem tantulam, quæ tam parabilis est, nosmet tantopere cruentamus, nosque anxii, laboribus et intempestivis curis conficimus.—Cum omnia, quæ quis improbo labore parat ad victum et cultum corporis referantur, sitque natura paucis contenta, insanam prorsus et prodigiosam hanc habendi inexplebilem cupiditatem esse, necesse est.—Deus os nostrum, in quod alimenta ingerimus, perangustum finxit: habendi cupiditas tamen tam late diffunditur, ac si os nostrum gurgitis et voraginis cujusdam instar, Jordanis fluvio uno haustu absorbendo idoneum esset; aut si Leviathanis os illis obtigisset, in quod plaustrum cum suis qui illud trahunt equis recipitur: ventriculus cum longitudine et latitudine vix sit palmaris, illi tamen farciendo ita omnes nervos suos intendit cupiditas acsi plus quam dolearis esset."

should also be assailed by earthly desires is the more to be
wondered at since "they know to walk before the living,"
since they are the nation of revelation, the only people on the
wide earth to whom God has given, in his law, a rule to regulate their conduct. Compare Deuteronomy iv. 5, 6 : "Behold I teach you to-day statutes and judgments, even as the
Lord my God commanded me : and ye shall keep them and
do them, for that is your wisdom and your understanding in
the sight of the nations, which shall hear all these statutes
and say, surely this great nation is a wise and understanding
people :" also Psalm cxlvii. 19, 20—"He sheweth His word
to Jacob, his statutes and his judgments unto Israel. He does
not deal so with any heathen, and his judgments, they know
the n not." The reverse of those who know to walk before
the living, are "the fools who do not know to go into the
city," (chap. x. 15) the heathen.

Ver. 9. מראה is universally the object of sight, that which
is seen : so in Leviticus xiii. 12,—"according to all the sight
of the eyes of the priest," that is, according to all that is seen
by the eyes of the priest. Seeing that man can so easily have
a sufficiency, it is better to rejoice in that which lies before
his eyes, however trivial it may be, than to wander away into
the clouds with our desires, (μὴ μετεωρίζεσθε, Luke xii. 29,) and
to vex ourselves with plans and hopes which very easily deceive, and even if fulfilled bring us no real happiness. The
Berleburger Bible says : "this is the wandering of the soul
which then runs about amongst the creatures, and like an
Esau hunts in the fields of this world for the good food which
wisdom finds only at home and in the calmness of contentment." Luther remarks,—"Solomon's opinion is, that it is
better to make use of that which lies before our eyes, that is,
of what is now at hand, than that the soul go wandering to
and fro. Solomon's will is that we make use of the present,
thank God for it, and not think of anything else—like the
dog in Æsop which snapped at the shadow and let the flesh
fall. What he intends then is that we should use that which
God has given before our eyes, that which is now here, and be
content therewith and not follow our own soul which is never
satisfied : as he said before. Let every Christian then abide
by that which he has, which God gives him just now : that

pleases him : but the godless are not so : on the contrary, all that they see is a torment to them, because they do not make use of the present, but their soul runs hither and thither and everywhere and is never satisfied. Consequently, when a godless man has money, it does not suffice him, he uses it not, but desires more : if he has a wife, he is not content, but wants another : if he has a whole kingdom he is unsatisfied : like Alexander the Great whom a world could not satisfy. Solomon therefore forbids the soul running to and fro, as it is said in the Hebrew, that is, we are not to be always weaving our thoughts together into plans. And the sum is this—use the present : for that also is vanity and vexation, to wit, when the soul wanders thus restlessly about."

Ver. 10. *What he is*—he, namely, to whom reference is here made—: *Long ago was his name named :* that we are told by the name long ago given to him. There is a reference here to Genesis v. 2,—" and he called their name *man*, on the day on which they were created." In this name is expressed the *impotence* of man. He describes men as *earthly*, because they are taken from the earth, (Genesis ii. 7,) and because they must return to it, (chap. iii. 19.) The article in התקיף which occasioned difficulty to the Masorite is quite regular. Hitzig remarks, " the meaning is not that a man cannot fight with a stronger (*e. g.* man,) but that, man cannot struggle with the particular person who surpasses men, namely, God." Paul appears to allude to this passage in 1 Corinthians x. 22, μὴ ἰσχυρότεροι αὐτοῦ ἐσμεν: the practical conclusion therefrom is the uncertainty of riches, the ἀδηλότης πλούτου ; and our duty, evidently is, not to set our hopes upon them but upon the living God, (1 Timothy vi. 17,) not to strive after riches, but to endeavour to stand well with our Creator. Inasmuch as man is absolutely dependent on God, he ought not to engage in many distracting occupations, he should not vex himself with cunning and violent modes of obtaining riches, because he cannot protect what he has gained, and knows not but that at any moment he may hear the call, "thou fool, this night will thy soul be required of thee." How foolish, then, to envy the heathen that wealth which may, like the flower of the field, so soon fade away, (James i. 10, 11.)

Ver. 11. *For there are many things that increase vanity.*

דברים in the sense of "words" does not suit the connection. More property, more vanity. That is as certain as that man is not the lord of his own life, but is absolutely dependent on a higher power. What did it help the Persian that he had subdued a great part of the world and had appropriated its treasures to himself? When Alexander came and violently assailed the two-horned ram of the Persian, Empire, (Daniel viii. 6,) it became evident that it had only increased vanity. The same thing takes place in great commercial crises. Cart-wright says—"quam ob rem animum ad studium pietatis convertamus, quæ ad omnia utilis est et promissiones habet præsentis et futuræ vitæ, (1 Timothy iv.") *What more has man?* The rich have not in reality more than the poor. For their advantages turn out, on a closer examination, to be mere delusion and vanity: and they vanish as soon as the judg-ments of God go abroad in the world.

Ver. 12. The question—*For who knoweth what is good for man in life?*—refers not only to earthly goods, but to eternal, to the true and real goods. (Luke xvi. 11,) whose possession is in all circumstances desirable. This is clear from the connec-tion with the foregoing enquiry—"what more has man?" (of these things?) For who knows what? The words—*for the number of the days of his vain life, which he spends like a shadow*—(מספר must be supplied with ב from בחיים; that the days can be counted, is a sign of the shortness of the duration of life; com-pare chap. v. 17,) are meant to teach us that the shorter our life the more important is it that we should not feed ourselves with wind and ashes. In this shadowy existence we should not hunt after unsubstantial shadows. The fleeting, quickly van-ishing shadow is an image of the transitoriness and short-lived-ness of man. Büchner remarks—" a shadow may stretch itself out as long as it can, but when the sun goes down it vanishes and leaves nothing behind it." Compare chap. viii. 13; 1 Chronicles xxix. 15,—"like the shadow are our days upon earth." Psalm ciii. 15,—"man is in his life like grass: as a flower of the field, so he flourisheth." Psalm cxliv. 4, "man is like to vanity: his days are as a shadow that passeth away." The words, " for who can tell a man what shall be after him under the sun?" contain the reason for the affirm-ation that riches are not to be regarded as a true good. Only

on one condition should we be justified in treating them as
important, namely, that we knew the future, and had it in our
power. Some accident or other may suddenly rob us of what
we have gathered with so much toil. Nay more, there may
come a great catastrophe which, like the flood, will sweep
everything away. *After him,* that is, after his present condition (compare chap. iii. 22 ; vii. 14.) Several have falsely
explained—"after his *death.*" The practical conclusion is, that
we should strive after true possessions : * and then that we
should be free from cares, covetousness and envy, content
with what we have, however little it may be : ἀρχεῖσθε τοῖς
ὀψωνίοις ὑμῶν (Luke iii. 14.) Rambach observes : "Ex quibus
omnibus apparet, nihil melius esse quam proscripta turpi avaritia præsentibus contentum esse, iisque cum pia et licita
hilaritate frui." Luther remarks . "the hearts of men strive
after various kinds of things : one seeks power, another riches :
but still they know not whether they shall obtain them. Nor
do they make use of God's present gifts, but their heart han-
kers alone and always after that which they have not, and
cannot yet see. He does not speak of that which will come
after this life, but means to say, that no man knows what
will happen to him after an hour, after a day, or after a year.
Julius Cæsar having put down the rest, thought that then he
had the game all in his own hands, and meant to set the
Roman Empire in fine order : but at the very moment when
he was revolving his plans, he was killed in the council at
Rome. Why then do we vex and torment ourselves with our
own thoughts, when future things are not a single moment in
our power ? We ought consequently to be content with that
which God gives us each moment, and commit all to Him
who alone is acquainted with, and is able to regulate both
present and future."

* As Paul Gerhardt sings :—
  " Aber was die Seele nährt
  Gottes Huld und Christi Blut
  Wird von Keiner Zeit verzehrt,
  Ist und bleibet allzeit gut.
  Erdengut zerfällt und bricht,
  Seelengut, das schwindet nicht."

CHAPTER VII. 1-10.

We have here a decalogue of instruction on the sufferings of the people of God and of consolation and admonition in regard thereto.   Attention is directed, on the one hand, to the fruit of righteousness which suffering brings, to its blessed termination ; and, on the other hand, God's people is warned not to permit itself to be drawn aside to murmurings.

Human existence is subjected to severe sufferings (ver. 1). But these sufferings must serve the best interests of those who love God (ver. 2-4).   The misery of the children of God is better than the happiness of the world, for the latter is the forerunner of impending ruin (ver. 5-7).   The people of God, on the contrary, if they are only patient and content with the leadings of their God, will receive the best at the end.

Ver. 1. *Better is name than good oil, and the day of death, than the day of one's birth.*   Ver. 2. *It is better to go to the house of mourning than to go to the house of feasting, for this is the end of all men, and the living lays it to heart.* Ver. 3. *Better is anger than laughter, for when the countenance looks sad, the heart becomes merry.   Ver. 4. The heart of the wise is in the house of mourning, and the heart of fools in the house of mirth.   Ver. 5. Better is it to hear the rebuke of the wise, than a man who hears the song of fools.* Ver. 6. *For as the crackling of thorns under a pot, so is the laughter of fools, and this also is vanity.   Ver. 7. For oppression maketh a wise man mad, and a gift destroyeth the heart.   Ver. 8. Better is the end of a thing than the beginning thereof : better the patient in spirit than the proud in spirit.   Ver. 9. Be not hasty in thy spirit to be angry, for anger resteth in the bosom of fools.   Ver. 10. Say not thou : what is the cause that the former days were better than these ? for with wisdom thou dost not inquire concerning this.*

Ver. 1. The first clause has no internal connection whatever with the second : the means adopted to point out such a connection have been plainly artificial and farfetched.   The point of comparison is simply this, that, in the first case, as well as the second, the one thing mentioned is better than the other. Just in the same way is the point of comparison external and general in chap. v. 2. טוב occurs oftener in this chapter than in any other chapter of the Old Testament. The first clause of the verse is based on Proverbs xxii. 1, "name is more to be preferred than great riches." Here, however, the sentence appears to be more pointed. שמן has a sound something like שם. From the fundamental passage it is evident that good oil is considered here as something very costly and precious. That there is an internal nexus between the words "ointment" and "name," we should be led to think by the passage in the Song of Solomon i. 3, where שמן and שם are in like manner connected: "In smell are thine ointments good, ointment poured forth is thy name." That in the first clause the great and lovely name is represented under the image of odorous ointments, is expressly said in the second clause. With smell is connected rumour (German, Geruch, and Gerücht): "odores," says Gesenius, appealing to Exodus v. 11, "sæpe ad famam transferuntur." The proposition which is here of primary importance is formed by the words: "and the day of death is better than the day of one's birth." By the day of death we are to understand the day when one dies: this explains the suff. The day of death is better than the day of birth—so speaks the author to such as mourn because of life's lost happiness. He does not wish to persuade them to feel what they do not feel: he allows that they are right whenever they have right on their side. "The world is a vale of tears, and everywhere care, trouble, fears:"—that is an undeniable truth about which we may not dispute with sufferers, and which, above all, we must concede, if we mean really and truly to comfort them. But this assertion, though perfectly true, is only a one-sided truth, and therefore the author does not rest satisfied with it; he goes further, and in connection therewith opens up afterwards points of view which throw light on the gloom and mystery of suffering. When he lays down this proposition, he does not deny that there dwells in man a natural love of life, and that life is in itself a good thing, (compare chap. ix. 4, xi. 7) he does not deny that the clear light of divine grace shines into the darkness of this earthly life (compare chap. ix, 7, 8) "go thy way, eat thy bread with joy, and drink thy wine

with a merry heart, for God hath pleasure in thy works:"
he does not deny the infinite value of suffering as a school
for the spirit ; he sees, on the contrary, as is plainly set forth
in verses 2 ff., ("the day of death is, indeed, better than the
day of birth, *but* yet it is better to go to the house of mourning, etc."), that it is the most important means of purification
and progress, that it is therefore disguised grace, and that it
constitutes the best preparation for a future existence, for the
day when the spirit shall return to God, who gave it (chap.
xii. 7). Sayings of similar import we find also in heathen
writers,* with this difference, however, that they possessed
no key to such sufferings, that they were unable to reconcile
them with the divine righteousness and love, and that they
were shut out from a knowledge of, and approach to, those
sources of consolation which are revealed in the Holy Scriptures. An amplification and illustration of this short saying
may be found in Job iii. and Jeremiah xx. Compare especially Jeremiah xx. 18—"Wherefore came I forth out of the
womb to see suffering and sorrow, that my days should be
consumed with shame ?" To seek happiness in this earthly
existence has been considered, ever since the day spoken of
in Genesis iii., as identical with gathering grapes from thorns
and figs from thistles. The right sense is mistaken by those
interpreters who suppose that death comes under consideration here, so far as it opens the way to eternal life, and who
compare Philippians i. 21, 23, and Revelations xiv. 13.
Amongst them is Melancthon, who remarks: "illa ethnica,
optimum non nasci aut quam celerrime aboleri aliena a
doctrina ecclesiæ :" and the Berleburger Bible, where we read
—"for although the day of death extinguishes the light of
this life, it kindles the light of eternal life and blessedness."

Ver. 2. That *the house of mourning* is one in which a

---

* Grotius: "Valerius Maximus ii. 6—'Thraciæ vero illa natio merito sibi
sapientiæ laudem vindicaverit, quæ natales hominum flebiliter, exequias cum
hilaritate celebrans, sine ullis doctorum præceptis verum conditionis nostræ
habitum pervidit.' Mela de iisdem Thracibus: 'Lugentur apud quosdam
puerperia, natique deflentur; funera contra festa sunt et veluti sacra cantu
lusuque celebrantur.' De iisdem Solinus: 'Apud plurimos luctuosa sunt puerperia denique recens natum fletu parens excipit : contraversum læta sunt funera
adeo ut exemtos gaudio prosequantur.' Hanc sententiam Euripides in Cresi-
phontem suam transtulit."

dead man is being mourned, is clear from what follows. אבל,
is generally used of mourning for the dead. הוא, "this"
namely, that one is mourned for, that one dies. The commentary to the words—"and the living takes it to heart"—
we find in Psalm xc. 11, 12. From the contemplation of
death we recognise "the power of the anger of God," and by
this knowledge we are led to regard with due earnestness
the sin which called forth such anger. The relation of this
verse to the preceding is as follows : Great, in truth, are the
sufferings of this life, as Israel must now, through painful
experience, acknowledge, but for him who knows how rightly
to use them, they will bear rich fruit. Israel was then in
the house of mourning, their heathen tyrants were in the
house of feasting : (compare chap. x. 19, where a description
is given of their wanton revels.) But, if they only know the
time of their visitation, the happiness is on their side, not on
that of their oppressors. If, in their mournful circumstances,
in the devastations which death had already made amongst
the people of God, they see the divine anger against sin, they
will gain a "wise and understanding heart" which is itself
the highest blessing on earth and the condition of all other
blessings. Times of misfortune are times of happiness for
the church. Melancthon says—" In rebus secundis fiunt
homines negligentiores, minus cogitant de ira dei et minus
expectant auxilium dei, deinde fiunt et insolentiores, confi-
dunt sua industria, sua potentia et facile impelluntur a dia-
bolo. Ideo ex illo fastigio postea ruunt in magnas calami-
tates, juxta illud : tolluntur in altum ut lapsu graviore
ruunt. Et contra ærumnæ sunt commonefactiones de nostra
infirmitate, et de petendo auxilio dei. Et sunt frenum mul-
tarum cupiditatum. Ideo ecclesia subjecta est cruci."

Ver. 3. With regard to כעס, "anger, indignation, chagrin,"
not "sorrow," compare what is said in Psalm vi. 8 ; x. 14.
Anger is here recommended : in verse 9, it is condemned.
The indignation which is usually called forth by sufferings, is
at once good and evil—*good* when it is directed against one's
own sin ; *evil* when it is directed against God and the instruments of His righteousness. Compare Lamentations iii. 39,
"Wherefore do the people murmur thus in life? Each one
murmurs against his sin." The anger which is here recom-

mended is in substance, in essence, repentance. It leads to
the confession, " We, we have sinned and been rebellious :
therefore hast thou not spared," (Lamentations iii. 42). רע פנים
which signifies strictly—" the badness of the countenance"—
is used in the sense of " sadness" only in one other place,
namely, in Nehemiah ii. 2, " Why is thy countenance sad,
seeing thou art not sick ? this is nothing else but sorrow of
heart," רע לב. Countenance and heart are put in contrast with
each other there also, but in such a way that the condition of
the latter is known from that of the former ; whereas here
the heart wears a different look from that of the countenance.
יטב when used of the heart, means always " to be joyful,
merry." This merriness, however, is one which arises from
improvement. By the contrast drawn between the countenance and the heart we are told, that sadness sits more on the
surface, takes possession of the outworks, whilst on the contrary
peace and joy reign within. The happiness which the world
gives causes the countenance to be radiant, but leaves the
heart in an evil state. True joy is only there where the
heart stands in a right relation to God and His commands.
Inasmuch, therefore, as suffering helps to put us into such a
relation :—as the Berleburger Bible says—" God's image is
often formed in suffering"—it is a means of attaining to true
joy. In consonance with this passage the apostle says in 2
Corinthians vi. 10—ὡς λυπούμενοι, ἀεὶ δὲ χαίροντες : and further
also in 2 Corinthians vii. 10—ἡ γὰρ κατὰ Θεὸν λύπη μετάνοιαν εἰς
σωτηρίαν ἀμεταμέλητον κατεργάζεται. If suffering works repentance it must also make joyful : for the heart becomes glad so
soon as it is in its true and normal condition.

Ver. 4. *The heart of the wise,* that is, of the genuine members of the kingdom of God, *is in the house of mourning,* that
is, the wise stay willingly, gladly, there. The *willing* assumption of the cross distinguishes the children of God from the
world. They are able to call the cross, " dear cross !" Whereas, to the world, suffering is a horror and an abomination.
Jerome institutes a comparison here with the beatitude of the
πενθοῦντες in Matthew v. 4. The sorrowful, however, are such
as have their hearts in the house of mourning. Others drive
it out of their minds and seek relief in dissipations.

Ver. 5. *Better is it to hear the rebuke of the wise,* as Israel was now compelled to hear the voice of its prophets, reproaching it with its sins on the ground of its misery. The rebuking wise man is set before us for example in Malachi, whose prophecies bear the inscription, "the burden of the word of the Lord," and further in this book also (compare chap. iv. 17; v. 5). That the rebuke found its point of departure in the suffering of him who was its object, and that in fact the rebuke was a kind of commentary on the suffering, was perceived even by S. Schmidt, who says, "intelliguntur sermones, qui a sapiente in domo luctus habentur." *Than a man who hears the song of fools.* The man must be conceived as himself also singing, as in fact, a member of a merry society of the children of this world. The Persians were at that time, the singing fools. That a distinction is to a certain extent made here between *the man* and *the fools,* would lead us to conclude that the thought is the following,—that Israel, although in suffering and compelled to submit to rebukes, is better off than if it luxuriated with the world in pleasure and mirth.

Ver. 6. The words—*For as the crackling of thorns under a pot, so is the laughter of fools*—are based on Psalm cxviii. 12, where Israel, being under the rule of the Persians, says— "They (the heathen) compassed me about like bees, they are quenched as the fire of thorns : in the name of the Lord will I destroy them." Between the happiness or good fortune of the heathen and the fire of thorns, the point of comparison is that both alike violently blaze up, and are quickly extinguished. In the fundamental passage just quoted we find אֵשׁ קוֹצִים. Here סִירִים is chosen because of the play on the word : like the play between שָׁמֵן and שֵׁם in ver. 1, where a passage found ready to hand in Proverbs is made somewhat more concise and pointed. More point is perhaps gained also by the description of the happiness of fools as laughter. Between crackling and giggling there is a certain similarity of sound ; there is significance therefore in the designation, "the *voice* of thorns." *Under the pot*, which J. D. Michaelis considered intolerable, serves to render the description more vivid and real, because thorn fires were usually made in such a position. See Psalm lviii. 9, "Before your pots can feel the thorns :" where thorns are evidently used for making a fire under the pots. *And also this*, namely, the laughter of fools, the happiness of the heathen, *is vanity*, like so much else in this world of illusions, and is consequently not a fit object of envy. Considered more carefully Israel is happier than the heathen world, "for the exultation of the wicked is short, and the joy of the impious is but for a moment. Though his greatness mount up to the heavens, and his head reach unto the clouds, yet he perishes for ever like his own dung, and they which see him say—where is he?" (Job xx. 5, 7). The words, "this also is vanity," have been historically fulfilled and confirmed in the utter and complete disappearance of the Persian monarchy, whereas Israel still blooms and flourishes on in the Christian Church. Luther remarks—"Virgilius says, fire in the stubble crackles very much, but has no force, contains no heat, and is soon extinguished. So also is the laughter and the mirth of fools: it looks as if it would last for ever, and blazes up high, but is nothing at all. One moment they have their consolation; the next comes a misfortune which casts them down to the ground: and so all the joy lies in the ashes. This, therefore, accords admirably with that which was said shortly before, "and this also is vanity." The joy and false worldly consolation of the flesh do not last long, and all such joy ends in sadness and evil."

Ver. 7. The reason is here assigned why the happiness of fools is so short. They work their own ruin. Sin deprives them of their understanding, and when that has vanished destruction cannot be far off. First the *mens sana* is lost, and then follows ruin. First the soul dies out, and afterwards the body is cast on the flaying ground. Parallel is Proverbs xv. 27, "he that is greedy of gain destroyeth his own house, and he that hateth gifts shall live." *For oppression maketh the wise man mad.* pwy, "oppression," as exercised by the Persian tyrants (Psalm lxii. 10). Oppression *befools, makes mad :* every tyranny has a demoralizing influence on him who wields it; it deadens all higher intelligence, and takes away consequently the preservative against destruction. "The wise man" here is not one who is still such, but who ought to be, and might be, and has in part been such. "The wise man"—so might the Persian still be designated at the time of Cyrus. *And a gift destroyeth the heart.* Under oriental tyrannies everything was to be had for presents. According to the parallel, "befools, makes mad," the *heart* is brought under consideration as the seat of the understanding : compare Jeremiah iv. 9, "and it shall come to pass at that day that the heart of the king shall perish and the heart of the princes," that is, they shall lose their prudence, their power of reflection.

Ver. 8. *Better is the end of a thing than the beginning :* The thought is quite correctly presented by Melancthon, " Quamquam enim multa patienda sunt tamen vincit tandem causa honesta :" "All's well that ends well," and whoso laughs the last, laughs the best. This is assuredly very consolatory for the people of God, for the end belongs to them so certainly as God belongs to them. The proposition is here expressed generally, that whoso has the end of a thing in his favour, for whomsoever the end of a business turns out well, is better off than he to whom the beginning belongs. The commencement of that which is here treated of was on the side of the heathen world, for in the present Israel served, and the heathens ruled. By *the end* we must understand a *fortunate happy end,* inasmuch as a bad end cannot be called an end at all. So also on the same subject in Psalm xxxvii. 37, 38, "mark the pious and behold the upright man, for a future has the man of peace. But the transgressors shall be destroyed together, the future of the wicked will be extirpated :" the meek man *has* an end, a future : whereas the wicked who are swept away in the half of their days, (Psalm lv. 23,) are violently robbed of their end or of their future. So also Proverbs xxiii. 17 ; Jeremiah xxix. 11,—"for I know the thoughts that I think towards you, thoughts of peace and not of evil, to give you an *end* and hope." The main passage in which an end is denied to the heathen is Numbers xxiv. 20, where it is said of Amalek,—"his end is destruction." "Behold, the end of the heathen is a wilderness, a dry land and a desert" says Jeremiah in chap. l. 12. The formula with which the prophets open their proclamations of redemption is based on the idea that only the beginning of the times belongs to the heathen world, the end on the contrary to the people of God. *Better is the patient in spirit than the proud in spirit.* Between רוח ארך, which occurs only in this place, and ארך אפים, βραδὺς εἰς ὀργήν, (James i. 19,) there is no difference, as is evident from the fact that its contrast in ver. 9 is *Anger,* כעם. Accordingly, we must understand by " patience of spirit " the opposite of

" passionate excitement," which bursts forth against God in
times of suffering and leads to arbitrary endeavours to help
oneself. The patient in spirit is the true Israelite : the
heathen is the proud in spirit. The former is better off, for
the patient man has the end as his portion : pride on the
contrary either comes before a fall or is unable to avert it.
If Israel have the end on their side, all they can do is to wait;
and he who can wait till the end must certainly attain redemption, (compare Lamentations iii. 24 ff.) As the heathen
power has no future it can effect nothing, notwithstanding
all its pride.

Ver. 9. Be not hasty in thy spirit to be angry. The *anger
or wrath* is to be conceived as directed against God and the
evil doers favoured by Him, that is, in this present case, against
the heathen ; compare Psalm xxxvii. 1, 2, 8. *For anger resteth
in the bosom of fools,* who only look at the present and at
once fall into error with regard to God and his providence if
things go otherwise than in their view they ought to do. It
is folly to fix the attention only on that which lies directly
before our eyes, to speak wisdom in presence of the good fortune of the wicked : "as grass shall they be cut down, and
as the green herb shall they wither," and, " evil doers shall be
rooted out, but they that wait on the Lord shall possess the
land." If we only do not make haste to be angry, the Lord will
in his own good time remove all occasions to wrath out of the
way. As the Berleburger Bible says : " blessed, on the contrary, is he who in all the events of life maintains a calm
patience, equips himself with a spirit of humble submissive-
ness and magnanimous contentment, accommodates himself to
good and evil times alike, and ever derives strength and
quickening from the petition,—" thy will be done."

*Ver. 10. Say not thou, what is the cause that the former
days were better than these,* meaning, "why is it so, how is
such a downfall of His people consistent with the love and
righteousness of God ?" Luther's remark, which starts from the
view that the words were directed against the " laudatores
temporis acti,"—" Say not thou, it has been better ; for it has
never gone right everywhere in the world,"—overlooks the
force of the expression, " what is it, that, *why,* is it so?"
Those whom the author had in view are described in ver. 16

of the Epistle of Jude, as γογγυσταί, μεμψίμοιροι.　The contemporary Malachi introduces them in chap. ii. 17, as speaking: "Ye weary the Lord with your words, and yet ye say, wherein do we weary Him? When ye say, every one that doeth evil is good in the sight of the Lord and He delighteth in them; or, where is the God of judgment?" So also in chap. iii. 14, 15, "ye say, it is vain to serve God, and what profit is it that we keep his ordinance and walk in filth before the Lord of Hosts. And now we call the proud happy, (that is, the heathen,) built up, (that is fortunate,) are the workers of iniquity, they tempt God and notwithstanding escape." *For with wisdom thou dost not inquire concerning this.* The wise man sees in the sufferings of the people of God the deserved punishment of their sins, and says, "It is the goodness of the Lord that we are not utterly lost, but the Lord does not cast off for ever, he has compassion again according to his great kindness." Wisdom at the same time recognises that afflictions are only temporal, *and* that temporal tribulations have a good *foundation.* Here, therefore, wisdom appears as the soul of patience.*

CHAPTER VII., 11-12.

Koheleth proceeds now to comfort Israel, by directing their thoughts to the treasure of wisdom left to them, which was a pledge of the restoration of that which had been lost. It is impossible that a people which can claim wisdom as its own possession should be for ever subjected to death.

Ver. 11. *Wisdom is good as an inheritance, and still better for those who see the sun.* Ver. 12. *For in the shadow of wisdom in the shadow of silver; but the excellency of knowledge is, Wisdom giveth life to him that hath it.*

Ver. 11. The words "wisdom is good," take up again the מחכמה of ver. 10. The mention of wisdom there occasions the

---

* Cartwright says, "Prov. iii., eodem modo patientiam sapientiæ appellatione describit. Nam cum v. 11, 12, ad patientiam in perferendis dei castigationibus cohortatus fuisset, v. 13, ad corroborandam hanc adhortationem subjungit, beatum esse qui sapientiam assecutus sit et Jac. i., ad patientiam exstimulans v. 5, subnectit, sapientiam hanc a deo ei petendam esse qui illa destituitur."

writer to seek to impress the soul of Israel with the excellence
of the possession which still remains.   To the word *inheritance* corresponds the word *silver* in ver. 12.   It is consequently the *property*.   As regards that, the children of Israel
were at a decided disadvantage compared with the world.
They were bondsmen in the land which the Lord had given
them, and strangers devoured its produce ; they were drained
by their heathen tyrants, they were an impoverished people.
For the inexperienced this must have been a source of severe
temptations.*   Against such assaults, Koheleth here offers a
ground of consolation.†   He reminds them that they still
have a great advantage over others in the wisdom which is a
privilege of the people of God, which can be found nowhere
on earth but only in God, (Job xxviii ; James i. 5,) and in
His word and law : compare Deuteronomy iv. 5-6, " Behold
I teach you statutes and judgments, as the Lord my God
commanded me :   and ye shall hold and do them, for this is
your wisdom and your understanding in the sight of the
nations :" also in Proverbs i. 7, " the fear of the Lord is
the beginning of knowledge :" further, chap. ii. 6, " the Lord
giveth wisdom, out of his mouth cometh knowledge and understanding ;" compare lastly, chap. v. 18, " rejoice in the wife
of thy youth," where by the wife of youth we are to understand *wisdom* which had stood in the very closest relation to
Israel from the first commencement of his existence, and chap.
ii. 16, where *folly* is brought forward as the strange woman,
the foreigner.   We may not follow the example of the Septuagint and Vulgate, and explain—" wisdom is good united
with possessions."   Such a rendering would not be consistent
with the posture of affairs at this time, when Israel was destitute of possessions, and with ver. 12, which represents wisdom and money as having different owners.   The word עם
rather expresses the idea that wisdom may enter into compe-
tition, or take rank, with property : and then with increased

---

* Melanchthon, " Scit ecclesia alias esse causas necis Abel et alias necis Ab-
salomis. Sed homines sine doctrina ecclesiæ turbantur his exemplis, ut dubi-
tent de providentia.

† This point of view is recognised also by Luther; he observes, "here Solomon
closes the admonition which he had given, to *strengthen* and to *comfort* those
who were in danger of being *impatient* because of the wickedness of the world."

force יוֹתֵר adds that, in fact, wisdom excels property. יוֹתֵר is properly a participle, and occurs in the sense "over, remaining," in 1 Samuel xv. 16, and in chap. xii. 9 of this book. Elsewhere it is always used as an adverb, in the sense of "more, very, too, too much, besides, moreover." So in chap. ii. 15 ; vi. 8-11 ; vii. 16 ; xii. 12. יוֹתֵר never signifies "advantage, gain." The meaning "more" is required further by the argument advanced in ver. 12, where the justice of its application to wisdom is more carefully pointed out. In Proverbs iii. 14, also, wisdom is represented as *better* than silver and gold.* The children of men are described in chap. vi. 5 ; xi. 8 also, as "those who see the sun."

Ver. 12. This verse is to be explained as follows,—"for, (if one is) in the shadow of wisdom, (one is also) in the shadow of money, not less safe than when one is protected by money." Threatening dangers may be averted quite as often by wisdom as by property. The reason is thus given for setting wisdom on an equality with property (ver. 11). Rightly Symmachus, σκέπει σοφία ὡς σκέπει τὸ ἀργύριον: falsely the Vulgate, "sicut enim protegit sapientia sic protegit pecunia." Because shadow affords protection against heat,—one of the greatest plagues of eastern countries,—it is used frequently as an image of .protection in general, and with the greater fitness since all tribulations are represented under the figure of heat.—In the second clause the reason of the use of the term "more" in respect to wisdom (ver. 11) is assigned. חִיָּה does not signify " to keep in life," a thing which would fall under the category of shadow, and which gold also in certain circumstances is capable of, but "to quicken, to call back to life." Israel had then fallen into the hands of death, but the treasure which they still retained, that wisdom from above which still dwelt amongst them, was the pledge of a joyful *resurrection.* Wisdom quickens, gives life, because the grace of the living and life-giving God rests on the wise man. The principal passage on this subject is Deuteronomy xxxii. 39, where, in regard to Israel's restoration after severe tribulations, it is said, " I kill and I make alive, I wound and I will heal." In the Psalms we

---

* Correctly Rambach : hac voce (יוֹתֵר) comparatio sapientiæ, cum hæreditate ita continuatur ut sapientia illi etiam præferatur."

find היה often used of the restoration to life of Israel when
fallen under the power of death, as also of a merely external
restoration : for example, Psalm lxxi. 20; lxxx. 18; lxxxv. 6;
cxix. 25, "My soul cleaveth to the dust, quicken thou me
according to thy word." In Hosea vi. 2, it is said, "he will
revive us after two days : on the third he will raise us up
that we may live before him." In opposition to the fundamental and the parallel passage, as well as against usage,
Knobel explains as follows,—" the advantage of wisdom consists therein, that it gives us a contented and cheerful spirit,"
Elster, " an inner power, a rich and full spiritual life." Compare besides, Proverbs iii. 18—" She (namely, Wisdom) is a
tree of life to them that lay hold on her, and happy is every
one that retaineth her :" according to which, the life which
wisdom gives, is identical with happiness.

CHAPTER VII. 13, 14.

This also was a comfort for Israel, that in their sufferings
no less than in their happiness they must recognize the arrangement of God,—one, too, proceeding from well considered
counsel.

Ver. 13. *Consider the work of God, for who can make that*
straight which he hath made crooked ? Ver. 14. *In the day*
of prosperity be joyful and in the day of adversity : behold,
God hath made this even as that, to the end that man should
not find anything which will come after him.

Ver. 13. *Behold the work of God;* most men see it not.
In adversity their minds remain fixed on the natural causes,—
hence their despair, their passionate excitement, and their
futile attempts to help themselves. He who sees God's work
attains at once the power of calm self-command and of quiet
submission ; he says, " I keep silence because thou hast done
it," (Psalm xxxix. 9). This summons to consider the work
of God is then justified and enforced by a reference to its lofti-
ness and significance : " for who can make that straight which
he hath made crooked ?" (עות, " to make crooked," chap. i. 15;
xii. 3). No one can withstand God or alter His determina-
tions. And because no one *can* no one therefore should *wish*

it. We ought to humble ourselves *with joy* beneath the almighty hand of God. For, as the *Almighty* One He is the sum and substance of all wisdom, all love, all righteousness. Almighty arbitrariness is inconceivable.*

Ver. 14. "On the day of good be in the good," that is, be inwardly in a good state when thou art outwardly prosperous, be joyful, בטוב = בלב טוב, chap. ix. 7, compare 1 Kings viii. The explanation, "be prosperous, occupy thyself with it, enjoy it," lays too strong an emphasis on the word היה. *And in the day of adversity behold,* instead of, "then also be thou content, for behold." The correspondence between the two phrases, "in the day of good," and "in the day of evil," plainly implies that what follows will teach, at all events, as to substance, how we ought to be in the day of adversity. This correspondence is unheeded by those who explain the Hebrew, "when misfortune befals thee, consider, weigh," namely, what follows. The words must be punctuated thus—"In the day of adversity, behold;" not, "In the day of adversity behold" —that is, a comma should be inserted after "adversity." Ewald also errs in the same way when he explains, "And the day of adversity look upon, consider it, calmly." To contentment in suffering we must surely be aroused by the consideration that it comes from the same God who sends us our prosperity, as Job says—"do we accept the good from God, and shall we not also accept the evil?" The sender being the same, there must be a substantial resemblance between the various things sent, notwithstanding external dissimilarity. God, when he lays the cross upon us, still remains God, still continues to be our heavenly Father, our Saviour, who has thoughts of peace concerning us; what He does is well done, and however heavily the burden may weigh upon us, it must prove wholesome in the end. But the author is not content with merely directing the mind to the ordering of God whose name is in itself a balsam for the wounds of the heart. He hints also at the motives which dictate the infliction of suffer-

---

* Cartwright says,—"Avis laqueo capta tanto arctius constringitur, quanto fortius ut se expediat luctatur. Si quis igitur dei laqueo irretitus teneatur, nihil illi tutius est, quam ut se totum dei voluntati permittat, maxime cum in summa illa potentia, qua instructus est, nihil non juste, nihil non sapienter facit, Iii. xxxiv. 12."

ings.   God causes evil days to alternate with gooɑ ones, *to the
end that man should not find anything which will come after
him*, that is, in order that he may not be able to fathom anything
which lies behind his present condition.   (*Afterhim*, so also chap.
iii. 23, vi. 12).   He is thus made thoroughly little, thoroughly
submissive to God : he is thus prevented from setting his
heart on transitory sources of happiness.   If man cannot be
certain of a single day of his life, he must surely be driven to
look up to the Lord of life.   על דברת which means strictly
"on a matter," occurs in the sense "by reason of," in chap.
iii. 18 ; viii. 2 ; here with a ש following it signifies "by reason
that = in order that."   With precisely the same force we find די
על דברת used in the Chaldee of Daniel ii. 30.   Out of Koheleth
there is no example in Hebrew of this usage.

CHAPTER VII. 15-18.

At the time of the author bitter complaints were raised
that Israel must suffer, despite his righteousness, and that
the heathen had the upper hand, notwithstanding their
wickedness.   He therefore proves that the righteousness
which complained so loudly and bitterly because of the
denial of its reward, was but another form of ungodliness alongside of a life of open sin ; he justifies God's with-
holding of redemption, and teaches that those whose aim it
is to become partakers of salvation must enter on a new way,
even that of a true and genuine fear of God.   Consolation and
admonition here go hand in hand.   There was nothing for
Israel but to err with regard to his God, and thus sink into the
abyss of despair, if he did not attain to a knowledge of the
true nature of his fancied righteousness.   If he did not learn
to murmur against his own sin, he must murmur against God.

Ver. 15. *All things did I see in the days of my vanity :
there is a just man that perisheth in his righteousness, and
there is a wicked man that maketh it long in his wickedness.*
Ver. 16. *Be not righteous overmuch, neither behave thou all
too wisely, why wilt thou destroy thyself ?*   Ver. 17. *Be not
overmuch wicked, neither be thou a fool, why wilt thou die
before thy time ?*   Ver. 18. *It is good that thou shouldest take*

hold of this, and also that from that thou shouldst not with-
draw thine hand: he that feareth God shall escape from all.

Ver. 15. *All,* is as to substance so much as "of all kinds, various." The word implies that sometimes strange enough things,
such too as one would scarcely have looked for, are true quid
pro quos. Then follows a remarkable illustration of the curi-
ous things one meets with in life. *In the days of my vanity:*
so Solomon describes the days of his life, because ever since
the fall human existence has been subjected to vanity. This
vanity is specially to be recognised in that which is adduced
directly afterwards;—namely, that so frequently a righteousness worked out with great labour produces notwithstanding
no fruit. Several interpreters have been of opinion that ב in
the words בצדקו and ברעתו is the causative ב, and that the
sense consequently is, "*through* his righteousness, *through* his
wickedness." In support of their view they appeal to ver. 16,
where righteousness is represented as the *cause* of destruction
—"Why wilt thou destroy thyself?" The word ברעתו, in the
sense—"through his wickedness," finds its explanation in the
fact, that the Persian secured the stability of his rule by a
wickedness, which esteemed all means to be good that served
his ends. But that we must rather explain "in, with, along
with his righteousness, or his wickedness," ב being often used
of the accompanying circumstances (Ewald, § 217, f. 3), is
evident, because the writer's intention is to advance a fact
patent to the world,—" I saw":—Such a fact was, the union
of righteousness and adversity, of wickedness and prosperity; not so, however, that in righteousness lay the cause
of adversity, and in wickedness, the cause of prosperity. This
is decided further by paralled passages in the contemporaneous
Malachi, which exhibit a remarkable agreement with this
verse—passages wherein Israel complains that he is unfortunate,
notwithstanding his righteousness, and that the heathen or
the heathenish tyrants are prosperous *notwithstanding* their
wickedness. Compare chap. ii. 17—" Ye weary the Lord with
your words, and ye say, wherein do we weary him? When
ye say: Every one that doeth evil is good in the sight of the
Lord, and he delighteth in them; or, where is the God of
judgment?" further, also, chap. iii. 13-15, " Ye do me violence
with your words saith the Lord, and ye say, what do we

speak then against thee? Ye say, it is vain to serve God, and what profit is it that we keep his ordnance, and walk in filth before the Lord of Hosts." (The righteous perisheth in his righteousness). "And now we count the proud happy, built up are the workers of iniquity, they tempt God, and *notwithstanding* escape:"—the זדים, "the proud," that is, the heathen tyrants, corresponding to "the wicked," in this place. From these parallel passages we deduce the conclusion that under "the righteous," Israel is tacitly referred to, under "the wicked," the heathen; and that the problem here discussed is the one so frequently and variously discussed and illustrated by Koheleth, namely, the sufferings of the people of God at the period of its oppression by the powers of the world, and specially under the yoke of the Persians. האריך signifies in 1 Kings iii. 14, "to lengthen;" elsewhere it is undeniably employed in the sense of "to last long, or, to abide." So in Deuteronomy v. 16, "in order that thy days may *last long:*" chap. vi. 2; xxv. 15. Numbers ix. 19, 22; and Koheleth viii. 12. There is no omission of ימים in the case, for even where it occurs, it is nothing more than the so-called *accusat. relativ.:* so in Deuteronomy xxii. 7, "And that thou mayest last long in respect of days." Allusion is here made to the promise of long duration for the people of God given in the Pentateuch. That which in God's word is spoken to His people by way of encouragement becomes, as things actually are, a ground of complaint against them with the heathen.—If the righteous man perisheth notwithstanding his righteousness, there must be a *fault* therein, and to point out that fault is the aim of the present section. We must not take the righteousness as merely imaginary; nor is the righteous man here spoken of one who deems himself righteous without reason. Even in Luke v. 32, where the Lord says οὐκ ἐλήλυθα καλέσαι δικαίους, ἀλλὰ ἁμαρτωλοὺς εἰς μετάνοιαν, the righteous are not merely such as fancy themselves to be righteous. But in the righteousness of the Pharisees, as it existed in the time of the author, there was a double fault. I. They laid a one-sided stress on the mere external accordance of their actions with the law of God, whereas the heart also was claimed and in the original record of that law, the evil word of the mouth, and the evil desire of the heart, are no less forbidden than the evil action. They failed to see that the law is *spiritual* (Romans vii. 14), that a man may, for example, give all his goods to the poor, and yet if he do it not from the impulse of love, he may be very far from true righteousness (1 Corinthians xiii. 3). Everything, even in the law itself, is repeatedly and expressly reduced back to *love,* (compare Romans xiii. 10). · II. They laid a one-sided stress on righteousness, forgetting that all human righteousness is characterised by imperfection, that the righteous man is at the best but a poor sinner. The first fault is closely connected with the second. If we empty righteousness of all deeper significance, it is easy to come to imagine ourselves to be absolutely righteous : such a fancy, however, disappears as soon as we consider more narrowly τὰ βαρύτερα τοῦ νόμου (Matthew xxiii. 23). In relation to publicans and whores the Pharisees were really righteous ; so also the Jews in relation to the heathen : but in many respects the righteous, οἵτινες οὐ χρείαν ἔχουσι μετανοίας (Luke xv. 7), are worse than open sinners, because they do not see the need of repentance and regeneration, because they are filled with pride and presumption and are universally inclined to judge others, and so forth. Those who in one sense are actually righteous, in another sense are only fanciedly righteous, reputedly righteous, righteous in their own eyes (Job xxxii. 1). The nature of such a false righteousness shows itself in a peculiarly mischievous manner in days of severe suffering. It is mainly at the bottom of discontent with God's leadings, and may very easily end in fatal error with regard to God, and an utter loss of Him.* The world presents a very perverted appearance. But when we examine more closely into *righteousness,* and into the *end of the wicked,* astonishment vanishes and we see that all is orderly. Even Isaiah proves (chap. lviii.) that a pretended righteousness cannot lay the same claims as the true, and teaches that the latter will at once be followed by deliverance.

Ver. 16. One is righteous overmuch, when one forgets one's own sinfulness, which calls for repentance, and when the prayer, ἰλάσθητί μοι τῷ ἀμαρταλῷ, (Luke xviii. 13,) which ought

---

* Following the example of Seb. Schmidt, Rambach observes: "Præceptum de fugienda impatientia adhuc continuari, ita ut occupetur perniciosissima opinio de propria justitiæ et sanctitate, quæ homnies sub difficultatibus et adversitatibus maxime reddit impatientes."

to express its prevailing feeling during this earthly life, dies
out in the soul. Behind the *plus* of such a pretended righteousness there lies concealed, a miserable *minus*. In Matthew v. 20, the Lord says—"unless your righteousness be
better than that of the scribes and pharisees ye shall in no wise
enter into the kingdom of heaven." To the admonition, "be
not righteous overmuch," Luke xviii. 11 forms the commentary : ὁ φαρισαῖος σταθεὶς πρὸς ἑαυτὸν ταῦτα προσηύχετο, ὁ Θεός
εὐχαριστῶ σοι, ὅτι οὐκ εἰμὶ ὥσπερ οἱ λοιποὶ τῶν ἀνθρώπων, ἅρπαγες, ἄδικοι,
μοιχοί, ἢ καὶ ὡς οὗτος ὁ τελώνης : Acts xxvi. 5, may also be compared, where Paul describes Pharisaism as the ἀκριβεστάτη
αἵρεσις τῆς ἡμετέρας θρησκείας. That the righteousness in which
as to substance we are not to do too much, is one characterised
by great defects, that further the author has not the least intention of recommending moral laxity, is clear even from the
parallel admonition—"be not wise overmuch"—that is, behave not as such, do not make a loud profession of wisdom,
do not employ all means in order to be considered a wise man,
like those who are said in Matthew xxiii. 7, to love καλεῖσθαι
ὑπὸ τῶν ἀνθρώπων, 'Ραββὶ 'Ραββί. Except here, the Hithpael form
of חכם, occurs only in Exodus i. 10, where it denotes "sapientem se gessit." Elsewhere the Hithp. of שמם means always
"to be alarmed, frightened, to be inwardly troubled:" here,
on the contrary, it means "to be outwardly disturbed," and
"to destroy." The signification of the mere word is the same.
In Kal also are the meanings of "to be outwardly disturbed,"
and "to be disturbed in spirit," of "vastatus, desolatus est,"
and "stupuit," connected with each other. But in what sense
does a one-sided handling of righteousness and wisdom produce
disquiet ? Had merely the words—"be not righteous overmuch," preceded, an exaggerated asceticism might be supposed
to be referred to : but this idea is prevented by the other
admonition, "be not overwise." What we must understand,
therefore, is the divine curse which it draws down on itself by
such perverted courses. Here we have the germ of the woe
denounced by the Lord in Matthew xxiii. against the Pharisees, and pharisaically disposed people, and of the detailed
threatenings which follow the often repeated woe ! Ver. 38
contains words corresponding most closely to the question,

" why wilt thou destroy thyself ? "—namely, ἰδοὺ ἀφίεται ὑμῖν ὁ οἶκος ὑμῶν ἔρημος.

Ver. 17. *Be not overmuch wicked:* a little follows, alas ! of itself, in man, who is born and conceived in sin, and whose thoughts and doings are evil from his youth upwards. According to ver. 20, there is not on earth a just man who doeth good and sinneth not. So much the more earnestly, therefore, should we be on our guard against crossing the border-line which separates the righteous man who is still subject to weakness and sin, from the sinner; so much the more carefully should we watch lest we get amongst the number of the ἅρπαγες ἄδικοι, μοιχοί, lest we fall into the evil company described in Psalm i. 1 ; so much the more earnestly should we strive to avoid the " path of the destroyer," (Psalm xvii. 4,) into which we may be so easily enticed if we do not walk with fear and trembling. *Why wilt thou die before thy time ?* The wicked may indeed *make it long,* when it is God's will to use him as an instrument for the accomplishment of wise and holy purposes, (ver. 15,) but judgment will notwithstanding come. "The fear of the Lord prolongeth days, and the years of the wicked are shortened," (Proverbs x. 27 :) " Men of blood and of deceit shall not live out half their days," (Psalm lv. 24.) The Egyptian, the Assyrian, the Chaldean, the Persian were compelled one after another to experience this.

Ver. 18. *It is good that thou shouldst take hold of this, and also that from that thou shouldest not withdraw thine hand:* "this," namely, not to be a *righteous* man in that condemnable sense, which was the specifically Jewish disease : " that," namely, not to lead a *life of sin,* which was specifically the disease of heathens; and was shared by all those who, having wandered into error concerning the God of Israel, now gave themselves up to heathen tendencies. Both alike must be carefully avoided : both alike are robberies of our gracious God, and both involve us in the judgments of the Righteous One. The Lord refers to these words in Matthew xxiii. 23. And from the words employed by Him in His rebuke of the Pharisees, viz., ταῦτα δὲ ἔδει ποιῆσαι κἀκεῖνα μὴ ἀφιέναι, we may judge that He regarded this passage as a reproof of the Pharisaic tendency then in germ. *Whoso feareth God escapes all that,* that is, all these dangerous things, the destruction which threatens on all hands. יצא with the accusative signifies "to go out of, or from, anything;" for example, יצא את העיר, "to go out of the city," then בְּנַי יְצָאֻנִי, "my children leave me," (Jeremiah x. 20 :) here it is used in the sense of "escape." By the fear of God we escape on the one hand the danger of Pharisaism, because firstly, it awakens in the heart a dread of all attempts to deceive God by the trappings of a heartless show of piety; and because further, an energetic knowledge of sin is inseparably bound up with a true fear of God, (Isaiah vi. 5 :) We escape, also, on the other hand, the danger of a life of sin, because we cannot really fear God without having also a keen dread of offending Him by our sins, (Genesis xxxix. 9,) and a lively wish to walk in the ways of His commands.

CHAPTER VII. 19, 20.

The good still retained by Israel, namely, wisdom, which, as an inalienable possession, accompanied the people of God even into the depths of their sufferings, (ver. 11.) is of greater value than the power which is on the side of the heathen world. For human sinfulness inevitably involves him in divine judgments who lacks wisdom. Wisdom, on the contrary, as was declared in ver. 13, gives life to him that hath it. For a parallel see, besides chap. vii. 12, 13, also chap. x. 14-18.

Ver. 19. *Wisdom is strong for the wise more than ten mighty men who are in the city.* Ver. 20. *For there is not a just man upon earth that did good and sinned not.*

Ver. 19. עז signifies not "to strengthen," but "to be strong." Wisdom is strong for the wise, proves itself strong for his best interests. We must think of the *mighty men* as attended by their *hosts.* In respect of mere power heathendom had then an infinite superiority.

Ver. 20. *For there is—sinned not :* hence the necessity for wisdom as a corrective. He who lacks wisdom will inevitably be guilty of that which will involve him in divine judgments. But only in the midst of Israel has it its abode : in the heathen world folly has pitched its tent, (Deuteron.

xxxii. 21.) In this fact is the pledge that Israel will finally be exalted to universal dominion.

CHAPTER VII. 21, 22.

The point of departure here also, is the misery of the people of God. In times of severe suffering it is of great importance to recognise that affliction is punishment which sin has merited. Light is then thrown on the otherwise dark providence of God: it stills also the tumults of the soul and awakens hope. When we see the footsteps of God in our tribulations, we gain a living confidence in his compassion.

Ver. 21. *Also take not to heart all words which they speak, so that thou mayst not hear thy servant when he curses thee.* Ver. 22. *For oftentimes also thine own heart knoweth that thou thyself likewise hast cursed others.*

Ver. 21. That this saying has a political reference is indicated by the word גַם, " also." It shows that the same subject is being handled as before, to wit, the sufferings of the people of God, only from a new point of view. In accordance with this גַם the Septuagint translation runs—οὒς λαλήλουσιν ἀσεβεῖς, that is, " the godless, the heathen," (see Isaiah xxv. 2, 5 ; 1 Maccabees iii. 15 ; ix. 73 ; Suidas—ἀσεβεῖς οἱ πολυθεΐαν ἢ ἀθεΐαν θρησκεύοντες.) The heathen tyrants mocked the miserably reduced Israelites because of their pretensions to be the people of God ; they said to them constantly—"where is now thy God ?" Their hatred, moreover, was stirred up by the presumption of the Jews, seeming, as it did, to judge by results, to judge by their actual condition, to be utterly groundless and sheer impudence. The nature of their speeches we may ascertain more closely from the words, " thy servant." The children of Israel let the heathen see that they looked upon them as, according to God and right, *servants ;* and this provoked them. *So that thou mayst not hear,* as thou certainly wouldest, if thou shouldest give thine heart to it ; which is as much as to say, " and avoid hearing therefore." If we turn our heart away from that which we perceive with the outward ear, it is as if we heard and yet heard not : for what is heard only with the outward ear is as good as not heard at all. In

Psalm xxxviii. 14, 15, David says, when describing his
patience under the assaults of his foes,—" and I as a deaf man
hear not, and I am as a dumb man that openeth not his
mouth.   And I am as a man that heareth not, and in whose
mouth is no reply."   Such is the passionless calm to which
every one attains, who sees in everything that befals him an
appointment or a judgment of God.   *Thy servant when he
curseth thee.*   The servant of Israel is the *heathen*, here as in
chap. x. 7,—" I saw servants upon horses, and princes walking
as servants upon the earth."   It is implied in the idea of the
people of God that it should have dominion over the world.
To give up this claim, is to give up itself.   A living piety
which has not this thought is an impossibility.   If the people of
God has a low conception of itself, it has at the same time
also a low view of its Lord.   According to Genesis xlix. 10,
" the obedience of the nations " is destined to the Shiloh, who
should go forth from Israel.   In Exodus xix. 6, Israel is de-
nominated " a kingdom of priests :" and because priests of
God who made heaven and earth, they are the legitimate lords
of the world.   " Thou shalt reign over many nations, but they
shall not reign over thee," it is said in Deuteronomy xv. 6.
According to Deuteronomy xxxiii. 29, Israel is a people " before which its enemies must play the hypocrite, and which
shall tread upon their high places."   In Deuteron. xxviii. 1,
we read—" and it shall come to pass, if thou shalt hearken
diligently unto the voice of the Lord thy God, the Lord thy
God will set thee on high above all the nations of the earth :"
and in ver. 13, " and the Lord shall make thee the head and
not the tail, and thou shalt be above and thou shalt not be
beneath."   Isaiah proclaims, in chap. xlv. 14, " thus saith the
Lord, the labour of Egypt, and the merchandise of Cushæa
and the Sabæans, the men of stature, shall come over unto
thee, and they shall be thine, and shall walk after thee ; in
chains shall they walk and fall down before thee, and make
supplication unto thee—only in thee is God, and there is no
God besides."   At the commencement of his Lamentations
Jeremiah complains—" she that should be *queen amongst the
heathen* must now serve," and in chap. v. 8,—" *Servants* rule
over them, and there is none that doth deliver out of their
hand :" on which we have the *annotat. uber.*, " qui nobis po-

tius si pii fuissemus, servire debuissent." The explanation—
"that thou mayest not be compelled to hear thy servant curse
thee,"—is inadmissible: we must rather render the Hebrew,
"that thou mayest not hear thy servant, who curseth thee."
No longer to hear that, is the reward of turning away our
heart from men, and returning to God. He who is without
God in the world has the great torture of being compelled
to bear the "killing in his bones" (Psalm xlii. 11). We
first become free from this pain when we have learnt livingly
to "wait upon God."

Ver. 22. If such is the voice of conscience we must recognise God's chastising hand in that which our enemies inflict
upon us. The heart then becomes tender towards those who
offend, and can receive their injuries with indifference: this
is the necessary and solid foundation of the love of enemies,
and of prayer for those who despitefully use us and persecute
us. We regard them as instruments of God, servants at once
of His righteousness, and of that pitiful love which chastises
at the right moment, to the end that it may not be compelled
to give us up to death: we say also, "let them curse, for God
has commanded it." אשר (where it happened) that, is used
here in the sense of "where, there where," as in 2 Samuel
xix. 25, and Genesis xxxv. 13, 15. Others, especially the
heathen, whom Israel had so often wounded to the quick, by
his haughty presumption and contempt of their prerogatives.

CHAPTER VII. 23-29.

Reviewing the course which he has pursued, Koheleth finds
that although in his struggle for wisdom he has made many
a gain, he still despite all remains far from his goal (ver. 23,
24). In his investigations concerning wisdom and folly he
arrives at the result that the most dangerous enemy of the
human race is *false wisdom* (ver. 25, 26). The difficulty of
attaining true wisdom may be estimated from the fact that
among men very few indeed have reached it, whilst among
women not a single instance is to be found (ver. 27, 28).
The reason whereof is, that men are no longer in their origi-

nal normal condition, but have fallen under the dominion of
arbitrary and lawless habits of thought (ver. 29).

Ver. 23. *All this I proved by wisdom; I said I will be
wise, and it was far from me.* Ver. 24. *Far off is that
which became* (ward), *and deep, deep, who can find it out?*
Ver. 25. *I turned myself with my heart to know, and to try,
and to search out wisdom and thoughts, and to know wickedness as folly, and foolishness as madness.* Ver. 26. *And I
find something which is more bitter than death; the woman,
which is nets and snares as to her heart, chains as to her
hands: whoso pleaseth God shall escape from her, and the
sinner shall be taken by her.* Ver. 27. *Behold, this found I,
said Koheleth, one after the other finding thoughts.* Ver. 28.
*After that my soul still seeketh, and I did not find it; one
man found I among a thousand, but among all these, a
woman have I not found.* Ver. 29. *And behold, this have I
found, that God hath made man upright, but they seek out
many inventions.*

Ver. 23. Koheleth having operated a considerable time with
wisdom begins now to reflect on his instrument. *All this*—
that is, not merely what has immediately preceded, but all
that has gone before from the commencement of the book—
I proved by wisdom. The attempt is to be regarded as a
successful one in relation to the results set forth: as an *un-
successful* one in relation to the final aim, which is, absolute
wisdom. In connection with all that he accomplished, there
remained in the writer's mind the humiliating consciousness
that he was still far distant from his goal: ἐκ μέρους γὰρ γινώσκο-
μεν καὶ ἐκ μέρους προφητεύομεν (1 Corinthians xiii. 9.) Of all
human efforts, however successful and blessed they may be,
the words of Phil. iii. 12, always hold good—οὐχ ὅτι ἤδη ἔλαβον,
ἢ ἤδη τετελείωμαι.

Ver. 24. *Far off is what became,* or "what is." The
preterite היה designates, a past stretching forward into the
present. That wisdom cannot reach its aim—see the words,
"it remained far from me," of the preceding verse—arises
from the difficulty of approaching its object, namely, *that
which is* (das Seyende). According to the Book of Wisdom,
chap. vii. 17, wisdom is τῶν ὄντων γνῶσις: according to chap. i.
13 of this book, wisdom has to do with all that happens

beneath the sun. If absolute being (das Seyende) is far off, difficult of attainment, unapproachable, then must *wisdom* also necessarily be far off. Parallel is chap. iii. 11 : " Man cannot find out all the work that God doeth, neither beginning nor end :"—to the words, " all the work," there, correspond the words, " what is," here : compare also chap. viii. 17, " man cannot find out all the work that is done under the sun . . though a wise man should think to know it, yet he findeth it not." Further may be compared Job xi. 8, where concerning the object of wisdom, namely, the nature and work of God, it is said—" deeper than hell what canst thou know ?"—and Romans xi. 33, where we read, ὡς ἀνεξερεύνητα τὰ κρίματα αὐτοῦ καὶ ἀνεξιχνίαστοι αἱ ὁδοὶ αὐτοῦ. שהיה מה in chap. 1. 9 signifies, as here, " that which was ;" in chap. vi. 10, it denotes, " that which is." To be rejected are the divergent explanations, first, of Luther and Stier—" it is far off, what will it be ?" then of Ewald—" far off is, what it may be," one cannot rightly see, what — ; and lastly of Hitzig, " what is far off and deep," which is inconsistent with the position of the words, and in opposition to chap. i. 9, where, as Hitzig himself is compelled to admit, " היה is itself predicate," whereas here he would make it out to be only copula. What man has to do, and what the Lord his God requires of him, namely, the directly practical, is " no longer far off," since the light of divine revelation has shined into the darkness of human existence (Deuteronomy xxx. 11) : rather on the contrary, as Moses says to Israel in ver. 14 of the same chapter, " is this word very *nigh* unto thee, in thy mouth, and in thy heart, that thou mayest do it." Of this, however, Koheleth does not here speak, but of the knowledge of things, and, in particular, of the deeper understanding of divine providence and God's method with His people on earth. That which in itself is clear seems in many respects dark to man because of his indwelling sin, so that he is unable fully to enjoy the gift of God.

Ver. 25. The words, *I turned myself and my heart,* are set in contrast to a merely *superficial* doing. No result is ever arrived at where ולבי cannot with truth be added. *To seek out wisdom and thoughts :* חשבון, " thought, musing, meditation," (compare chap. ix. 10, where *thought* is con-

nected with *work*, the former being the spiritual element
from which the latter proceeds forth) is put in opposition to
the blind impulses and passions by which the common man
allows himself to be led.   That we must render the Hebrew
—*wickedness as folly*, and so forth—is clear even from the
article in הסכלות.   To judge from the parallel passages (chap.
i. 17 ; ii. 12, 13 ; x. 13) רשע might stand in the place of
כסל, and סכלות in place of הוללות.   כסל and הסכלות too might be
omitted without any material alteration of the sense—*and to
know wisdom and folly*—in agreement with the first half of
the verse, where the writer speaks merely of the knowledge
of wisdom and thoughts.   This verse forms merely the *introduction* to verse 26, where the author communicates the important result at which he arrived in the course of his studies
on wisdom and folly.

    Ver. 26. There can be no doubt that by the *woman* spoken
of here, we are not to understand a common prostitute, but
an *ideal person*, to wit, *false wisdom*, which kept constantly
undertaking excursions and sallies from her proper home, the
heathen world, into the territory of the Israelites.   It does
little honour to the exegesis of the present day that it has so
frequently mistaken this plain and evident truth.   The feeling for the allegorical element in Scripture is still, alas ! very
little developed ; and a false occidental realism largely prevails no less amongst certain orthodox, than amongst rationalistic interpreters.   A woman in the common sense does not
suit the connection : whereas the ideal does.   Before and
afterwards Koheleth speaks of the great difficulty of attaining to true wisdom.   The ground whereof is specially that
alongside of the wisdom that is from above, the σοφία ἄνωθεν
κατερχομένη, there is a fleshy wisdom, the ἐπίγειος, ψυχική,
δαιμονιώδης (James iii. 15), which entangles men in her snares
and is the mother of the "inventions" alluded to in ver. 29.
Then further, it must be remembered, an ideal female person,
namely, Koheleth the Assembling One, is here speaking : and
if this person warns us against another female, as the most
dangerous enemy of the human race, we may reasonably pre-
sume that the latter is also ideal.   But what is quite decisive
in favour of the view now advocated is, that it alone enables
us to account for the feminine connection of the word Kohe-

leth, which occurs nowhere else in the whole book. Everywhere else, the reference to the incarnation of the wisdom which is from above in the person of Solomon gave rise to the masculine connection; here, however, a change is made on account of the opposition in which wisdom is set to philosophy and wanton seduction. And finally there can be no doubt that the woman here is identical with the (female) "stranger," the "foreigner," who is introduced in Proverbs as the dangerous foe of true wisdom: this can be the less questioned, since, as has been already shown, Koheleth refers back to Proverbs. But now there are strong grounds for thinking that the woman of the Proverbs is the personification of heathenish folly, putting on the airs of wisdom and penetrating into the territory of the Israelites: she is no other than the φιλοσοφία and κενὴ ἀπάτη of Colossians ii. 8, and the ψευδώνυμος γνῶσις of 1 Timothy vi. 20, which renewed its old attempts at invasion in the very first beginnings of the Christian Church. The key to Proverbs ii. 16, 17: "to deliver thee from the strange woman, the foreigner which maketh smooth her words; which forsaketh the friend of her youth, and forgetteth the covenant of her God,"—is Jeremiah iii. 4, 20, according to which the friend of youth is no other than the Lord. This Gentile wisdom, so far as it found disciples amongst the people of God, was chargeable with *forgetting* the Lord. In Proverbs v., the evil woman must needs be regarded as an ideal person because of the opposition in which she is set to the *good* woman, Wisdom. Chr. B. Michælis remarks: I. dehortatur a falsi nominis sapientia s. potius μωρίᾳ sub schemate mulieris adulteræ, ver. 1-14; II. Commendat veram sapientiam sub schemate castæ dulcissimæque conjugis, ver. 15-23. In fact, verses 15 and 16 there—"drink waters out of thine own cistern, and running waters out of thine own well. Let thy fountains be dispersed abroad, and rivers of waters in the streets,"—are without meaning on the literal view of them. Bertheau, who adopts the literal view, finds himself in such perplexity that he wishes to alter the text and interpolate a negation—"let them *not* flow abroad." The cistern, the fountain, is the native Israelitish wisdom. Out of that one ought to draw living waters and communicate thereof to the heathen world, but not busy oneself with *their* wisdom which, more closely inquired into, is *folly*. Further, if wisdom in chap. vii. 4, 5, —" say unto wisdom, thou art my sister, and call understanding thine acquaintance. That she may protect thee from the strange woman, the foreigner, who useth flattering words,"— is an ideal person, her opponent must be so also. In the 9th chapter again the evil woman is put in contrast with wisdom. See Ch. B. Michaelis, who says, " Partes cap. duæ sunt. Describitur enim I. sapientia, missis circumquaque famulis ad epulas a se paratas invitans, ver. 1-12. II. Opposita mulier stultitiæ suas e contrario delicias commendans et offerens, ver. 13-18." The *explanation* is in fact plainly given in the words of ver. 13—" there is a woman of folly, clamorous, who is simple and knows nothing." The woman is personified wisdom. Last of all, in Proverbs xxii. 14, we read—" the mouth of the foreigner is a deep pit : he that is abhorred of the Lord falleth therein." That the writer treats here of *doctrines*, *teachings*, and that foreign doctrines, (seductions always came from foreign countries, as may be seen in the example of Israel in the desert, and then also in that of Solomon himself) are personified as foreigners (female) is clear from the mention of the *mouth*. Nahum iii. 4, presents an analogous instance of such personification. There, Nineveh, the wielder of the world's sceptre, is represented, on account of her arts of deception, as a whore, who plunges the nations into ruin by her seductions. That which is true of heathen *politics*, is true also of heathen *wisdom*, of the philosophy and hollow deceits of the world. To the woman here, corresponds in Revelations ii. 20, " the woman Jesebel, which called herself a prophetess to teach and seduce my servants to commit fornication, and to eat things sacrificed to idols." Jesebel there, is a symbolical person, a personification of the erroneous doctrines of the heathen. Against strange teachings and heathenish wisdom, Koheleth warns his fellow-countrymen also in chap. xii. 12. Numerous parallels to the words, "more bitter than death," (Cartwright—" cujus nefariam consuetudinem vel morte redimere utile fuerit,") may be found in Proverbs. See, for example, chap. vii. 26, 27, where it is said of " the stranger," " she hath cast down many wounded, and numerous are her slain. Her house are ways to hell, going down to the chambers of death :" and chap. ix. 18, " he knoweth not that the dead are there, and that her guests are in the depths of hell." It is simplest to take לבה as an accusative—"which is nets and snares as to her heart (accoiding to her heart)." *The wisdom of the world offers peculiarly strong temptations in times when the world has the dominion;* as may be seen in the example of the Maccabæan period.

Ver. 27. *This found I*, namely, that which has been set forth in the previous part of the book (ver. 23). *One for one,* which is as much as, " one by one, one after the other," so that on each occasion he only undertook one subject, and thoroughly investigated that. Compare לאחד אחד, " one after the other " (Isaiah xxvii. 12) and, εἷς καθεῖς (John viii. 9). In this way alone can anything be effected in the struggle for knowledge. As the Berleburger Bible remarks — " knowledge grows by slow degrees." *Finding thoughts :*—in the later usage the infinitive with ל is frequently employed to describe a condition, a state, in this respect resembling the participle, (see Ewald, § 237 c. 280 d).

Ver. 28. The word אשר standing at the commencement indicates that the searching and not finding refer to the matter mentioned in the previous verse, namely, wisdom, speculation. In regard to the word, see Ewald, § 181 b. There is the same correspondence between the words, " my soul still seeketh and I have not found it," and the words in ver. 23,—" I said I will be wise and it was far from me :" as between ver. 27 and the first part of ver. 23. Compare further chap. viii. 17. Many a result has been arrived at, but the full possession of wisdom has not been gained. How difficult that is of attainment is proved by the fact that amongst men only an extremely small number has succeeded, and among women not a single one. The phrase, " one of a thousand," is borrowed from Job xxxiii. 23. Elihu says there that a man who can enlighten his brother on God's ways, one therefore who is in full possession of divine wisdom, is very seldom to be found, is " one among a thousand." The select few of this class consist of such men as Moses, David, Isaiah, the same that the author of the Greek " Wisdom of Solomon," had in view, when in chap. ii. 27, he says of wisdom, κατὰ γενεὰς εἰς ψυχὰς ὁσίας μεταβαίνουσα φίλους Θεοῦ καὶ προφήτας κατασκευάζει. Himself the author does not reckon amongst these chosen few, without thereby giving up the claim to canonical authority which he expressly makes at the close of the book. In connection with the declaration—" one woman have I not found under all these," that is, amongst the possessors of wisdom, the fact must be taken into consideration, *that no writing by a woman is to be found in the entire Old and New Testaments.* That which was vouchsafed only to the chosen few amongst men,—and be it remarked that we do not here speak of that general participation in wisdom to which the entire people of God, as " the wise nation," (Deuteronomy iv. 6,) was called, but of an independent, pioneering, and productive possession thereof,—we should not at all expect to be con'erred on woman, who is the " weaker vessel," (1 Peter iii. 7.) It lies beyond the degree of woman, whose characteristic is in these respects predominantly receptive, not productive, and whose real sphere of independent action is quite another. Luther says—" Women are created by God for their own kind of work, namely, for the management of the house, and the bringing up of children ; and each one of us accomplishes that best to which God has created and called him. A woman lays hold of a child better with her little finger than a man with his two fists. Therefore let each one stick to the work to which he has been called and appointed by God." Nothing but a complete misapprehension, confounding the woman here with the one in ver. 26, when they have nothing whatever to do with each other, could have given rise to such explanations as that of Hitzig—" among a thousand men I found an upright man, but not one good woman." " Uprightness," in Hitzig's sense, is not once treated of in this entire connection. What is discussed is wisdom, the fathoming of the nature of things, of the depths of the Godhead. The author only denies to women, what he does not attribute to himself. But undoubtedly it is not his intention to renounce all claim to the honour of being an " upright," " good" man. Whoever has made himself acquainted with the general features of the Scripture mode of viewing things will at once acknowledge that Hitzig's view is an impossible one. Luther observes, " amongst the heathen there was a saying—tria mala, mala pessima, ignis, aqua, femina, that is, there can be nothing

worse than what these three can do, to wit, fire, water, woman.
But these and many of the like sayings against the female
sex have been vomited forth by the devil out of pure hatred
and venom towards God and His work, meaning in this way
to disgust every man with the married state, and with God's
word." The practical point of view has been well hit upon
and described by Cartwright,—"Quod fœminas admoneat, ut
modeste se gerant, et consciæ imbecillitatis suæ caveant, ne
sibi et suo ingenio confidant, sed se suis quibus subsunt gu-
bernatoribus regendas et moderandas tradant, et ante omnia
Deum sollicite precentur, ut suæ imbecillitatis misertus viri-
bus illos accingat, quibus in officio contineantur."

Ver. 29. But whence does it arise that wisdom is so difficult for man to reach? The fault lies not in God, but in man,
whose original nature has degenerated. *God made man upright :* יָשָׁר means "upright," (not "sincere," as Luther translates,) and designates the normal state, the state which is in adequate correspondence with the divine standard. Were man still
in the condition in which he was created, wisdom would be easy
of approach to him, for the possession of wisdom is part of
the normal condition and character of man, *But they sought
out many inventions,* (arts.) חִשְּׁבֹן occurs only here and in 2
Chronicles xxvi. 15. There it is used of artfully devised war
machines :* and by way of explanation there is added הִשֵׁב
מַחֲשֶׁבֶת that is "devised by the meditative." The word designates here, properly, that which is "thought out," "excogi-
tated," "subtilty," not *malas artes,* such as, "intrigues,"
"machinations," as Hitzig would explain it. The question in
hand relates not to *practice* but *theory,* not to *evil doing* but
to perverse *thinking.* The word describes rather those so
often plausible and brilliant reasonings of the natural understanding, which perplex the heart and lead away from the
wisdom that is from above, those speculations of a heart turned
away from God, which are perpetually penetrating into the
Church from the world, those βεβήλους κενοφωνίας καὶ ἀντιθέσεις
τῆς ψευδωνύμου γνώσεως, against which the Apostle utters his
warning in 1 Timothy vi. 20. Since the fall man has forgotten

* Gesenius,—" cf. ingenium, quod media latinitate ballistam pr. machinam
ingeniose fabrefactam notat, unde dicebant ingeniare urbem, i. e., machinis oppug-
nare, ingeniosus, ingeniator, gall. ingenieur."

that he should in the first instance take up a receptive position, in relation to the ἄνωθεν σοφία, and that such a position is the only right one ; but instead of that, he goes hunting after his own phantastic and high-flown thoughts. The only way of throwing off this severe disease, and of escaping from the bonds of one's own thoughts and imaginations, is to unlearn the serpent's lesson—" ye shall be as God, knowing good and evil,"—to return to our dependence on God, to renounce all self-acquired knowledge, and, " leaving all our own fancies and conclusions to sink in Lethe's stream," to accept the divine teachings alone, according to our Lord's saying in Matthew xi. 25,— " I thank thee, O Father, that thou hast hid these things from the wise and prudent, and hast revealed them unto babes."

CHAPTER VIII. 1-8.

Here too again the point of departure is the mournful condition of the people of God. After an introductory eulogy of wisdom, (ver. 1,) the author admonishes his fellow-countrymen not to allow themselves by any means to be diverted from obeying their heavenly King, or to be seduced to evil courses, seeing that their Lord is *almighty* both in action and in punishment, (ver. 2-4.) If the people of God only continue steadfast in obedience their sufferings will one day be removed from them : men, however mighty they may seem, are far too impotent to be able to hinder the course of the judgments which God at His own appointed time decrees for the good of His children, (ver. 5-8.)

Ver. 1. *Who is as the wise man ? and who knoweth the interpretation of things ? A man's wisdom maketh his face to shine, and the harshness of his face is changed.* Ver. 2. *I; observe the mouth of the king, and that because of the oath of God.* Ver. 3. *Be not hasty to go out of his sight, stand not in an evil thing, for he doeth whatsoever pleaseth him.* Ver. 4. *Because the word of the king is ruler, and who can say to him, what doest thou ?* Ver. 5. *Whoso keepeth the command shall experience no evil thing, and a wise heart discerneth both time and judgment.* Ver. 6. *For every desire of man has a time and right ; for the adversity of man is heavy upon him.* Ver. 7. *For he knoweth not that which shall be, for who can show to him how it will be?* Ver. 8. *There is no man that hath power over the spirit, to retain the spirit: neither hath he power over the day of death, and there is no discharge from that conflict, nor does wickedness deliver him that hath it.*

Ver. 1. As in chap. vii. 23-28, at the close of a series of wise sayings, the author institutes a consideration of wisdom itself, so also here, at the beginning of a new series of such sayings, he extols the high importance of wisdom, in order to prepare the spiritual ear for the reception of his utterances. *Who is as the wise man?* No one is equal to the wise man : wisdom is the one precious pearl with which no possession on earth can be compared (Job xxviii. 18 ; Matthew xiii. 45, 46.) The ground of the importance of wisdom is assigned in the words—*and who knoweth the interpretation* (פֵּשֶׁר the Hebrew word, occurs only here ; elsewhere the Chaldee form פְּשַׁר is used, and that only in Daniel) *of things?* דָּבָר, corresponds to the expression, "that which is," employed in chap. vii. 24 to designate the object of wisdom. Wisdom leads us into the nature, the essence of things, and thus furnishes a basis for right practical conduct. J. D. Michaelis says—"By the solution of things, we are to understand nothing but the explanation of all that which is done in the world and of the design thereof: the evils of the world appear to us like letters without meaning, unintelligible ; but as soon as we consider their good results, their interpretation will be plain, we shall see why God permits them." The cross, whose dark depths are illuminated by wisdom, is no doubt, according to what follows, a special aspect of the general question which is here principally brought under consideration ; but J. D. Michaelis has had it too directly and exclusively in view. The statement of the high advantages of wisdom is continued in the words—*a man's wisdom maketh his face to shine.* By the *illumination of the face* several commentators understand "the instruction and good guidance which wisdom confers on its possessor." That, however, is against usage, according to which the illumination of the countenance can only signify "to cheer, to enliven." The cognate phrase, "enlighten the eyes," means usually "to make

brisk and cheerful :" misery and pain cause the eyes to be
dull, gloomy, languid.   Compare Psalm xix. 9, where " en-
lightening the eyes" is set in parallelism with "rejoicing the
heart."   To the cheering of the countenance has reference the
phrase האיר פניו, used of God : God's face *beams, is radiant,* in
relation to those towards whom he is gracious.   This expression is not elsewhere employed of men ; yet in Proverbs xvi.
15, it is said, " in the light of the king's countenance is life."
The reason of the joy afforded by wisdom may be found in
the insight it gives into the nature of things, specially, into
the providence of God ; and in the assurance and decision
with which, as a consequence, we can regard the practical
questions of life.   *And the strength of his countenance is
changed.*   According to usage, " the strength of the countenance," can only mean, " hard and rigid features," as the expression of boldness and impudence.   In Deuteronomy xxviii. 50,
עז פנים גוי is " a bold and impudent people."   In Daniel viii.
23, a king עז פנים is a bold, impudent king.   העז פנים or בפנים,
" to make the face strong," is used of " boldness, impudence,"
in Proverbs vii. 13 ; xxi. 29.   Consequently, the rendering,
" rage, chagrin at the repugnant circumstances of life," must
be rejected as erroneous.   Jerome has given substantially the
correct view—" Omnis hæreticus et falsum dogma defendens
impudenti vultu est."   So also the Berleburger Bible which
says—" In order that the rigidness of his countenance, that is,
his savage unfriendly crabbed stubborn nature, his wrinkled
forehead and impudent face, may be changed ; that man may
be no longer so harsh, so difficult of approach, nor be, as
hitherto, refractory to human and divine commands.   When,
through the transforming power of wisdom, a heart of flesh
has taken the place of the heart of stone, the inward pliancy
and docility, the soul's fear of God and his commands, which
then follow, become discernible in the *countenance.*"

Ver. 2. The simple " I" standing alone, is as much as, " I
counsel thee," or, " wilt thou listen to my advice, then."   At
first sight the author seems here to be admonishing his fellow-
countrymen to obey the *secular authorities,* that is the heathen.
Even Jerome remarks, " videtur præcipere juxta apostolum
regibus et potestatibus obsequium ;" but rightly adds, " this
explanation is however to be rejected."   Against this explana-

tion there is at the very outset one objection, namely, that scarcely a passage is to be found in the Old Testament where obedience to the heathen tyrants is represented as a religious duty. Jeremiah xxix. 7, is not to be reckoned amongst them. Romans xiii. was written at the time of the dominion of the Romans, and therefore in essentially different circumstances. What the Apostle says there of the authorities, as the guardians of law and right, is inapplicable to oriental monarchies, as is satisfactorily enough proved by this very book. The characteristic which distinguished the Romans from other heathen nations, namely, their sense of justice, is prominently referred to in 1 Maccabees viii. The king here, for whom obedience is claimed is rather the *Heavenly one*, as in chap. v. 8 : compare also Psalm xx. 10 ; v. 3 ; x. 16. The author intentionally abstains from saying expressly that he means the heavenly king. Wisdom loves to speak in " dark sayings," (Proverbs i. 6). It pursues its aim of sharpening the intellect even at the risk of misunderstanding. But prudence also rendered it advisable not to express himself here more clearly. The mouth being the organ of speech, it stands here for the *words* which proceed from it (compare chap. x. 13). שמר is the standing term employed to denote the observance of the commands of God : compare שמר מצוה in ver. 5. There is a difference between the words here and the phrases usually employed in relation to the heavenly king, *e. g.,* עבר פי יהוה (Num. xiv. 41, and elsewhere), and מרה את פי יהוה (Numbers xx. 24, and frequently besides). *And* (indeed) *because of the oath to God.* A person's oath is, in all cases, either that which he makes (Psalm cv. 9 ; 1 Chronicles xvi. 16), or which is made to him (Habakkuk iii. 9, where " oaths of the tribes," are oaths which were made to the tribes, promises of God to Israel confirmed by oath, Genesis xxiv. 8 ; Joshua ii. 17, 20 ; 1 Kings ii. 43), which therefore belongs to him, either as giver or receiver. Accordingly, in this place, " the oath of God" can only be the oath *which is made to God,* and the explanation, " the oath by God," must therefore be rejected. But this does not prevent the words being referred also to earthly authorities. For in fact every oath *by God* must be looked upon as an oath *made to God :*—one swears to God, to perform this or that thing to this or that man. Compare Exodus xxii. 10——

"the oath of the Lord shall be between them both :"—and 2
Samuel xxi. 7; 1 Kings ii. 43. The subject-matter in hand,
however, forbids us referring the words to such an oath of
allegiance : we can only think of the oath which bound the
people of God to obedience to their heavenly King. Nebuchadnezzar, it is true, made Zedekiah take an oath of faithfulness to himself (2 Chronicles xxxvi. 13) : but there is nowhere
to be found the slightest trace of an oath taken by the *nation*
to its heathen tyrants. To their heavenly King, on the contrary, the Israelites stood notoriously pledged by sacred covenant and oath to obey His laws and commands. In Deuteronomy xxix. 12-15, it is said, "thou shalt enter into the covenant of the Lord thy God, and into his oath, which the Lord
thy God maketh with thee this day.—Neither with you only
do I make this covenant and this oath : but both with those
who are here this day, and also with those who are not here."
Ezekiel says, in chap. xvi. 50, to Judah—"I will deal with
thee even as thou hast done, which despiseth the oath and
breakest the covenant," on which Michaelis remarks, "quo te
devovisti paciscens cum deo." It is of special importance, however, to compare a passage which refers to the same period as
the one now under notice, and is remarkably allied therewith,
namely Nehemiah x. 30, where it is said of the people, "they
entered into an oath and *curse* to walk in God's law, which
was given by the hand of Moses, the servant of God, and to
observe (לשמר) and do all the *commandments* (מצות, compare
ver. 5) of the Lord our God, and his judgments and his
statutes."

Ver. 3. Be not hasty to go out of his sight; compare
Genesis iv. 16, "and Cain went out from the presence of the
Lord ;" Jonah i. 3, "and Jonah rose up to flee to Tarshish
from the presence of the Lord ;" and Hosea xi. 2, where מפני
הלך is used of apostasy from the living God (John vi. 66).
When severe suffering befalls a man he is tempted to turn
away from God: compare Job ii. 9, "then said his wife unto
him, Dost thou still retain thine integrity? Bless God and
die." Job answers thereto—"As one of the foolish women
speakest thou. Do we take good at the hand of God, and
shall we not receive the evil?" "In all this," we read, "Job
sinned not," although his circumstances rendered him exceed-

ingly liable to sin." In chap. xxxvi. 13, Elihu speaks of the "impious, who heap up wrath," when God binds them, that is, when He visits them with heavy sufferings. "Their soul," says he, "dies in youth, and their life is among the degraded." Psalm xxxvii. 1, admonishes us not to "fret ourselves because of evil-doers," and warns us against being seduced into apostacy from the living God, and into wicked courses, by the sight of the prosperity of the wicked and of the power which they wield. "O man, though thy cross press thee without end, though thy sufferings be ever so severe, become not a rebel against God:" thus would the writer address the covenanted people groaning beneath the hard yoke of the heathen world. *Stand not in an evil thing.* Several commentators explain, "remain not therein." But "remain" does not suit the connection. The idea evidently is, that we should not allow ourselves to be seduced by suffering into the paths of sin, into despair of God, into infractions of his sacred ordainments, and endeavours to work out our own deliverance in our strength and way : compare Psalm xxxvii. 8—"cease from anger and forsake wrath, fret not thyself in any wise to do evil:" on which J. Arnd remarks—"many of them do evil things in wrath, revenge, and impatience, of which they repent in eternity." עמד must consequently be understood here as in Psalm i. 1—"*Stand not in the way of sinners:*" sin is represented as an evil spot on which we should not take our post. *For he doeth whatsoever pleaseth him :* into a worse situation it is impossible to be betrayed, than to make *omnipotence,* in the person of God, our enemy, as we inevitably do when we suffer ourselves to be carried away, by impatience, to evil things, instead of following the counsel, "Be silent to the Lord, and wait patiently for him." Referred to an earthly king, no satisfactory explanation can be given of this verse. How little even the very first words suit such an application is evident from the frequent attempts which have been made to alter their sense, as, for example, by Knobel : "Be not hasty to *revolt* from him." Very few persons indeed ever got to see the face of an eastern king, and when they did, to go away or to remain, lay not in their choice. "Apud Persas," says Justinus i. 9, "persona regis sub specie majestatis occulitur ; Xenophon says in his Agesil. ix. 1, ὁ μὲν Πέρσης τῷ σπανίως ὁρᾶσθαι ἐσεμνύνετο ; according to Aristotle, " de Mundo," the Persian monarch was παντὶ ἀόρατος,—compare Esther iv. 11—and on this passage, Baumgarten, "de fide hist. libri Estheræ," 82. Moreover, an Israelite cannot say of an earthly monarch—"he doeth whatsoever it pleaseth him." It would be a denial of God on high. Nebuchadnezzar, it is true, says to Daniel's three companions—"Let us see who that God is that shall deliver you out of mine hand" (Daniel iii. 15): but they answer, "Behold, the God whom we honour is able to deliver us from the burning fiery furnace, and out of thine hand, O king, will he deliver us." Overwhelmed by facts Nebuchadnezzar himself was forced to say of Jehovah—" his dominion is an everlasting dominion, and his kingdom is from generation to generation," (Daniel iv. 34).

Ver. 4. Because the word of the king is ruler. שלטון is used to denote "ruler" in the Chaldee portion of Daniel : see chap. iii. 2, 3, " all the rulers of the provinces." The rank which they vindicate to themselves belongs, truly regarded, to the word of God. שלטון must be regarded here and in ver. 8 as introduced with the marks of quotation. It is employed *ironically. And who can say to him, what doest thou ?* S. Schmidt remarks on Job ix. 12—"'est interrogatio in jus vocantis v. auctoritate superiore prohibentis. Describitur enim hic summum dei imperium et independentia a superiore." Knobel is compelled to observe, " The formula which constitutes the second clause is never used except to glorify the divine power." Compare Job ix. 12, " Behold he robbeth, and who shall drive him back, who shall say unto him, What doest thou?" and chap. xxiii. 13, " and he is one, and who shall drive him back ; and what his soul desireth, even that he doeth." See also the " Book of Wisdom " xii. 12, τίς γὰρ ἐρεῖ τι ἐποίησας ἢ τίς ἀντιστήσεται τῷ κρίματί σου ; Isaiah xlv. 9 ; Jonah i. 14.

Ver. 5. Whoso keepeth the command, that is, as much as, " whoso standeth not in an evil thing," (ver. 3). מצוה is to be taken as a kind of nomen proprium, signifying, the command absolutely, the divine command ; compare שמר מצוה, used in 1 Kings xi. 34, of the observance of the divine commands. *Shall experience no evil thing :* whoso avoids the evil of *guilt,* shall be spared the evil of *punishment.* Knobel's explanation יָדַע " to know," " to make the acquaintance," דְּבַר, " of moral culpability," does not suit the second clause. He may fall into great sufferings, as the pious in Israel were now compelled to experience,—by way of consolation for the bearers of the cross are the words spoken—but only into such sufferings as are *blessings,* when more carefully examined, and as shall have a joyous termination : compare Romans viii. 28, οἴδαμεν δὲ, ὅτι τοῖς ἀγαπῶσι τὸν Θεὸν, πάντα συνεργεῖ εἰς ἀγαθόν. *And a wise heart discerneth both time and judgment.* According to chap. iii. 1, " the time " can only be the time of the interference of God. " Judgment" consequently must refer to God's exercise of judgment and right. Time and judgment taken together, signify that God will judge at his own time. The meaning of the entire verse is as follows : As certainly as God in his own time shall judge righteously—a thing which is known to the wise heart—so certain is it, that those who hold God's commands, and therefore have God on their side, cannot be really and lastingly unhappy.[*]

Ver. 6. *For to every desire—*(of wise and believing hearts after the establishment of the Kingdom of God,)—*there is time and right, because the adversity of man is heavy upon him.* Behind *man* lies concealed the *monarch of the world.* The ground whereof is, that the means of human chastisement in God's hand are very powerful, רַב " great,' see on chap. vi. 1. With all his power man is still not *independent,* but subject to the heavy blows of fate. Men therefore can oppose no resistance when God proceeds to exercise judgment for the good of His people.

Ver. 7. *For he knoweth not that which shall be :* before one who does not know that, we should not be afraid ; to his temporary prosperity we should attach little importance. To-morrow it may be all over with him, however glorious and brilliant is his appearance to-day. If we only have God on our side, we may be calm and contented even in the midst of oppression.

Ver. 8. *There is no man that hath power over the spirit,*

[*] Gousset, " scit judicium postea venturum certum et inevitabile et ideo patiens est, si injuste a magistratu tractatur, v. si interea, dum summi regis mandata servat, aliquid adversi ei contingat."

to retain the spirit. In this point also the monarch of the world lies hidden behind man. When the hour of death appointed by God comes, he must away. In Psalm cxlvi., which was composed during the time of the Persian dominion, it is said, (ver. 3, 4,) "Put not your trust," (the Psalmist is addressing the world, the great nation,) "in princes, in the son of man, in whom is no help. When his breath goeth forth he returneth to his earth : in that very day his thoughts perish." Jerome writes—"non est ergo lugendum, si . . . sæpe ab iniquis potentioribus opprimamur, quum morte omnia finiantur, et superbus et potens qui cuncta populatus est, non valeat animam suam retinere quum rapitur." *And there is no discharge in the conflict,* which God carries on with man. When God has once begun the strife with any one, He does not let him free, He does not desist, until He has brought him to ruin. Illustrative of these words is the example of Pharaoh. The *discharge* does not refer so much to the *imprisonment,* as to the strife, the conflict itself : compare Genesis xxxii. 27, where one of the wrestlers addresses to the other the word שלחני, "let me go." *Wickedness delivereth not him that hath it,* notwithstanding that it puts powerful and apparently irresistible means at his disposal. They have only importance until God's time and judgment draw nigh. The Berleburger Bible remarks, "he will not succeed in freeing himself in this matter, as he succeeded in freeing himself from God's law."

CHAPTER VIII. 9-13.

Here also again the author finds the occasion for his utterances in the sufferings of the people of God, in the tyranny with which they were burdened. The consolation, which is offered under a twofold head, (ver. 9 and 10, and ver. 11-13,) is the following—"Look to the end, (Psalm lxxiii. 17,) in good time God's judgment will overthrow the wicked, and exalt the righteous."

Ver. 9. *All this saw I, in that I applied my heart to every history that takes place under the sun : there is a time when man ruleth over men to their misfortune.* Ver. 10. *And then saw I the wicked buried, and they came, and from the place of the holy, they went forth. And they were forgotten in the city, who had thus done. This also is vanity.* Ver. 11. *Because a sentence is not pronounced, the work of wickedness hasteneth: therefore the heart of the sons of men is fully set in them to do evil.* Ver. 12. *Let a sinner do evil an hundred times and long endure! Yet surely I know that it shall be well with men that fear God, which fear before him.* Ver. 13. *But it shall not be well with the wicked, neither like the shadow shall he long endure, which feareth not before God.*

Ver. 9. *All this*, that is, all that can be classed under the same head as that which is specially mentioned immediately after, and which can be represented thereby ;—facts namely, which, when superficially examined may easily prove a stumbling block in the way of *faith* (compare chap. vii. 15.) Jerome says—" Dedi inquit cor meum, ut omne quod sub sole geritur intuerer, et hoc vel maxime, quod homo accepit in hominem potestatem, ut quoscunque vult affligat atque condemnet." The suffix in לֹ refers of course to the second mentioned man. The present verse sets forth the stumbling block : the following verse shows how it is to be removed. That a hint concerning the latter cannot be contained in the present verse is clear from the word בכן in ver. 10, alone.

Ver. 10. *And then saw I the wicked buried.* ראיתי serves here, as in ver. 9, to render the description more vivid and palpable. It is to be noted that Solomon here speaks, and not the author. They are experiences like those which are alluded to by Asaph in Psalm lxiii., such as took their rise from the conflict between evil and good which raged in the midst of the covenant people itself. In the background however stands the thought : thus will the Persian Empire also one day be borne to the grave. בכן " under such circumstances," or since things are thus situated : as a Hebrew word it occurs, besides here, only in Esther iv. 16. Not to be buried, is frequently represented as a punishment of the godless : compare on chap. vi. 3. The untimely comparison of these two passages has led many commentators into the error of supposing that burial, which, on their own authority they have here converted into an honourable one, (Cartwright, for example, who says, " sepulturam, et illam quidem amplam

et dignitatis plenam consequi, in benedictione dei jure numer-
atur,") is represented as an advantage enjoyed by the wicked.
But the wicked condemned by God are buried in Ezekiel
xxxii. 23-24, xxxix. 11, also : so too the godless rich man of
the Gospels, (Luke xvi. 22.) *And they came. Whither,* may
be learnt from the preceding קברים; namely, *into the grave :*
and thus an end is put to all their prosperity, their wealth
and their efforts to injure the righteous. *And from the
place of the holy went they forth.* יהלכו forms the contrast to
באו. They come·into the grave and are thus removed from the
place where their presence gave such offence. Worthy of note
is it that מקום stands in the *stat. constr.* It is not said, " from
the holy place," but, "from the place of the holy," that is, the
place to which the holy belong : " the holy" must here be regarded as ideal persons. They must leave the place in which
their existence and presence is something abnormal. The
Holy are the true members of the Church of the Lord, (compare the remarks in my Christology on Isaiah iv. 3.) Parallel is Isaiah lii. 1, "put on thy festival garments, O Jerusalem,
thou holy city, for henceforth there shall no more come into
thee the uncircumcised and the unclean :" and chap. xlix. 17,
" thy destroyers and those that laid thee waste shall go forth
of thee." *And they were forgotten in the city, who had
thus done.* Compare Proverbs x. 7, " the memory of the just
is blessed, but the name of the wicked shall rot :" also Psalm
lxxiii. 19, 20, " how are they brought to desolation in a
moment, they are utterly consumed with terrors. As a dream,
when one awaketh, so dost thou in the city despise their
image." Many commentators have been led into an entirely
mistaken view of the whole verse by the translation—" who
have done justice," or, " who have rightly acted." It may
still be fairly doubted whether כן ever, as a neuter, signifies
" rectum," and adverbially, " recte." In most of the passages
adduced in favour of this rendering, the common and therefore the simplest meaning " thus," is plainly the most suitable.
Even in the two which seem most in its favour, namely in
Numbers xxxvi. 5 ; xxvii. 7, the translation "thus,"—" *thus*
speak they of the tribe of Joseph : *thus* speak the daughters,
etc."—is rendered probable by a comparison of Matthew xxvi.
25, and John xviii. 37. When any one who is solicited for

a decision, speaks of the petition as reported or as being inquired into, *consent* is implied. Here, however, in any case must כן be taken in its usual meaning on account of the unmistakable reference to the foregoing בכן. *This also is vanity*, to wit, that man should rule over man to his misfortune,—the doings of tyrants. It is vanity because of the sudden catastrophe which befals it,—vanity because it suddenly comes to nought and ends in horror. In regard to the prosperity of the wicked, of the heathen tyrants, it is said also in chap. vii. 6, "this also is vanity." The Berleburger Bible says, " O how foolish are men not to prove and judge such things more wisely, not to see how vainly they act ! " Faith receives here as in Psalm lxxiii. the victory, in that by the grace of God it discerns that the prosperity of the wicked as well as the sufferings of the righteous are only transitory.

Ver. 11. *Because a sentence is not pronounced*—that is, because the heavenly edict is delayed—*the work of wickedness hasteneth :* that is, because they go unpunished the wicked are confirmed in their wickedness : compare Isaiah xxvi. 10, " Let favour be showed to the wicked yet will he not learn righteousness. On the earth, where one should do right, he commits iniquity." פתגם, signifying " word " in general, and then specially " mandate, edict," is probably of Persian origin, and it seems to have been used, as it were technically, for the edicts of the Persian kings : compare Esther i. 20 ; Ezra iv. 17 ; vi. 11 ; Daniel iii. 16. The only passage where the word elsewhere occurs in Hebrew is the one in Esther just quoted : otherwise it is only found in the Chaldee of Daniel and Ezra Here, as also in Daniel iv. 14, it is then transferred to the decrees of heaven. We must consider it as introduced with signs of quotation. פתגם occurs in connection with עשה in Esther i. 20 also: " the edict of the king which he makes." Since אין means " it is not," נעשה can only be a participle. פתגם is here therefore treated as a feminine. The explanation— " the judgment on the work of wickedness,"—is contrary to the accents : besides פתגם is never elsewhere employed with the genitive of the object, and it is questionable whether it can be so employed. מהרה is properly a noun, signifying " haste : " it is so used in chap iv. 12 : see too Psalm cxlvii. 15, במהרה. " in haste." It is best to take it in this sense here also—"Haste," for, "hasty." The adverb "hastily," might very fitly take the place of the adjective : see Ewald, § 296 d. *Therefore the heart of the sons of men is fully set in them to do evil*, in that they are purposed to drive out violence with violence, and, falling into error concerning God, seek to secure prosperity for themselves, by the same means as the fortunate wicked. The "children of men" are those who suffer at the hands of prosperous wickedness, with special reference to Israel as oppressed by the fortunate powers of this world. How the wicked are confirmed in their wickedness by their prosperity, and how the suffering are thereby tempted to apostatize from God, is vividly and to the life described in Psalm lxxiii. The "heart becomes full" of evil inclinations, so full that they violently break forth in deeds of wickedness : compare the remarkably similar passage in Esther vii. 5 : then also Acts v. 3.

Ver. 12. The author does not however let himself be deceived by that which is now visible. We may have to wait for God's righteous decision, but in its own time it will certainly come. אֲשֶׁר, "(be it) that," which is as much as to say, "May it, let it, even" (be). A cognate use of the word is found in Leviticus iv. 22 ; Deuteronomy xi. 27 ; xviii. 22, where אֲשֶׁר, signifies, "(supposing) that." To מְאֹד, must פְּעָמִים be supplied. For remarks on הַאֲרִיך compare chap. vii. 15. לוֹ is the dat. comm. The word כִּי assigns the reason why the writer does not grudge the wicked his prosperity.

Ver. 13. Inasmuch as long duration is a relative idea, the long duration previously attributed to the wicked does not contradict the assertion made here, that he will not endure long. Of the Persian Empire, which the author has here primarily in view, both assertions held at the same time good,— it lasted long, and yet it lasted a short time. All depends on the standard applied. *As the shadow :* fleeting, transitory as the shadow which vanishes with the setting sun, and leaves not a trace behind (compare Psalm cxliv. 4 ; Book of Wisdom, ii. 5.)

CHAPTER VIII. 14-17.

The sufferings of the people of God constitute still the point
of departure, as in verses 1-8 and in verses 9-13.   Instead of
racking our brains over their fate, we should rejoice at the
good gifts of God which remain.   Speculation and questioning
conduct to no result, for the divine counsels are incomprehen-
sible by man.

Ver. 14. *There is a vanity which is done upon earth, that
there be just men to whom it happeneth according to the work of
the wicked, and that there be wicked men to whom it happeneth
according to the work of the righteous : I said that this also
is vanity.   Ver. 15.   And I commended mirth, that nothing
is better for man under the sun than to eat, and to drink,
and to be merry, and that abides with him in his labour
through the days of his life, which God giveth him under the
sun.   Ver. 16.   When I applied my heart to know wisdom,
and to see the travail which takes place on the earth, that
neither day nor night doth he see sleep with his eyes.   Ver.
17.   So I beheld the whole work of God, that man cannot find
out the work that is done under the sun, for the sake of which
man labours to seek it out, and findeth it not; yea, further,
though a wise man should think to know it, he cannot find it.*

Ver. 14. That the lots of the righteous and the wicked are
not seldom mixed up with each other, is a *vanity,* and is *intended* to be a vanity.   Taking man to be what he now actually is, these things go to constitute the best world we can
conceive ; and Elster's remark, that "facts cannot fail to make
a bitter and gloomy impression," holds good only of the natural man in the believer : the spiritual man judges quite differently.   Righteousness would too soon disappear if its reward were bestowed on it immediately, and, as it were, piece
by piece.   Godliness perishes as soon as it becomes a matter
of trade : it is not meant that the righteous should find their
satisfaction in an open and manifest recompence.   If there
existed nem righteous as they should be, righteous throughout,
of one piece, then the experience here set forth would of course
be suspicious.   But as things actually are, whilst sin dwells

even in the righteous, so long as they need to be punished and guarded, so long as they wander too readily from the right path, and especially, so long as they are prone to serve God for hire, the facts under consideration offer no difficulty to those who stand really in righteousness. They may be and are not seldom fiercely perplexed and harassed thereby, but that is all. Really meant complaints at such experiences proceed only from such as, without authority or right, reckon themselves among the righteous ;—as may be clearly seen in Malachi. Without doubt, however, as is proved by a considerable number of declarations even from this book, the resemblance between the fate of the righteous and that of the wicked, is but an *external* and *partial* one. All things must finally work together for the good of those who love God : the end will separate the righteous from the wicked. *I said that this also is vanity;* " this also"—this doubtful condition of the pious and the ungodly. *Vanity,* that is, it is to be counted as part of the misery and wretchedness of this life, to which even believers are subject and with which they must put up. He is, of course, a poor fool, who devotes himself to righteousness in order to become rich and honoured, in order to lose none of his family or friends, and so forth.

Ver. 15. This *mirth,* is the cheerful enjoyment of those gifts of God which do not fail us even in circumstances of need, and is put in contrast to the habit of looking out for an open and splendid reward of righteousness—the consequence of the non-bestowal of which is gloomy discontent. Jewish speculators in righteousness thought that they must at once rule the heathen with a sceptre of iron ; and when they found that the exact contrary was the case, they hung their heads, refused to find anything more to their liking, and grew dissatisfied with God and the world. The " mirth" spoken of here is quite consistent with the deep earnestness in life recommended by Koheleth in chap. vii. 1 ff. It is a joy which is the direct outflow of a piety that thankfully accepts what God gives, and refuses to be disturbed in its enjoyment thereof by unfounded pretensions. The Berleburger Bible remarks— " Mirth, that is, a godly joyfulness and cheerfulness of heart ; in that, namely, the righteous, when he has anything to endure amidst the vanities of the world, which are universal,

and are saddled on all alike, maintains and displays by faith
in God a spirit calm and free from cares ; and in all the divine
arrangements proves himself prompt and lively. *That he
should eat and drink and be merry*, that is, that he calmly
and with fitting cheerfulness enjoy what God bestows on him.
This had been already said in chap. ii. 24; iii. 12, 22 ; it is
here again repeated, and not without reason, but to serve another purpose, namely, as an answer to the objection just
urged."

Ver. 16. The *travail* here mentioned is that into which
those fall who seek to fathom, and rack their brains about, the
ways of God : wherein those are usually the most zealous
who are endowed with least capacity to answer the questions
raised. The problem is in itself an exceedingly difficult one,
but the solution becames enormously more difficult when at-
tempted by those who lack knowledge of the depths of human
sinfulness. And this was a characteristic fault of the author's
age : hence was there so much murmuring and racking of
brains. The author turns his heart to know wisdom, and (in
spirit) to see (in the light of wisdom) the travail. עִנְיָן can
only mean " travail," " torment," not " business," as may be
seen on comparing chap. ii. 26, and especially chap. iii. 10.
What " travail " is meant, we are informed in the words—
" that he does not see ;" namely, that man, who is spoken of
both before and afterwards, is unable to fathom the divine
counsels in the distribution of fates, even though he apply
himself earnestly to the work. Knobel explains quite incorrectly—" man who is restlessly busy, and through sheer
activity gets no sleep."

Ver. 17. The " travail " proves itself to be useless. We
walk by faith and not by sight, and blessed are they that see
not and yet believe. Therefore should we leave off worrying
our minds. Blessed is the man who takes without questioning what God sends him, in the firm confidence that, however perverted it may appear, it is the right thing, and that
all things must work together for the good of those who love
God. Jerome says—" Subostendet tamen esse causas rerum
omnium et justitiam, quare unumquodque sic fiat : sed in
occulto eas latere et non posse ab hominibus comprehendi :"
and Cartwright, " si enim opera, quæ fecit Salomo, sapientem

reginam Sabæ in admirationem ita abripiunt ut non esset
amplius in illa spiritus, quanto magis opera dei, omnem nostram intelligentiam superantia, nos in admirationem ejus ad-
ducant? Ut enim quisque est, ita sunt ejus opera." *Then
saw I the whole work of God :* in what aspect he sees it and
knows it, to wit, in respect of its *unsearchableness,* we are
informed by the words—*that man cannot find,* etc. In the
Berleburger Bible we read—"O ye poor blind men, who
think by your philosophy to fathom the grounds of the divine
leadings, ye are justly cheated! Ye disapprove of all that
are beyond human comprehension, when ye ought rather to
confess that the higher they transcend your conceptions. so
much the diviner are. they. The more pains you take to
fathom the secrets of wisdom by your reflection, the farther
are you from reaching your aim. Of the possession of true
wisdom the best sign is when a man is assured that he cannot
comprehend the mysteries of the divine dealings with souls."

CHAPTER IX. 1-10.

This section falls into two parts, the *temptation* which
assails (verses 1-6), and the *alleviation* and comfort, (καὶ ἐκό-
πασεν ὁ ἄνεμος, καὶ ἐγένετο γαλήνη μεγάλη Mark iv. 39), (ver. 7-10).
The temptation, in regard to which the author appears as
the representative of the tone of mind then prevailing amongst
the people, takes its rise in the same fact as that which was
considered in the foregoing section, namely, in the sufferings
of the people of God. Since God looks calmly on whilst the
wicked swallows up him who is more righteous than himself
(Habakkuk i. 13), it seems as if there were no retribution to
be found on earth, as if the righteous were deprived of
their reward (verses 1-3) : furthermore, the gloom and sadness which must take possession of the soul in consequence
of such thoughts are deepened by the prospect of that which
awaits us after this life (verses 4-6). Against such dark
discontent, however, the *spirit raises its voice* in verses 7-10,
and answers that God has pleasure in the works of his people,
and that in good time the now failing retribution will come.
In view of the glorious future the eye should be turned away

from the gloomy present, and we should be joyful through hope. Above all, should we not give ourselves up to a despairing inactivity, but call forth all our powers to fulfil the task which is set us for the present life.

Ver. 1. For all this I took to heart and (indeed) *thereby I fathomed all this—that the righteous and the wise, and their works, are in the hand of God ; neither love nor hatred doth man know, all things are before them.* Ver. 2. *All things as to all : one event to the righteous and to the wicked ; to the good and to the clean and to the unclean ; to him that sacrificeth and to him that sacrificeth not : as the sinner, so the good : he that sweareth is as he that feareth an oath.* Ver. 3. *That is evil among all things that are done under the sun, that there is one event to all : yea also the heart of the sons of men is full of evil, and folly is in their heart while they live, and after that* (they go) *to the dead.* Ver. 4. *For who is preferred ? In all the living one may trust, for a living dog is better than a dead lion.* Ver. 5. *For the living know that they shall die, and the dead know nothing at all : neither have they any more a reward, for the memory of them is forgotten.* Ver. 6. *Their love and also their hatred and their envy is vanished : neither have they any more for ever a portion in anything that is done under the sun.* Ver. 7. *Go thy way, eat thy bread in joy and drink thy wine with a good heart ; for God hath pleasure in thy works.* Ver. 8. *Let thy garments be always white, and let thy head lack no ointment.* Ver. 9. *Look upon life with the wife whom thou lovest. all the days of thy vain life, which he giveth thee under the sun : all the days of thy vain life, for that is thy portion in life, and in thy labour which thou takest under the sun.* Ver. 10. *All that thy hand findeth to do by thy power, do, for there is no work nor device, nor knowledge, nor wisdom in the hell whither thou goest.*

Ver. 1. The word " for" points to the connection between this discussion and that of chap. viii. 14-17. A further confirmation is here set forth of the result there arrived at, to wit, of the unsearchableness of the ways of God. The righteous and the wise are in the hand of God, in His power, so that He does with them what He will. No one, by his own intentions and his own acts can determine his fate. That acts are not spoken of here, in themselves, as acts, as if we were compelled, without any exercise of will, to do what God pleases ; but with regard to their results, in so far that *the saddest fate may follow on the best deed,* is clear from the whole context, in which only what befalls man, not what man does, is considered.   Ver. 2 especially, which may serve as a commentary to the present one, proves this.   For the same reason what is said of *love* and *hatred* cannot be referred to human affections, —as Hitzig does.when he writes, " Inasmuch as man has not his acts in his own power, he does not know whether he will love or hate,"—but only to the good and evil providential arrangements in which God's love and hatred seem to embody themselves.   J. D. Michaelis justly observes, " In this world we cannot tell by the events of life whether God loves us or hates us, because to the righteous it happens as to the unrighteous ; nor can we even know whether God means to show us love by sending prosperity, or hatred by sending adversity." In all the last sections the historical occasion of the Author's words was the miserable fate of the people of God at the time of his writing,   We read in Malachi i. 2,—" I love you, saith the Lord, yet ye say, wherein dost thou love us ?" " God loves us not, although we are worthy of His love,"— that is the reproach against God, which the Prophet exposes at the very beginning ; and which we may therefore judge to have been a kind of watchword at the time.   The translation of the Vulgate—" nescit homo, utrum amore an odio dignus sit," has quite missed the right sense.   Complaints were raised that he who was worthy of the divine love did not experience it in God's leadings.   *Man,* that is, in accordance with what precedes, more precisely, " the wise and righteous man :" a similar usage is found in Psalm xxxvi. 8, where the connection shows that by *the children of men,* we are to understand, the citizens of the kingdom of God.   *All things are before them,* that is, may happen to them : the righteous man is not assured against anything.   J. D. Michaelis remarks, "All things have they before them, that is, there is the same probability that a man will be loved as that he will be hated, that in prosperity he will experience proofs of God's grace, or in adversity proofs of his disfavour.   The one experience is as easy to be conceived as the other."

Ver. 2. The expression—*all things as to all*—presents no
difficulty when it is borne in mind that in ver. 1, " Man," is
used instead of, *the wise and righteous,* by way of intimating
his absolute dependence on the heavenly powers.   " All things"
(happen to the wise and righteous,) " as to all," that is, as to
the rest : they have no peculiar fate, such as was promised to
Israel, who, in the Books of Moses, is represented as being put
under God's most special providence and care ;—they share
the universal destiny.   A commentary on this intentionally
short and enigmatical saying is furnished by what follows.
Knobel has a specific against the temptations and difficulties
which assailed the author so terribly, and with which believers
of all times have to wage fierce warfare, namely, " we must
distinguish between the physical and moral order of the world ;
physical evils are experienced by all without exception ; the
pious cannot evade them because of their morality, and yet
they have not to endure the special punishments of immor-
ality."   But if we make the " physical" independent of God,
and thus strip God of his true Godhead, and we ourselves at
the same time fall into semi-atheism, the remedy is worse
than the disease.   *Event* or accident, is not set in opposition
to the divine ordainment, but to independent action on the
part of the righteous, (compare ii. 14, 15 ; iii. 19.) טוב is
prefixed to טהור with the design of showing that the terms
" clean, unclean," are to be taken not in the juridical or levit-
ical sense, but in the moral sense.   A sufficient evidence of
this is, that elsewhere one only is set in opposition to the
other : besides, טוב occurs again, to show that in the first instance it serves the purpose of explaining or defining more
clearly that which follows.   *He that sweareth*—(under certain
circumstances, be it observed, a man may swear and yet not
be what is meant by the designation " swearer,") refers here
to one who swears in a *frivolous* manner.   The words stand
in remarkable parallelism to Matthew v. 34.   To fear an oath,
is to look upon it with holy awe, so that only in cases of
necessity and at the command of *love* can we be induced
to take one upon ourselves.   It is evident from chap. viii. 2,
that the author has no intention whatever of rejecting oaths
altogether.   Cartwright says, " notandum etiam adjunctum,
quo describit improbum, nempe quod jurat, id est juramentis

assuetus est. Cujus igitur ori juramenta et nominis divini usurpatio familiaris et trita est, illum improbum esse constat: contra etiam observandum est, pium non eum appellari, qui non jurat, sed qui a juramento sibi metuit."

Ver. 3. Regarding things from the point of view of natural reason and in a rough matter of fact way, judging them by the vulgar empirical method which he afterwards rejects, the author goes on to say, " that is evil ;"—he thus " sins with his tongue," as it is said in Psalm xxxix. 2. Parallel is Psalm lxxiii. 1 6, where in reference to the same fact it is said —" and I considered in order to know it : a pain was it in mine eyes." But the Psalmist speaks thus only until he comes to the sanctuary of God : then a light suddenly breaks in upon him such as the natural reason cannot supply. Cartwright compares Malachi iii. 1 4, ff., where the Jews are introduced as complaining, that it is in vain to serve God, and as resting their charge on the fact that they who fear God are unhappy and the heathen are prosperous : his remarks are as follows—" certe, si vere judicare velimus, hac tam impia et blasphema voce Deum esse negant. Nam qui illi justitiam suam adimit, is Deum a mundo tollit, nec enim Deus est nisi justus." The manner of the Scriptures is to let doubts and murmurings have free and full expression, and then to vanquish them in open conflict with the sword of faith. Scepticism and despair cannot possibly bring forward anything stronger than what we find in the Holy Scriptures. And, in fact, this openness and candour in setting forth doubts is one of the best means of overcoming them. Knobel is of opinion that this verse shows " that Koheleth did not believe in immortality and in retribution after death ; for had he held such a faith he might easily have taught that the recompence that was not made here would be made on the other side the grave." He, however, who has surrendered this world, has ceased to attach much importance to the world to come : if God's ways here cannot be justified, we shall not be able really and livingly to believe in a future retribution. The author therefore takes exactly the right course, when he, as the representative of his tried and tempted contemporaries, fights and strives above all things with the scepticism which envelopes in darkness the ways of God in the present world.

This task accomplished, the future becomes plain and clear of itself. The words—*amidst all that is done under the sun*, point out that so far from being exceptional it is the usual course of this world that all things should come alike to all. With the expression—" the heart of the children of men is full of evil"—compare chap. viii. 11, according to which by the "children of men," we are to understand those who up to that point had striven after better things. Parallel also is Psalm lxxiii. 10, " therefore turns he, (namely, the wicked,) his people hither;" by his impunity from punishment and his prosperity he induces others to leave the right way and to come over to his manner of thinking. It is a melancholy consideration that external sufferings only too easily exert a demoralizing influence. *And folly is in their heart :*—their heart is filled with foolish thoughts about God's government of the world, and with foolish proposals to help themselves by wrong, when God leaves them in the lurch. On the word אחריו compare chap. vi. 12; vii. 14 : after that he, namely, the righteous, has been thus visited by evils which, though external, bring alas! moral ones also in their train ; *behind themselves*, that is, after such a mode of existence.

Ver. 4. *For who is preferred ?* The reason is given for the words—" And after that to the dead :" for death is the lot of all mortals, and the righteous forms no exception to the rule : as Gesenius renders, " quis enim qui electus sit, *i. e,* moriendi sorte exemtus." As the vowels belong to the man ginal reading, and as the Pual does not elsewhere occur, it is better to point as for Niphal, which is frequently employed in the sense of " chosen out, preferred :" see, for example, Jeremiah viii. 3. The unnecessary Masoretic conjecture offered by the marginal reading is most simply explained by Rambach and others as follows, " qui adsocietur, v. adsociari velit sub mortuis." The words, "who is excepted " (from this sad lot ?) " are dictated by the feeling that the lot of death is a sad one, and the reason for such a view is assigned by the author when he affirms that " in all the living one may trust." The verb בטח is used in conjunction with אל, to designate one in whom confidence is placed, in Psalm iv. 6, xxxi. 7. בטחון is not " hope," but " confidence, abandonment," see Isaiah xxxvi. 4. Only the living are capable of doing anything.   To be no object of confidence is a miserable condition.   On the words — "for the living dog," (or strictly, "as far as the living dog is concerned, so is he") "better than the dead lion," Cartwright remarks — "hæc vox pecudis potius quam hominis dicenda est." This observation agrees with Psalm lxxiii. 22, where the writer brings against himself the charge of having behaved like the cattle, when the prosperity of the ungodly exposed him to temptation.   Nor indeed can it be otherwise: when God vanishes from the present world the future is changed into a dismal night of death, by whose darkness all are alike covered.

Ver. 5. The advantage of the living over the dead consists in his, that the former have *consciousness*.   This consciousness is here individualised, and one of the forms in which it expresses itself is used to describe the whole.   The living have consciousness ; they know, for example, that they shall die, which in comparison with utter unconsciousness is unquestionably a good, however sad may be the object of knowledge.   Such is the language of natural reason, to whose eye all seems dark and gloomy that lies beyond the present scene, because it fails in this world to discern the traces of divine retribution.   The Spirit says on the contrary : " the spirit returns to God who gave it."   *Neither have they any more a reward :* that God should recompense them is impossible, inasmuch as the righteous who are dead have no self-conscious personality.   To what extent this is the case is indicated by the words—"for their memory is forgotten ;" so little power have they to make good a position for themselves, so entirely are they deprived of all means of expressing their life, so completely have they disappeared.

Ver. 6. Alongside of the *hatred* which is condemned, there is one that is allowed, and not only *allowed,* but even commanded (see Psalm xxxi. 7, and Revelations ii. 6).   Hatred is indeed to be condemned, but still his condition must be regarded as a degraded one who is unable to hate.

Ver. 7. The voice of the flesh is here opposed by the voice of the spirit.   It is exactly so elsewhere ; as, for example, in Psalm xxxix, where the Psalmist first strives with God and impatiently demands of Him to know the end of his life and

sufferings, but afterwards rises up and casts down discontent
and doubt to the ground. Here also we might say that
in verses 1-6 the author speaks as the representative of the
then prevailing spirit of the people; not, however, as though he
appropriated views that were utterly strange to his own
mind, but such as he also himself in his hours of weakness
had been compelled to sympathise with. Now, on the contrary, the writer sets himself in God to oppose the popular
views and feelings. Calvin's remarks on Psalm xlii. 6 hold
good of this place also : " David represents himself to us as
divided into two portions. So far as he rests by faith in
God's promises, he rises in arms, with a spirit of unconquer-
able valour, against the feelings and will of the flesh, and condemns at the same time his own weak and yielding conduct."
Here, just as there, it is the spirit which is strong in God
that enters the lists against the "weaker vessel," the timid
fearful soul, which in the book of Job is introduced under the
personification of Job's wife. There is undoubtedly a reference to individual men, but still it is the "man Judah" of
Isaiah v. 3, who is, in the first instance, addressed. This
is evident from the entire context, of which the sufferings of
the *people of God* form the point of departure. *Eat thy bread
in joy and drink thy wine with a good heart.* " Joy and
good heart," stand in opposition to the gloomy discontent
which led them formerly to say, " Every one that doeth
evil is good in the eyes of the Lord, and he delighteth in
them, or where is the God of judgment ?" (Malachi ii. 17).
The contrast to eating bread and drinking wine is presented
in such passages as 1 Samuel i. 7, where it is said of Han-
nah, " she wept and ate not ;" Psalm xlii. 4, " My tears are
my meat day and night ;" Psalm lxxx. 6, " Thou feedest them
with the bread of tears, and givest them tears to drink in
great measure," (" Bread of tears," signifies bread that consists of tears), and Psalm cii. 10, Job iii. 24. *God hath pleasure in thy works,* (רצה with the accusative means, " to have
pleasure in anything,") and, therefore, in His good time thou
wilt see the reward which thou now missest, and " ye shall
discern again the difference between the righteous and the
wicked, between him that serveth God and him that serveth
him not," (Malachi iii. 18). We have in this verse the dis-

tinct negation of verse 1. There, by a hasty conclusion
drawn from the fact of the temporal sufferings of the righteous, it was affirmed that man does not at all know whether
he has grace before God or not, whether he may or may not
expect love from God. The great sting of temporal suffering
is, that we very easily get to fancy that it will last for ever,
and that it is apt to lead us into erroneous thoughts about
God's grace. We can only overcome this temptation by
rising in faith above the present. In Psalm lxxiii. 17, " till
I come to the sanctuaries of God, then will I look on their
end." The thing first mentioned stands to the second
in the relation of cause to effect. Having entered into the
sanctuary of God, the Psalmist sees that the prosperity of the
wicked and the sufferings of the righteous are only transitory, and thus he attains to an unbounded confidence in
God's help and redemption. A real, if not a verbal, parallel
to the words, " God has pleasure in thy works," may be found
in the commencement of Psalm lxxiii: " only good is God to
Israel, to those who are of a pure heart." God is good, and
not evil as the righteous may well fancy when they are
plagued continually, when they are chastened every morning,
whilst the wicked live in prosperity. Luther remarks on the
verse, "He means to say something like this—thou livest in
the world where there is nothing without that, for there is
much sorrow, heart suffering, misery, there is death and much
vanity : make use then of life with love, and do not make
thine own life sour and hard with anxious and fruitless
cares. Solomon says what he says not to the secure and
godless children of the world, but to such as truly fear God
and believe. These he comforts, and would fain see them
comfort themselves and rejoice in God. To them he gives the
exhortation, to be glad ; he does not bid those to drink wine
and eat, etc., who were beforehand too secure, and being godless and lost, spent their lives in indolence and debauchery."

Ver. 8. Let thy garments be always white. **White** is in
Scripture the colour of serene splendour symbolically shadow-
ing forth glory: (compare my Commentary on Revelations
iv. 4.) The Angel of Mark xvi. 5 appears in white clothes,
as a sign that the rank of the angels is the same as that of
the "saints," who are the glorious. The clothes of Christ be-

came white in His transfiguration, (Matthew xvii. 2, Mark ix. 3, Luke ix. 29.) White clothes are borne by the glorified in Revelations iii. 4, 5, vii. 9, as a symbol of glory. In this place white clothes were to be put on *to express the confident hope of the future glory of the people of God.* Spener, in testimony of his hope of a better future for the Church, caused himself to be buried in a white coffin. The adoption of white clothes signifies here the anticipation of the future victory of the people of God. Analogous is Revelations vi. 11, where in answer to their prayer, which could not yet be perfectly fulfilled, each of the slaughtered receives provisionally a white garment. There also the white garment has an *anticipatory* significance. Hand in hand with the white garment goes the *oil on the head.* This oil is the "oil of joy" mentioned in Psalm xlv. 8, and in Isaiah lxi. 3. In joyful circumstances, on festive occasions men were accustomed to anoint themselves: such oil was an embodiment of festive joy, on which account the oil of gladness is opposed to sadness in Isaiah lxi. 3. The true members of the people of God ought always to be in a festive, joyous mood, inasmuch as they rise by faith above the gloomy present to the glorious future awaiting them.

Ver. 9. Look upon life, which is as much as to say, be happy, in that thou turnest away thine eye from the sad present and fixest it on the glorious future, and in that thou enjoyest those little pleasures which God offers thee in the midst of this vain existence, and which thou mayest not sour and embitter by cares and vexatious questions. The woman appears here not as the source, but as the companion of joy; and the words, "with the woman whom thou lovest," may to a certain extent be regarded as a parenthesis. אשר before נתן refers to the days of life, (chap. vi. 17.) The connection is the following, "look upon life . . . all the days of thy vain life, which He giveth thee under the sun, all the days of thy vain life." By the repetition of the last words we are expressly taught that, in the midst of the vanity and travail with which human existence is burdened (Genesis iii.), we are pressingly summoned not to seal up the sources of enjoyment which still remain open to us. הוא, "this," namely, to see life, to be pleased.

Ver. 10. Despair carries with it the danger of a sluggish inactivity. Against this, men are here warned. Luther remarks, "an admonition to the lazy. For when they see that so much pains and toil are lost, they are minded to do nothing but to let everything stand quite still." As to substance, Hebrews xii. 12 presents a parallel, where to the severely tried and tempted it is said, διὸ τὰς παρειμένας χεῖρας καὶ τὰ παραλελυμένα γόνατα ἀνορθώσατε. "Sluggish hands" are ascribed to the suffering even in Job iv. 3, and Isaiah xxxv. 3. The saying, "my hand finds something," signifies, "I am capable of something," "I am in a position for something," "I have opportunity for something:" (compare Judges ix. 33, 1 Samuel x. 7, xxv. 8.) According to the accents, and the sense, בכחך belongs not to עשׂה, but to what goes before. The duty of doing all that it is in any way possible to do is based, in the second part of the verse, on the consideration that what is here left undone never is done, that the tasks appointed by God for this life which are here unaccomplished remain unaccomplished, and that the gifts and powers lent for this life should be used in this life. *For there is no work, nor device, nor knowledge, nor wisdom, in the hell whither thou goest:—* it is not so in the intermediate kingdom, nor is it so in the kingdom of glory, (1 Corinthians xiii. 8). There are forms of knowledge and work which belong only to the present life, and he who does not employ them, has buried his talent in the earth, and thus committed a heavy sin,—a sin, the consequences of which will stretch into eternity. Even Jerome compares the saying of our Lord in John ix. 4, ἐμὲ δεῖ ἐργάζεσθαι τὰ ἔργα τοῦ πέμψαντός με ἕως ἡμέρα ἐστίν· ἔρχεται νὺξ, ὅτε οὐδεὶς δύναται ἐργάζεσθαι. That there is a reference to the verse now under notice, can scarcely be called in question. It begins at once with the words "for no *work*." Even Lücke, although this passage was not in his mind, felt that the Lord made partial use of an already existing expression. "Day and night mark the fixed and bounded time of the earthly career of the earthly activity of our Lord." Feeling that death shortly awaited Him, Christ says, "there comes for me the night, when, *as it is said*, no man can work." What Jesus spake, alluding to the present verse, holds good for all believers.

VERSES 11, 12.

When the position of the people of God is a sad one, whilst on the contrary, the world triumphs, what we should do is to bear in mind that the destinies of men are decided in heaven, that their fortunes are not determined according to might, or according to weakness, and that a sudden catastrophe often lays low that which was highly exalted. To have God as our friend is the main thing; all depends at last on that; and that alone decides.

Ver. 11. *I returned and saw under the sun that the race is not to the swift, nor the battle to the heroes, neither yet bread to the wise, nor yet riches to men of understanding, nor yet favour to men of skill: but time and chance happeneth to them all. Ver. 12. For man also knoweth not his time, as the fishes that are fallen in an evil net, and as the birds that are caught in a snare: like them are the children of men snared at the time of misfortune, when it falleth suddenly upon them.*

Ver. 11. The words, *I returned and saw under the sun,* indicate that the writer takes up again the consideration of sublunary things, which had been interrupted, and turns his attention to a new subject. Compare iv. 1, 7. In the two passages just quoted ואראה is used; here we find the Infinitive, which is more accurately defined by the verb. finit. which precedes. After the words, *under the sun,* we must mentally add, "and indeed I saw." The point of departure here, also, is the tribulation of the people of God, but considered from a new point of view. *The race is not to the swift,* for they may be hindered by something or other,—sometimes even by the very slightest obstacle, so that the less swift shall arrive sooner than they. *Nor the battle to the heroes.* This same view, which Rationalism looks upon as "fatalistic," (Knobel) David gave utterance to in the presence of Goliath, himself furnishing a living illustration of the affirmation of the text. See 1 Samuel xvii. 47, "the battle is the Lord's, and he gives you into our hands:" further also, Psalm xxxii. 16, 17, "the king is not saved by his great hosts, a hero is not delivered by much strength. A horse is a vain thing for safety, neither doth he deliver by his great strength." Jahaziel the Prophet says in 2 Chronicles xx. 15, "Be not afraid nor dismayed by reason of this great multitude, for the battle is not yours but God's." The point of view in these passages, (compare besides Jeremiah xlvi. 6, where speaking against Egypt the Prophet says—"the swift will not escape, nor the hero be delivered :" Proverbs xxi. 30, 31), as well as in the one we are now illustrating is that of *consolation :* if it depended on human strength the people of God must succumb. "Favour" means much the same as "preference, popularity." In connection with the words, *for time and chance happeneth to them all,* whose import is, "they all are subject to the influence of time and chance," compare Psalm xxxi. 16, "my times are in thy hand, deliver me from the hand of mine enemies, and from my persecutors." That the fates of the Psalmist, as indeed of all men, are in God's hand, is represented there as the ground of their hope of deliverance, as the light in the dark night of adversity. *Chance* here is not to to be regarded as a power alongside of and opposed to God : chance is that which happens to man without his co-operation, and the idea of the verse is that of Romans ix. 16—ἄρα οὖν οὐ τοῦ θέλοντος, οὐδὲ τοῦ τρέχοντος, ἀλλὰ τοῦ ἐλεοῦντος Θεοῦ· If everything depends on time and chance, we ought not to despair in view of the seeming omnipotence of the world, supposing God to be our friend. For to the friends of God belongs the future. All things human, let them be as proud and splendid as they may, let them boast and be puffed up as they may, are but loose chaff, which the wind of divine judgments will sweep away.

Ver. 12. The general assertion, that everything mighty and distinguished is subject to chance, is grounded on the particular fact which is here brought specially under notice, the fact, namely, that no man is able to escape a catastrophe coming over him. In the background stands the thought— *the Persian also in his time will fall under such a catastrophe, and in fact the powers of this world generally :* their apparent omnipotence will not deliver them. When Alexander came, the seal of divine confirmation was set to this declaration. According to the context, the "time" of man

must mean here, the time of his downfal : elsewhere "day" is
used in the same sense (Job xviii. 20). Man's ignorance
of his time is brought here under consideration so far as it is
determined by a power standing absolutely above him *Trap
or snare* is quite a common image of the divine judgments :
Net is used for this purpose in Hosea vii. 12, " I will spread
out my net over them ;" in Ezekiel xii. 13, " and I spread out
my net over him, and he is taken in my snare;" Ezekiel xxxii.
3, " and I spread over thee (Pharoah) my net in the assembly
of many peoples, and they draw thee up with my snare."
With regard to יקוש the part. Pual compare Ewald, § 169 d.

VERSES 13-18.

In the midst of all their misery one high prerogative has
remained to the people of God, to wit, *wisdom,* which is
a nobler possession than the strength in which the world
temporarily rejoices.   That this wisdom is despised because it
is in the form of a servant, detracts nothing at all from its worth.
Were its voice only heard it would exert a wholesome and
preservative influence even on the heathen world ; it would
become a salt to it ; whereas now the heathen states being
under the rule and direction of folly hurry unrestrainably to
ruin.   In the background, however, stands the conviction that
the nation which possesses wisdom must of necessity in due
season rise again to supremacy.   In verses 13-15 a parable is
set before us : in ver. 16 we have its interpretation.   In verses
17-18 the thought is carried out into further detail.

Ver. 13. *This also saw I as wisdom under the sun, and it
seemed great unto me :*   Ver. 14. *A little city and few men
within it, and there came a great king against it and be-
sieged it, and built great bulwarks against it.*   Ver. 15. *And
he found therein a poor wise man, and he by his wisdom
delivered the city, yet no man thought of this same poor
man.*   Ver. 16. *And I said, Wisdom is better than strength,
nevertheless the wisdom of the poor man is despised and his
words are not heard.*   Ver. 17. *The words of the wise heard
in quiet are better than the cry of him that ruleth among*

fools. Ver. 18. *Better is wisdom than weapons of war; and one sinner destroyeth much good.*

Ver. 13. Even Luther and Mercerus saw that in verses 13-15 a parable is presented to us, and not an historical occurrence. The poor man with his delivering wisdom is an image of Israel. The words, " this also saw I," as well as those just noticed, " I returned and saw ;" (ver. 11) introduce a new subject of consideration. It is not allowable to explain the words, " this also," as if they signified, " along with other evidences of wisdom which occur in the world," for no allusion has been previously made to such exhibitions of wisdom. Nor may we adopt the rendering—" this also saw I, (namely) wisdom under the sun ;" for the closing words describe the sphere of vision generally. The best explanation is rather the one given in the text, namely, "this also saw I as wisdom." חכמה thus defines more closely the quality of that which, along with other things, he saw ; and the meaning would be, " this also saw I under the sun,—a wisdom which seemed to me great." Luther remarks, " he calls it here a great wisdom, for it is in truth a great wisdom, to deliver a little and poor city possessed of few resources from great and powerful enemies."

Ver. 14. מָצוֹר from צוּר signifies in chap. vii. 26, (מצורה in chap. ix. 12,) " the implement of hunting, of snaring, the net ;" here it is used of " siege-works."

Ver. 15. The subject of מצא is, the Great King : Rambach remarks, " contra omnem opinionem expertus est."

Ver. 16. This verse contains the practical application of the parable. On the words, *And his words are not heard,* Hitzig remarks, " In this particular case they had, it is true, not despised his wisdom, and they had listened to his words. But it was an exceptional case, necessity drove them thereto, and afterwards they forgot him." Cartwright says, " viri humilis conditionis sapientia, tametsi splendeat maxime, tamen paupertate tanquam nube interjecta ita obfuscatur, ut levi temporis momento omnium oculos a se aversos habens memoria excidat."

Ver. 17. Attention is called, on the very face, to the close connection between this verse and the last, by the catchword נשמעים. The author's great aim throughout this whole connection being to console, he could not possibly rest satisfied

with the little consolatory matter advanced in ver. 16. Moreover, the close connection referred to is required by the parallel passages, which allude to wisdom as the jewel still remaining to the people of God, and as the pledge of a joyful termination of their present experiences. *Heard in quiet :*—that
is the condition of their wholesome influence. Israel would
have proved a salt to the heathen world if ear had only been
given to the voice of wisdom dwelling in his midst. Hitzig
remarks justly, that "the quiet hearing of words, promises their
fulfilment, a thing which is here implied." In opposition to the
passive state of quietly listening to the words of wisdom is set
the activity developed in our own crying. He that ruleth
among fools, namely, the world-monarch, is himself to be conceived as a fool. This is shown by his conduct in vehemently
crying instead of calmly listening. Compare Isaiah xlii. 2,
where it is said of the servant of God, " he shall *not* cry, nor
call, nor cause his voice to be heard in the streets," in contrast
to the clamorous and passionate conduct of a worldly con-
queror, who thinks of nothing but carrying through his own
will, and who blusters and rages when he meets with opposition.

Ver. 18. *That wisdom is better than weapons of war,*
would show itself in the example of the powers of the world
if they only lent an ear to its voice, and it will one day be
proved in the experience of the nation whose privilege it is to
possess wisdom, in that day when, notwithstanding its defenceless impotence, it is raised to universal dominion. *One sinner,*
for example, the heathen world-monarch, *destroyeth much
good ;* מובה is not good in the moral sense, but " possession,
property, prosperity," as in chap. v. 10-17 ; vi. 6. The truth
of this assertion was first made clear in the wretched decline
and sudden downfal of the Persian Empire.

CHAPTER X. 1-3.

Resuming the subject touched upon in the second half of
chap. ix. 19, the writer cheers the people of God, groaning
under the tyranny of the world, by directing attention to the
fact that their enemies, (in the first instance the Persians,)

were given up to folly and its destructive influences. Where folly rules, destruction cannot be far off, as it is said, "thou didst hide their heart from understanding, therefore shalt thou not suffer them to remain exalted," (Job xvii. 4.)

Ver. 1. *Dead flies cause through putrefaction, the oil of the perfumer to stink : the glorious in wisdom and honour, a little folly.* Ver. 2. *A wise man's heart is at his right hand and a fool's heart is at his left.* Ver. 3. *Yea also in the way which he goes is his heart lacking, and he saith of every one, he is foolish.*

Ver. 1. Not without significance is it said, "Flies of death," and not "dead flies," although these are meant. The effect described is not produced by flies as such ; but is so entirely connected with death, that instead of flies any other dead thing might have been mentioned. "Dead flies," are only specified because they find their way first of all to the salve pot, and because the author wished to adduce some small thing. Physical death is the more prominently referred to as its correspondent, in spiritual things, is folly. The employment of the singular of the verb יבאיש calls special attention to it. When special emphasis is meant to be laid on the second word in the *stat. constr.*, the verb is accommodated to it. That the singular depends on מות was recognised even by Symmachus, μυιῶν θάνατος σήψει ἔλαιον εὐῶδες μυρεψοῦ. The oil of the perfumer is mentioned as being a costly, noble substance. יביע is added subsidiarily, for the purpose of indicating more distinctly the cause : "in that they cause to putrify," in consequence of the process of putrification which they commence. But that it serves only a subsidiary purpose is evident, because יבאיש does not suit any but the second clause. "To make to stink," is used elsewhere for "to make contemptible" in Genesis xxxiv. 30, (compare Exodus v. 21,) and in this sense it is to be repeated in the second clause. יקר signifies originally "dear, costly," and then "excellent," glorious, noble." Compare Jeremiah xv. 19, where יקר "excellent" is opposed to זולל "contemptible ;" and Lamentations iv. 2, "the sons of Zion, the glorious," (Psalm xlv. 10 ; Proverbs iii. 15 ; vi. 26.) מן is used here causatively. At its commencement under Cyrus, the Persian kingdom was glorious in wisdom and honour : its praises were sounded not only by the profane, but also by the sacred writers. Geier remarks with regard to the two terms " wisdom and honour," "duo hæc vocabula duplicem pretii causam indicant, sapientiam et honerem, *i. e.*, partim internam culturam partim externam hominum existimationem opes aut felicitatem gloriosam." *A little folly :* that is, folly which is little in proportion to the entire system and edifice of which it proves the ruin. Corresponding to the active cause here, namely, " the little folly," stands that which is acted upon, namely, "the much good" in chap. ix. 18. In the New Testament also the leaven is called little, not in relation to a greater quantity thereof, but to the whole mass (ὅλον φύραμα :) see the parallel passages 1 Cor. v. 6 ; Galatians v. 9 Folly, sin, is so little and insignificant that on a superficial consideration it is scarcely noticed, or at all events, is looked upon only as a *bagatelle, a peccadillo.*

Ver. 2. The right hand being "the principal one, the dearest, the strongest hand, with which we chiefly grasp, work, wield our weapons, and so forth," we say of that which is as it ought to be, that it is at the right, whilst of things that are no longer in their normal state, we say that they are at the left. A comparison has rightly been instituted between this expression and our saying, "his heart is in the right place." Attention is drawn to the heart here, so far as in it are the roots of the understanding, which is always determined and guided by *inclination.*

Ver. 3. *On the way which he goes,* in his actions. When the heart has taken a perverse turn, the hands are unable to lay hold of anything rightly. *He saith of every one, he is foolish.* By a strange confusion of places, he speaks thus especially of those on whom God has bestowed the gift and privilege of wisdom. Hitzig says, "Himself he dare not hold for a fool: for therein would lie some truth, and a beginning of understanding would have been made."

CHAPTER X. 4.

In the difficult circumstances in which they are placed, the people of God should be on their guard against *irritability,* which would inevitably tend to increase their sufferings: and further, they should carefully guard that precious treasure of *calmness of soul* which is his portion who sees the hand of God in everything, even in that which is hardest to bear, and resigns himself patiently and humbly to the Divine will.

Ver. 4. *If the spirit of the ruler rise up against thee, leave not thy place, for yielding pacifieth great offence.*

The spirit of the ruler, to wit, of the foolish one, (chap. ix. 17, x. 1-3,) of the sinner, (chap. ix. 18.)   Hitzig remarks, "the ruler here is one who, when angered, is capable of committing great offences" *against thee.*   The author addresses the covenant people, against whom the minds of the heathen ru!·rs were greatly irritated, because they had got wind of the pretensions made by them to the privilege of wisdom, and to the future possession of the throne of the world.   What the *place* is for the people of God, is plain from the *yielding,* from the retiring gentleness, mentioned in the second clause, which is exclusively found amongst those who commit their cause to God.   Through it Jacob overcame Esau, and David Saul, (1 Samuel xxvi.)   The contrast to מרפא is in Proverbs xiv. 30, קנאה "anger, passion."   *Great sins,* into which a passionate tyrant inevitably falls, when he meets with resistance. To rage against the people of God is a great sin.   Cartwright says, "hæc igitur animi submissio et patientia turbulentissimas perturbationum et animi motuum tempestates serenat tumidissimos et maxime inflatos affectuum fluctus tranquillat, et ex leone agnum reddit.   Quamobrem connitendum, ut hac virtute imbuamur, qua cum deo, tum hominibus placeamus, etiam his, qui a pietate et humanitate procul remoti sunt."

CHAPTER X. 5-10.

The humiliation of the people of God, and the triumph of the world, is a heavy stone of stumbling.   But in His own good time God will remove this offence out of the way: those who have used violence will meet with recompence: and it is the less possible that they should escape ruin as they are utterly destitute of the corrective and preservative element of wisdom.

Ver. 5. *There is an evil which I saw under the sun, as an error which proceedeth from the ruler :*   Ver. 6. *Folly was set on great heights, and the rich sit in low place.* Ver. 7. *I saw servants on horses and princes walking on foot as servants.* Ver. 8. *He that diggeth a pit shall fall into it : and whoso breaketh through a wall, a serpent shall bite him.* Ver. 9. *Whoso looseneth stones shall be hurt therewith, and he that cleaveth wood shall be injured thereby.* Ver. 10. *If the iron has become blunt, and he has not whetted the edge, he must put to more strength, and wisdom has the advantage of amendment.*

Ver. 5. *The Ruler*, absolutely is the heavenly one, even as in chap. v. 8, and chap. viii. 2, 4, *the king* is the heavenly king. Of the heavenly ruler, שׁלִּיט is used in Daniel iv. 23, v. 21, also. The correct view is given by Jerome as communicated to him by the Jew of whose assistance he availed himself, "Hebræus potentem et principem a cujus facie, ignoratio videatur egredi, Deum exposuit, quod putent homines in hac inæqualitate rerum illum non juste et ut æquum est judicare." The ב before שׁגגה is of great importance. It is not really an "error," *it only has the seeming of one;* it bears this appearance only to those superficial minds whose eyes are fastened on the present, and which are unable to survey the whole and take the end into view.

Ver. 6. This verse sets before us "the evil," the apparent "fault" in providence. The matter treated of is the downfall of the people of God. According to what precedes, the "folly" spoken of must be that of the heathens, especially that of the Persians. By the "rich" we cannot understand such as are now actually so, for then they would not be sitting in a low place, but such as by right should be so. According to the divine destination, Israel was a *rich* people. To him the promise had been given, "there shall be no poor among you—(אביון forms a strict contrast to the word עשׁיר employed here)—for the Lord will bless thee," (Deuteronomy xv. 4:) and further, "thou shalt lend unto many nations, and shalt borrow from no one; thou shalt reign over many nations, but they shall not reign over thee," (Deuteronomy xv. 6, xxviii. 11.) The prosperity meant for the Israelites was prefigured in the opulence which, through the divine blessing, was enjoyed by their forefathers, who walked in God's ways: compare Genesis xiii. 2. "And Abraham was very rich in cattle, in silver, and

gold." It is true that the promise given in the law rested on
the expressly specified condition of faithfulness in fulfilling
the divine commands; and failure therein must of course lead to
suspension of the promise. But still the promise might not
be for ever revoked; and because this seemed to be the case,
it looked as if there were a fault in the divine government.
This appearance is done away with by what follows. In
connection with בשפל compare verse 23 of Psalm cxxxvi.
which was written during the dominion of the Persians, "who
remembered us in our low estate, בשפלנו." שֵׁפֶל is only used
in these two passages.

Ver. 7. A world turned upside down : Servants ride and
masters walk.   *Servants,*—such, by right and by God's
appointment, were the heathen ; for Israel was called to universal dominion : him were the nations meant to obey,
(Genesis xlix. 10.)   The Jews were a kingdom of priests,
(Exodus xix. 6;) before them their enemies would be compelled to play the hypocrite, and they should tread on their
high places, (Deut. xxxiii. 29 ;) through them all nations were
to be blessed, and as the dispensers of blessing, the latter must
by consequence take up towards them the position of dependent petitioners, (Isaiah xliv. 5 ; xlv. 14.)   "Thou shalt be
above only and thou shalt not be beneath," (Deuteronomy
xxviii. 13-43 :)   So ought it to be according to their true idea,
and so must it some time really be : compare Daniel vii. 27,
" and the kingdom and the dominion, and the power over the
kingdoms under the whole heaven shall be given to the people
of the saints of the Most High :" compare also Isaiah lxi. 5,
" and strangers shall stand and feed your flocks, and the sons
of the alien shall be your ploughmen and your vine-dressers."
And so in fact it is now as to the essential features : in
Christ and His Church Israel has attained to dominion over
the world.   At the time, however, when the author wrote, the
idea and the reality stood in most glaring contrast to each
other.   "We are servants," it is said in Ezra ix. 9.   In
Lamentations v. 8, exactly as here, those are styled servants
who by right should be such, although they actually are not—
"servants rule over us and there is none that delivereth out
of their hand," on which Ch. B. Michaelis remarks, "qui nobis
potius si pii fuissemus servire debuissent, Deut. xxviii. 48.

Princes : that is, by right and according to God. The passage of chief authority on this point is Lamentations i. 1 where Israel is called " the princess over the provinces."

Ver. 8. The writer now proceeds to advance considerations which may prove a consolation in such abnormal circumstances. But *whoso diggeth a ditch* (גומץ is a pure Aramaic word) *shall fall into it.* It was the custom to dig ditches, which were covered with branches of trees, in order to catch lions and other wild beasts, and it might come to pass that a man should fall unwittingly into the ditch which he himself had dug. That which may happen in the external sense, does always and inevitably happen when any one digs a ditch in the moral sense. He who prepares mischief for his neighbour will himself be overtaken by ruin: the conquering kingdoms of this world prepare their own downfall by that which they do to others ; but above all do they expose themselves to inevitable divine vengeance who deal unfairly by the people of God. That is a sweet consolation for those who suffer wrong. Passages of greatest weight in relation to this matter are Psalm vii. 16, 17, " he hath made a pit and digged it, but he falleth into the ditch which he maketh. His mischief returns on his own head, and his wrong cometh down on his own pate." Psalm lvii. 7, " A net have they prepared for my steps, they bent my soul, they digged before me a ditch, they fell into it themselves," (compare besides Proverbs xxvi. 27, Sirach xxvii. 29). *Whoso breaketh through a wall, a serpent shall bite him.* Serpents often lurked in walls (Amos v. 19). He therefore who breaks through a common wall may easily get bitten by a serpent. That which happens sometimes physically, takes place always morally. He who breaks through a wall in the moral world, he who makes attacks on the property of his neighbour, is bitten by the serpent of divine righteousness, so certainly as that God has spoken, "thou shalt not remove thy neighbour's landmarks " (Deuteronomy xix. 14), and "cursed is he who removes his neighbour's landmarks " (Deuteronomy xxvii. 17). The snake is used as an image of divine judgment also in Amos ix. 3. גדר and גדרה designate in particular the walls built to protect vineyards and other property.

Ver. 9. *Whoso looseneth stones* (compare הסיע אבנים " to

break stones loose " in 1 Kings v. 31) *shall be hurt therewith*
(LXX., διαπονθήσεται ἐν αὐτοῖς,) *whoso cleaveth wood shall be injured thereby,* סָכַן in the Chaldee, "periculo se exposuit," in
Hithpael, "in periculo versari," connected with מסכן "poor"
in chap. iv. 13, ix. 15, 16 ; with מסכנות "poverty," in Deuteronomy viii. 9 ; and with מסכן "impoverished" in Isaiah xl.
20. In common life one may easily receive injuries whilst
engaged in occupations requiring violent exertion. But he
will inevitably receive injury who in the moral sphere carries
on occupations involving violence, who does works, which in
respect of force resemble the breaking of stones, and the
splitting of wood.

Ver. 10. The misery of the heathen world is that it does
not possess in wisdom a corrective, that, in fact, it has nothing on which the iron of their understanding may be
whetted when its edge has become dull. In this respect the
people of God has an infinite advantage over it. Whoso
possesses such a corrective must be exalted, however deeply
he may have sunk : he who possesses it not, must perish,
to whatever height he may have risen. *When the iron has
become dull.* קהה is only another mode of writing כהה. Piel,
however, is used there undeniably in an intransitive sense :
and that the iron must be the subject here is clear from
what follows : "and he," to wit, he whom it concerns, the
owner of the hatchet ; whereas this could not well be if this
owner did not already form the subject to קהה. פנים signifies
first "face" then "edge :" so in Ezekiel xxi. 21. קלל " to be
light," in the Pilp. form, "to make light," then "to sharpen ;"
for this latter meaning we need adduce no examples, seeing
that "to sharpen" is simply "to make light." חילים occurs
elsewhere also in the sense of "powers ;" and נבר in that of
"to strengthen," (Zechariah x. 6, 12). He puts to, applies,
more strength, but without attaining a satisfactory result.
This holds good both of the physical and the spiritual sphere.
The verb כשר is used in the sense of " to be right " in Esther
viii. 5 ; the substantive כשרון in that of "capacity, ability,"
in chap. ii. 21, iv. 4 of this book. On this ground we are
justified in attaching to the word הכשיר here, the meaning,
" to make right, to amend, to correct,"—a meaning, moreover,
which suits the connection admirably. Others have adopted

the less appropriate explanation, " ea est sapientiæ præstantia, ut prosperum eventum consiliis suorum spondeat," appealing to the fact that כשׁר occurs in the sense of "prosper" in chap. xi. 6, and בשׁרון in that of "gain, advantage" in chap. v. 10.

CHAPTER X. 11-20.

In order to quicken in the minds of his fellow-countrymen the hope of an imminent termination of the rule of their tyrants, the author points out that their character is such as to render it impossible for them to continue long their present courses. Of that character wickedness and folly are fundamental features, (ver. 11-15.) The king and his nobles are given up to drunkenness and debauchery, (ver. 16, 17.)

The system of state is utterly destitute of moral vigour : speedy ruin is promised by the prevailing rottenness and sensuality, and by the omnipotence of gold, (ver. 18, 19.) In ver. 20, the author indicates the reason why, when treating of the events and relations of his time, he limits himself to gentle and enigmatical hints—a character which for the sake of clearness we have not kept up in our exposition of the contents of the book.

Ver. 11. *If the snake bites without enchantment, so has the man of an evil tongue no advantage.* Ver. 12. *The words of a wise man's mouth are gracious, and the lips of the fool swallow up himself.* Ver. 13. *The beginning of the words of his mouth is foolishness, and the end of his mouth mischievous madness.* Ver. 14. *And the fool maketh many words; man knoweth not what shall be, and what will happen after him, who could tell it ?* Ver. 15. *The labour of the fool wearieth him, because he knoweth not how to go to the city.* Ver. 16. *Woe to thee, O Land, whose king is a child, and whose princes eat in the morning.* Ver. 17. *Blessed art thou, O Land, whose king is a son of the noble, and whose princes eat in due season, for strength and not for gluttony.* Ver. 18. *Through great rottenness sinketh the beam, and through idleness of the hands drippeth the house.* Ver. 19. *Eating change they into laughter, and wine maketh glad the living, and money answereth all things.* Ver. 20. *Even in*

*thy closet curse not the king, and in thy bed-chamber curse
not the rich, for the birds of heaven carry the voice, and that
which hath wings shall tell the matter.*

Ver. 11. When suffering under the evil tongue of the
heathen, Israel is exhorted to look to the divine retribution,
which will come not only on the works of the *hands,* but also
on the works of the *tongue,* (Matthew xii. 36, 37.) He will
thus see that the man who is sinned against with the tongue
is in a better case than the man who sins with his tongue.
The snake is here the *spiritual* snake, to wit, the man whose
poisonous wickedness causes him to resemble the snake.   In
the New Testament the wicked pharisees are styled ὄφεις,
γεννήματα ἐχιδνῶν.   To the snake corresponds, in the second
clause, the "owner of the tongue."   *Without enchantment ;*
this is never applied when it is foreseen that it will be *fruitless.*
To enchantment, in the case of ordinary snakes, correspond
supplicative prayers in the case of spiritual snakes.   The main
passage on this point is Psalm lviii. 5, 6 : " Poison have they
(the wicked) like the poison of snakes : like a deaf adder
stoppeth he his ear.   Which hearkeneth not to the voice of
the charmer, of the enchanter, who can enchant well."   The
commentary to the words *has no advantage* is supplied by the
declaration of ver. 12, "the lips of the fool swallow up himself," and by that of ver. 8, " he that diggeth a ditch shall
fall into it."   The connection, referring as it does to serpents,
defines *the* tongue, more precisely, to be the *evil poisonous*
tongue.   Psalm cxl. 12, supplied the foundation for the expression, " the possessor of the tongue ;"—"the man of the
tongue will not prosper in the land."   The man of the tongue,
is put there in contrast to the man of wicked and violent
deeds.   In ver. 3 of the same Psalm we read, " they sharpen
their tongue like the serpent ; adder's poison is under their
lips :" and this passage, along with Psalm lviii, serves as a
commentary on the figurative description of enemies as snakes.

Ver. 12. חֵן is the grace that wins favour. Compare Proverbs xxii. 11, " He that loveth pureness of heart, for the grace
of his lips, the king is his friend." Psalm xlv. 2, " grace was
poured out over thy lips." Luke ii. 52 ; iv. 22, " and all bare
him witness, and wondered at the gracious words, (ἐπὶ τοῖς
λόγοις τῆς χάριτος,) which proceeded out of his mouth." In

Christ was fully verified the saying, " the words of the wise, that is, of the true Israelites, are grace :" by his grace, in which each of his servants participates, he draws the whole heathen world to himself. The lips are used to represent speech, discourse, in the second clause. The lips of the fool, of the heathen in his natural condition, and specially of the heathen tyrant and dominant nation, swallow them up, because they set them at emnity with God and man. Their thought was to swallow up others. to destroy others by their mischievous discourse : (compare Psalm v. 10, " their throat is an open sepulchre :") but instead of swallowing up others they swallow up themselves. Compare Proverbs xviii. 7, " A fool's mouth prepares him horror, and his lips are a snare to his soul ;" and Psalm lxiv. 9, " and they are cast down, over them cometh their own tongue," so far, namely, as it draws upon them the punishment and judgment of God.

Ver. 13. In the proportion in which we bring before our minds the entire extent of the foolishness of our enemy, in that proportion will our hope of final victory be lively. Such as are every inch fools cannot be far from ruin. *The end of his mouth,* which Hitzig rightly explains, " the end which his mouth makes with its discoursings." *Mischievous* madness, that is, madness which is hurtful first to others, but afterwards also to himself, so certainly as there is a divine retribution. He is not a good-natured, harmless, but a *mischievous,* fool.

Ver. 14. *And the fool maketh many words :*—words such as those of which James speaks in chap. iv. 13, of his Epistle, (compare also Luke xii. 18-20,) to wit, plans for the future, what he will then do, how he will live in splendour and merriness, how he will spread himself out in all directions and humble all his foes. That this is the more precise import of the words is evident from what follows. It is, furthermore, of the nature of the " fool," to talk of such matters ; this therefore by itself would justify the explanation given. To all the high flying thoughts and proud words of the Persian the lie was all at once given on the appearance of Alexander. That event proved the author of this book to be a *wise man.*

Ver. 15. True religion affords fine culture. Even Moses described the people of God as, by divine grace, the wisest among the nations, (Deuteronomy iv.,) and the heathen as a foolish people, (Deut. xxxii.)   That which in Genesis xlix. 21, is spoken primarily of Naphtali—" he giveth goodly words" —is but an individualization, and holds good substantially of entire Israel.   The Persians appeared as coarse barbarians in comparison with the people of God : and it was impossible that the supreme power should remain long in the hands of such blunderers.   Where the mind, the spirit is, there in the long run must be the authority.   *The work of the fool wearies him;* and for the simple reason, that we can only carry on that business with pleasure and love, for which we have spiritual capacity.   עָמָל is treated as a feminine for the sake of avoiding the violation of euphony which would be presented in the verb by the third masculine.   *Because he knoweth not how to go to the city:* compare Proverbs xiii. 16; xiv. 8, "the prudent man in his wisdom understandeth his way," and ver. 5, "the prudent man understandeth his step."   *Here,* as ver. 3 shows, he cannot even find his way—he is at sea regarding it.   The way into the city is specified, as being the most frequented.   He who is unable to find that, must be sadly ignorant of the bearings of a district.*

Ver. 16. Woe to thee, O Land, whose king is a child.   Out of a prudent regard to his position and circumstances the author here uses indefinite and general language, (compare v. 20 :) at the same time it is clear enough from the context, (specially from ver. 19,) that he had in view the state of the Persian Empire.   It is in reality as if he said—" Woe to thee, O Land of Persia, because thy kings are children ?"   That נַעַר refers, not to *age,* but to *boyish childish character,* is plain both from the context, (Geier says, " a stultitia absolute considerata pergit ad certam ejus speciem, ratione peculiaris subjecti, nempe in magistratu constituti ;") from the parallel passages *here,* and from the contrast drawn in ver. 17.   In precisely the same manner is Rehoboam called נַעַר in 2 Chronicles xiii. 7, although when he ascended the throne he was already forty-one years old : so also in Isaiah iii. 12, are bad rulers described as women and children, (compare further 1 Corinth. xiv. 20.)   Not only had Xerxes a boyish character, but,

---

* Rambach says, "Similitudo desumta est a viatore, qui ad urbem facturus iter rectam ignorat viam atque proinde errabundus per avia et invia circa urbem vagatur."

according to the Israelitish standard, according to the standard
of God's law, even the better Persian rulers were more like boys
than men. *And whose princes eat in the morning,* that is, at
the time which ought to be devoted to serious and important
business.

Ver. 17. "A noble," not merely by birth, but in disposition
and customs. The words *for strength and not for drunken-*
ness, (or gluttony,) show clearly enough what the writer has
in mind. He does not refer to invigoration, but to intemper-
ate drinking, and the pleasures connected therewith.

Ver. 18. Luther remarks—"he introduces a proverb, as if
he meant to say,—in such a kingdom or land, where the great
lords and mighty men seek their own profit, and the king is
without sense, things go on as they do in the house of an idle
man, who might frequently repair his roof and protect it
against the weather for a penny, but lets the rain come through
till at last the entire building is damaged. For where the
master of a house is not industrious, always building and
repairing, one damage is sure to follow on the heels of another."
The house is the edifice of state. *Double rottenness,* is great
rottenness, as Kushan Rishataim, "double wickedness," means
great wickedness; in Ezekiel xlvii. 9, "the double stream"
means "the strong stream," and as in Jeremiah l. 21, מרתים
"double apostacy," signifies great apostacy. שפלות "low place,"
designates here, a miserable reduced condition.

Ver. 19. *Bread they make to laughter.* Here it is quite clear
that the author is not giving general observations, but depicting things as they really and truly existed. Hitzig says,
"That which in ver. 16 was not affirmed, to wit, that the
home of the speaker was such an unhappy country, is here
added." *Laughter* is used in chap. ii. 2, for extravagant merriment. Elsewhere לשחק always means "to laughter," and
consequently may not in this place be translated, "amidst
laughter." If היה לשחק signifies, "to become laughter," then
will עשה לשחק mean "to make to laughter,"—to laughter, not
in the passive, but in the active sense. Besides, עשה along
with ל is employed in other places to designate that into
which anything is made: compare Isaiah xliv. 17, "the re-
mainder he maketh to a God," לאל עשה שאריתו. Bread, which
should serve to give strength, serves them only as a vehicle of

laughter. Their meal times are scenes of excess. *And wine maketh glad the living.* This is plainly a dictum taken from the mouths of the "merry carousers." It is a compendium of Isaiah xxii. 13, (compare 1 Cor. where the godless say, "let us eat and drink, for to-morrow we die." *And money answereth all things:* ענה with the accusative signifies "to answer," (Job xxxi. 35,) and then "to be answerable for," (Job. xxxiii. 13.) Money is the answer to all charges, the apology for all crimes: he who has money may allow himself any liberty. ענה cannot signify "to afford, to confer."

Ver. 20. The author now assigns the reason why, in the part immediately preceding, and in fact throughout the whole book, he had spoken of the circumstances of the Persian Empire in such a vague and indistinct manner. Openness under a tyrannical government is dangerous and ruinous. Ewald renders the sense as follows, "as well on account of the great danger of treachery, as in consideration that *duty*, (chap. viii. 2,) forbids it, we should never permit ourselves to curse our rulers even in the greatest secrecy." The advice, however, is rather a simple rule of prudence, and may be subsumed under that saying of our Lord's, γίνεσθε φρόνιμοι ὡς οἱ ὄφεις. Only a false explanation can find, in chap. viii. 2, a reference to the duty of which Ewald speaks. Nothing is said of such a duty in the entire book: on the contrary, the writer says the strongest possible things against the heathen tyrannical rule— covertly, however, and so that he could nowhere be laid hold of. It would, in truth, have been perverse to judge an Asiatic tyranny by the principles laid down in Romans xiii;—principles which even in our own day do not hold good for Greeks in relation to the Turks. The word מדע belongs to the language in its post-exile period, and occurs elsewhere only in the sense "insight, understanding:" so also the Chaldee מנדע from which it is derived. Here it is usually explained by "consciousness, thought." This meaning, however, besides being uncertain, does not appear to suit the connection; the word קול shows that the writer is not treating of mere thoughts,—besides that, the sphere of thoughts is not accessible to espionage, which is here the sole subject of consideration. It is the simplest course to understand by מדע, "study;" just as in Latin, *studium* is used both of studies, and of the place where studies are carried on. The mention of "the study" cannot surprise, if we examine chap. xii. 12 : it is moreover very suitably employed in connection with "bed-chamber," of which mention is made also in 2 Kings vi. 12, "Elisha, the prophet, telleth the King of Israel the words which thou speakest in thy bed-chamber." The rich man is the Persian, (compare chap. v. 11.) On the words, "for the birds of heaven, etc," the Berleburger Bible remarks, "it may come out by no visible medium, as quickly and marvellously, as if a bird flying by or seated before the window had picked it up."

CHAPTER XI. 1-3.

In view of the threatened judgments of God, which should soon cast down the proud tree of the Persian Empire, it behoved them not to fix their hearts on uncertain riches, but rather to seek by compassionate and benevolent conduct to gain the favour of God who is able to deliver his children from their troubles :—such is the admonition addressed by the author to his narrow-hearted, avaricious, and sordid contemporaries.

Ver. 1. *Send thy bread on the water, for thou shalt find it after many days.* Ver. 2. *Give a portion to seven and also to eight, for thou knowest not what evil shall be on the earth.* Ver. 3. *If the clouds be full of rain they empty themselves upon the earth ; and if the tree fall, be it toward the south or be it toward the north, in the place where it falleth, there it shall be.*

Ver. 1. In the presence of great catastrophes, earthly possessions are of very little value, for they may easily be overwhelmed therein ; on the contrary, that God should be gracious towards us is of the last importance. This the author admonishes us to secure by benevolence, and by putting completely away that covetous narrow-heartedness, which, in times of distress, so easily creeps into the heart. The image is borrowed from sea-trading. In that, the temporary sacrifice of one's property brings in a rich reward, even though after a long interval : (according to 1 Kings x. 22, Solomon's vessels returned from Tarshish once in three years, bringing with them rich cargoes). So is it also in connection with benevolence: in His own good time the Lord restores that which may have been given to sufferers for His name's sake. If one casts one's bread on the water in the usual external sense, it may very easily itself become water should the ship perish; it is in fact but a mere experiment: but when we cast our bread on the water in the spiritual sense, a return is certain; that which we have staked is sure to come back again, even though after a long season. Jerome says, "cum dies judicii advenerit, multo amplius quam dederat recepturus:" and Cartwright, "tametsi enim non raro fit, ut deus compensationem in longum tempus rejiciat, tandem tamen mercedem in hac vita, certe quidem in futura reponet." We have here, in an abbreviated form, the comparison so frequently made, and which is, "whoso giveth alms is like a merchant who sends his property over the sea." Verse 2, which gives the real substance, the idea, contained in the figurative representation, shows that we must not limit our attention to the common kind of trade. מים פני על is used of navigation also in Job xxiv. 18, where it is said of pirates—"swift is that one on the mirror of the water." Parallel in point of significance are the following passages:—Psalm xli. 1, 2, "Blessed is he who acts prudently towards the wretched: in the day of adversity shall the Lord deliver him. The Lord will preserve him and keep him alive, he is blessed in the land, and thou mayest not deliver him unto the will of his enemies:"—Proverbs xix. 17, "he that giveth to the poor lendeth to the Lord, and his gift will he pay him again:"—and 1 Timothy vi. 18, 19, where the apostle prescribes to the rich, εὐμεταδότους εἶναι, κοινωνικούς, ἀποθησαυρίζοντας, ἑαυτοῖς θεμέλιον καλὸν εἰς τὸ μέλλον. Luke vi. 38, xvi. 9; Galatians vi. 9.

Ver. 2. *Give a portion,* that is, of thy bread (compare Isaiah lviii. 7, 10.) The addition of the words, "also to eight," serves the purpose of indicating that the number seven did not mark the limit of the extent of our benevolence:—not, "at the utmost, seven," but, "seven and more." *For thou knowest not, etc.,* and there, all depends on making to thyself friends of the unrighteous mammon. Cartwright observes, "Ad hanc autem munificentiam te excitare debet rerum om-

nium Europæa veluti inconstantia et incertitudo, quid aut de
te, aut divitiis, quas possides, fiet: ut illud merito in lucro
deputes, quod in pauperum subsidium conferendo veluti e
flamma et incendio eripueris." In point of thought the following passages may be adduced as parallels; Psalm cxii. 9,
"he disperseth, he giveth to the poor, his righteousness en-
dureth for ever, his horn is exalted with honour,"—words
which, by the way, belong also to the period of the rule of
the Persians, and which teach the Jews that if they were pervaded by a liberal spirit, they would at some future time certainly rise to honour:—and then further Matthew v. 42, τῷ
αἰτοῦντί σε δίδου.

Ver. 3. Clouds and *rain* are a usual image of the judgments of God, and of the troubles sent by him. Compare in
respect of "clouds," Isaiah xix. 1; Psalm xcvii. 2; Psalm
xviii. 10; Nahum i. 3; Jeremiah iv. 13; Revelations i. 7:
in regard to "rain," compare Song of Solomon, ii. 11; Isaiah
iv. 6; Matthew vii. 24, 25. Clouds and rain are employed
as designations of troubles also in chap. xii. 2. The thought
is identical with that expressed in the words of the Lord—
"where the carcase is, there will the eagles be gathered together." When the measure of sin is filled up, and the clouds
of divine wrath are therefore gathered together, the storm will
inevitably break; in the day when such an outbreak is imminent, every one should ask earnestly in his heart, "how
shall I receive thee, and how shall I meet thee?" in order that
he may not be swept away by the wickedness of the world.—
The connection between the first and second part of the verse
is to be explained from the fact that in heavy storms trees
are not unfrequently cast down by the lightning and gusts
of wind (compare Psalm xxix.) The tree is here that of the
Persian Empire. No human power will be in a position to
delay its fall when it has once begun, or to raise it up again
after it is down. He who is judged by God remains judged.
Trees are a common symbol of the mighty. In Isaiah x. 18,
the trees of Assyria are its great men. Nebuchadnezzar the
king of Babylon is represented under the image of a proud
tree in Daniel iv. 19—"the tree art thou, O king." In
Ezekiel xxxi. 3 ff., Assyria is introduced as a cedar of Lebanon,
with goodly foliage, and its top reaching unto the clouds. See
also Revelations vii. 1.

VERSES 4-6.

The author now enters the lists to battle with the temptation to despairing inactivity which arose out of the circumstances of the time. Their unfavourableness should move us on the contrary to redoubled activity.

Ver. 4. *He that observeth the wind shall not sow, and he that regardeth the clouds shall not reap.* Ver. 5. *As thou knowest not what is the way of the wind, like the bones in the womb of her that is with child; even so thou knowest not the work of God who maketh all.* Ver. 6. *In the morning sow thy seed, and in the evening withhold not thine hand: for thou knowest not whether shall prosper, either this or that, or whether they both shall be alike good.*

Ver. 4. The unfavourable circumstances of the time exerted a crippling influence. Men were dejected, and gave themselves up to listlessness and despair—they were inclined to lay their hands in their bosom and wait for better times. Against this the author here raises his warning voice. Under all circumstances we should do our duty and let God care for us. Sowing and reaping are employed here after the example of Psalm cxxvi. 5, to designate *activity.* To the wind, which may easily blow away the seed, and to the clouds which threaten to injure the harvests, correspond the unfavourable circumstances of the time. In explaining the abbreviated comparison used by the author, Cartwright says, "whoso layeth his hands in his bosom, because the circumstances of the time are unfavourable, perinde esse acsi agricola sementem facere recusaret, quia ventus paulo vehementius flat: unde fit ut de die in diem sementem proferens seminandi tempus præterfluat." With a special application to the preaching of the word, Jerome remarks, "opportune, importune suo tenore Dei sermo est prædicandus, nec fidei tempore, adversariarum nubium consideranda tempestas.——Absque consideratione ergo nubium et timore ventorum in mediis tempestatibus seminandum est. Nec dicendum, illud tempus commodum, hoc inutile, quum ignoremus, quæ via, et quæ voluntas sit spiritus universa dispensantis."

Ver. 5. Things turn out very often quite otherwise than

the understanding of men anticipated. For this reason we should avoid puzzling our minds much with the circumstances of the time, we should do what God commands and leave results to him.   There is no doubt that our Lord alluded to the first words of the verse, when he said in John iii. 8, of the wind οὐκ οἶδας πόθεν ἔρχεται καὶ ποῦ ὑπάγει.   *Like the bones*, or, in other words, as it is with the bones.   The only point of comparison is the invisibility.   The principal passage in this connection is Psalm cxxxix. 15, "My bones were not hid from thee when I was made in secret, when I was wrought in the depths of the earth."   Bone is in the Hebrew so designated from the strength which it has, and, as the most important part of the body, is used to represent the whole.

Ver. 6. Be incessantly active!   Precisely in troublous and wretched times should we be most restlessly active, for then many things that we do may fail of success.   The more doubtful the results of our undertakings, the less should we be disposed to lay our hands in our bosom.

VERSES 7, 8.

Better to be dead!   So were people exclaiming on all hands at the time of the author.   He, on the contrary, insists on the importance of life as a noble gift of God, and warns against thanklessly regarding it in a mistaken light.

Ver. 7. *And sweet is the light, and a pleasant thing is it for the eyes to see the sun.*   *Ver.* 8. *For if a man live many years, let him rejoice in them all ; yet let him remember the days of darkness that they shall be many : all that cometh is vanity.*

Ver. 7. However great are the sufferings of this life, however manifold is the vanity to which the world has been subjected since the day spoken of in Genesis iii., however sad are the circumstances of the time, it still remains true, that life is a good thing ; and when a gloomy and depressing mood gets the upper hand in the Church, it is the task of the word of God to impress upon it this truth.

Ver. 8. Christ has brought life and immortality to light For him who is in Christ the argument has no longer the

weight it had under the old covenant : we can no more allow
the light of this life to be darkened by the shadow of Sheol.
To be weary of life is, however, still a sin, even under the new
Covenant.   A pious heart will seek out the bright sides of
our earthly existence, and contemplate them with sincere
thankfulness.

CHAPTER XI. 9.—CHAPTER XII. 7.

At a time when dark discontent had got the mastery over
the minds of men, the Spirit of God exhorts them through the
writer of this book to enjoy cheerfully divine gifts, admonishing them, however, in order to prevent carnal misunderstand-
ings, to keep in view the account they will have one day to
give to the Holy God, of all their doings :—he warns them
to remember their Creator, who alone has the power to render
their life prosperous and happy.   In depicting the joylessness
of the age, he shows how fitting it is to enter betimes on this
path of self-surrender to the Creator, to consecrate even the
bloom of youth to Him, lest when we arrive at the end of our
days, after a miserable and curse-laden life—(and apart from
fellowship with God there is nought but misery and curse)—
we should be compelled, looking back on a wasted existence,
to cry in despair, "too late."   The whole concludes with a
reference to the judgment awaiting men after death.

Chap. xi. 9. *Rejoice O young man in thy youth : and let
thy heart cheer thee in the days of thy youth, and walk in the
ways of thine heart, and in the sight of thine eyes : but know
that for all this God will bring thee into judgment.*   Ver.
10. *And remove discontent from thy heart, and put away
evil from thy flesh : for youth and the dawn of life are vanity.*
Chap. xii. 1. *And remember thy Creator in the days of thy
youth, before the evil days come, and the years draw nigh,
of which thou shalt say, I have no pleasure in them.*   Ver. 2.
*Before the sun be darkened, and the light, and the moon, and
the stars, and the clouds return after the rain.*   Ver. 3. *In
the day when the keepers of the house shall tremble, and the
strong men bow themselves, and the grinders cease because they
are become few, and those that look out of the windows be*

darkened.   Ver. 4. *And the doors are shut in the streets, in that the sound of the grinding is low, and he riseth up at the voice of the bird, and all the daughters of song are bent down.* Ver. 5. *Also they are afraid of that which is high, and terrors, (are for them,) in the way, and the almond tree flourisheth, and the locust becometh burdensome, and desire faileth, because man goeth to his everlasting home, and the mourners go about in the street.* Ver. 6. *Before then the silver cord be removed, and the golden bowl haste away, and the pitcher be broken at the fountain, and the wheel be dashed to pieces at the cistern.* Ver. 7. *And the dust returneth to the earth as it was, and the spirit returneth to God who gave it.*

Chap. xi. 9. The writer directs his discourse to the *youth* because he has still to *choose* his path in life, and good advice is consequently most appropriate in his case. *Let thy heart cheer thee:* the heart is mentioned because it is the fountain from which cheerfulness is, as it were, diffused over the whole man : compare Proverbs xiv. 30, "a sound heart is the life of the body:" and chap. xv. 13, "a merry heart maketh a cheerful countenance."* Many of the older commentators look upon this summons to cheerfulness as *ironical;* so that it would be substantially a dissuasion therefrom.† There is, however, no satisfactory reason for taking such a view, especially when we bear in mind that the disease of the age was not *excess,* but dull *melancholy.* It is furthermore inconsistent with a whole number of parallel passages, in which men are exhorted to the cheerful enjoyment of God's gifts. And lastly, in verse 10, to a very forced explanation of which that view would lead, by כעס, we should then be compelled to understand "passionateness," to which youth is specially inclined, and by רעה "badness" in general.‡ The

---

* Geiersays : "Ex corde vel animo de amore dei certo redundet pia ac honesta refectio in totum corpus."

† For example, Cartwright also observes : "In priore dehortatio adhibetur, primum tropo ironias exornata : et deinde simplici oratione exposita. Nec enim oleum igni addit sed contra frenum juveni injicit."

‡ The fundamental idea of the book, to which the present verse owes its origin, was quite correctly perceived and admirably presented by Witsius in his Essay on chap. xii. 1, in the Misc. s. ii., p. 165, "toto libro nil nisi virtus docetur, non fucata illa, austera, tetrica, quæ ex sordibus et illuvie ac ἀφειδία τοῦ σώματος, laudem captat. : sed ingenua, liberalis, hilaris quæ deprehensa rerum cæterarum inanitate felicitatem suam quærit et invenit in conscientia

words, "*walk in the ways of thine heart and in the sight of thine eyes*," would be at variance with the passage, Numbers xv. 39, to which allusion is probably here made—"ye shall remember all the commandments of the Lord and do them, and ye shall not follow after your own heart and your own eyes, after which ye use to go a whoring"—were they not defined and limited by the succeeding warning—"but know, etc."* There is undoubtedly a difference between the two passages. In the one only unallowed merriness is *forbidden* : in the other permitted merriness is recommended,—to a generation, namely, which had lost its joy in life, which was consumed by a murmuring disposition, and which tried to force God to redeem it by means of a gloomy and rigid asceticism. Cheerfulness, here, is not merely permitted : it is commanded, and represented as an essential element of piety. Emphasis must be laid equally on the word "walk" and on the word "know." Even in Leviticus xiii. 12 and Deuteronomy xxviii. 34, מראה עינים signifies that which we see with our eyes. The Masorites wished to change the plural, which refers to the multiplicity of the objects of sight, into the singular, because they falsely supposed מראה to denote the "act of sight." To walk in that which we see with our eyes is to be mentally occupied with it, to have pleasure in it, in contradiction to either a strict and gloomy asceticism or a discontented dullness and insensibility. *Into the judgment,* which will be carried on according to the standard of God's revealed law. Whatever is in opposition to this must inevitably be expiated by punishment,—by punishment, too, which is executed not only in the future world, but affects the whole of our present life. For God is angry every day (Psalm vii. 12).

Ver. 10. The last verse exhorted to a divine cheerfulness : this verse dissuades from that which stands in its way. כעס signifies "discontent," that is, with God and his leadings. That poor age was rich in this particular (compare chap. vii.

tranquilla ac læta et usu bonorum ex favore divino provenientium. Ita tamen ut memor fluxæ hujus ac lubricæ vitæ et imminentis judicii omnia cum reverentia summi Numinis peragat."

* Jerome says, "rursum ne putaretur hæc dicens hominem ad luxuriam provocare et in Epicuri dogma corruere, suspicionem hanc abstulit inferens: Et scito, quoniam super omnibus his adducet te deus in judicium. Sic inquit abutere mundi rebus, ut scias te in ultimo judicandum."

9). We meet with it also in the contemporary Malachi : see chap. iii. 14, " ye say, it is vain to serve God, and what profit is it that we keep his ordinances and walk in filth before the Lord of hosts ?" *And put away evil from thy body.* Discontent has the effect, at the same time, of rendering the body wretched (Psalm vi. 8). Schmidt remarks, " afflictiones et ærumnas, quæ ex tristitia animi in corpus redundant carnemque consumunt." To this we must add the mortifications resorted to in order to extort redemption from God : compare the passage from Malachi just quoted and Isaiah lviii. 3, " wherefore do we fast, and thou seest not, wherefore do we afflict our soul and thou knowest not ?" The exhortation, not wilfully to rob themselves by dark melancholy of that which God graciously presents to them, is grounded on the consideration that youth, the time when men are most capable of enjoyment, is vain and quickly passes by. שׁחרות, " the time of dawn," "youth," occurs only here, and is a word that was probably formed by the author himself. This is rendered probable by the preceding term ילדות, which serves as an explanation.

Chap. xii. 1. *And remember thy Creator in the days of thy youth.* The Berleburger Bible remarks, " in the noble time of youth turn betimes to God, and do not sacrifice its bloom to the devil : do not devote merely the dregs of thy years to God and put off till late the work of conversion." In order to be happy, it is not enough that we form the resolution to be cheerful (chap. xi. 9), and to put away discontent, (chap. xi. 10). With such a determination, a hearty piety must go hand in hand. Man could not be considered as bearing the image of God if it were possible for him to spend a joyous existence without remembering his Creator. Truly rejoice can he only who is in his true element ; and man is only in his true element when he gives himself up to devotion, and thus returns to the origin and source of his being. To this must be added, that whoso apostatizes from his Creator becomes necessarily involved in the divine judgments ; for the Lord must have his due from all who bear his image, either in their destruction or their voluntary return to himself. Divine condemnation renders cheerfulness impossible. The summons to "remember our Creator" does not stand in contrast to that other one, " let thy heart cheer thee :" they rather go hand in hand with each other. Their relation might be expressed in this way— " and *in order* that thou mayest be able to rejoice, and to put away discontent, remember thy Creator." Ewald renders wrongly—" *yet* think." The words, " thy *Creator*," give the reason why we should *remember*. It is unnatural not to think of Him in whom we live and move and have our being ; and such unnatural conduct brings its own punishment,—misery is its inseparable companion. In the Berleburger Bible we read, " When the Preacher says, ' Remember thy Creator,' it is more than if he had merely mentioned *God*. He indicates quite distinctly the right that God has to man, the benefits which God has conferred on man, and ma, 's consequent duty to recognise and act according to his entire dependence on God." The plural in בוראיך, in the same way as that in " Elohim," draws attention to the fulness and the wealth of the divine nature, to God's majesty and glory. For remarks on such plural designations of God, (as for example, Joshua xxiv. 19, where God is called קדשים, and Proverbs ix. 10), see chap. v. 7. *Before the evil days come*, etc. What we are to understand by the " days of evil or suffering," is made clear by the following verses. They stand for a *joyless old age*. If we fail to remember our Creator in youth, the period between it and old age, the time when we are most capable of happiness, is taken up with misery, and after our susceptibility to pleasure has ceased, we are forced to look with sorrow on a wasted existence. Cartwright mistakes the right point of view when he says—" before old age reaches thee, which by reason of numerous weaknesses and burdens is less fitted for the learning or exercise of piety." As is expressly said, age is here brought under consideration, not because then the spiritual powers are deadened, but because it brings on the " days of evil," because all joy in our earthly existence is then irrecoverably lost if not previously gained possession of—a thing which is impossible apart from the fear of God. Knobel's observation however is quite incorrect:—"that we must not connect the second part of this verse exclusively with the admonition to fear God, but more particularly with the summons to enjoyment about which Koheleth is here chiefly concerned, ' enjoy thyself before, etc., but not in such a way that thou make thyself a fool.'" To such violent explanations are men driven who are incapable of grasping the thought, that Jehovah is the Alpha and Omega of our earthly existence, and that a right relation to him is the condition and foundation of all happiness and all joy. In the following verses a picture is presented of a joyless old age drawn in the lively colours of youth, in order that the exhortation to remember the Creator in the days of youth might sink the more deeply into the heart. How mournful a thing must it be to pass into the ranks of those who are here described, without having tasted of the feast of joys prepared by the Creator for all those who remember Him.

Ver. 2. In the first half of this verse, age is brought forward as the time when sun, moon, and stars become dark. The lights of heaven really shine only for the *happy*. When the eye is no longer sunlike, the sun is, as it were, gone down. For this reason in Old Testament delineations of adversity we so often read of the destruction of the heavenly lights. Isaiah, for example, when describing in chap. v. 30, the heavy sufferings which were about to fall upon the land because of its alienation from God, says—"the light is darkened in the heavens thereof." Jeremiah in chap. iv. 33, picturing the judgments which threatened Judah, says, "I beheld the earth, and lo, it was without form and void, and the heavens they had no lights :" (compare Ezekiel xxxii. 7, 8 ; Amos viii. 9, 10 ; Micah iii. 6 ; Revelations vi. 12.) With the sun is connected " the light," the Scripture symbol of salvation and happiness, for the purpose of indicating why the sun, moon, and stars are introduced, and what is their significance. In the second half of the verse, age appears as the time when clouds return after rain, that is, when one trouble succeeds to the other. Dark clouds are often used as an image of troubles : so also rain in Ezekiel xiii. 11-13 ; xxxviii. 22 ; Song of Solomon ii. 11. Luther observes that, "the Holy Scriptures call consolation and prosperity, *light*, and troubles, *darkness* or night. The author means therefore to say—before the age comes when neither sun nor stars shall shine on thee, when the clouds shall return after rain, that is, when one trouble shall follow on the heels of another. For young boys, for young men, for men who are in the very prime of life, there is still a measure of joy : in their case it is still a fact that, after rain comes beautiful sunshine; that is, in other words, although they have times of trouble, they have also again days of joy and consolation.   But age has no joy : clouds come after the rain : one misfortune succeeds another, one storm follows another."   The power to suffer is exhausted in old age, the heart is already broken : that is however not the only consideration here : God's will is to melt down his own people completely before the end of life, and to give to the wicked a foretaste of hell.   That which is here said of age in general, holds especially good of the age of the godless, which the author had principally in view.*   It did not, however, accord with his purpose, to mention, that as the lights of this world grow dark, the celestial divine light shines all the more brightly on a godly old age.†

Ver. 3. The body in which the spirit dwells is elsewhere, also, represented under the image of a *house :* (see Job iv. 19 ; 2 Corinthians v. 1.)   The *watchmen* of the house are the *arms*, by which everything inimical and destructive is warded of.   יזע in kal occurs only here and in Esther v. 9 : in the Chaldee it is frequently used.   The *strong men* are the feet. These are introduced as the seat of the strength of a man, also in Psalm cxlvii. 10, "he delighteth not in the strength of a horse, he hath no pleasure in the legs of a man,"—and in their strength,—as we may add, supplementing from the first clause of the verse.   The *millers*, (feminine,) or *the grinders*, are the teeth.   The feminine form was chosen because grinding (with the handmill) was usually an occupation of women, (Exodus xi. 5 ; Isaiah xlvii. 2.)   The teeth *make holiday* or *cease*, that is, are no longer able to fulfil their task, because they *have become few :* if they are to be properly active, their number must be full.   בטל as a Hebrew word, " to cease to make holiday," occurs only in this place : in Aramaic it is frequently

---

* Cartwright says, " quod quidem, ut fere senibus omnibus evenit, ita potissimum his, qui luxu et libidine juventutem transegerunt.   Effœtum enim corpus et nauseabundum senectuti tradunt : ita ut in illis pluviam excipiat nubes, nubem grando, grandinem gelu, donec eum deus ad barathrum condemnationis detruserit.

† Cartwright observes, " tametsi visibilis sol illis occidit, tamen sol justitiæ Christus illorum in animis adolescentiæ exoriens, in senectuti altior in hujus vitæ hemispherio assurgens, lumen suum duplicabit.   Prov. iv. 18."

found, (see for example, Ezra iv. 24.)   The Piel of מעט is only
used here, and that with an intransitive meaning.   The Piel
denotes *enhancement, very few.*   *Those that look out of the
windows,* are the eyes.   Hitzig remarks, "as at first, two
masculines, which in conception belong to each other, namely,
arms and legs, are connected ; so in the next place, two feminines, to wit, teeth and eyes ; as also in portions of the law,
(Exodus xxi. 24 ; Deuteronomy xix. 21,) eyes and teeth, hands
and feet, are co-ordinated with each other."

Ver. 4.   By *the doors in the streets,* some organ must here
be designated, which is the medium of intercourse with the
external world,—one, too, which is divided into two parts, as
is clear from the use of the dual דלתים.   The mention of the
eyes, which goes immediately before, would at once suggest
the thought of *ears :* this moreover suits admirably the connection with the voice—" in that the voice of the mill becomes
weak"—they are less able to hear, and to make themselves
intelligible.   According to others, the *mouth* is intended, and
the dual form דלתים is chosen with reference to the two lips—
a form which is used also of the jaws of the Leviathan in Job
xli. 6.   See the Berleburger Bible, where we read—"through
the mouth man's heart goes forth and is seen and known by
means of what he utters."   The image of doors is used also of
the mouth in Micah vii. 5, "preserve the doors of thy mouth."
On this view the words, "in that the voice of the mill becomes
weak," would assign the reason for the closing of the doors, as
much as to say, "they scarcely open the mouth any more because it has become difficult for them to speak."   But it is
more appropriate to apply the description *being shut* to that
hardness of hearing, which is so characteristic of old age
that it can scarcely be absent.   If the teeth are the *grinders,*
the mouth must be the *mill.*   שְׁפַל is *Infin. nominasc.* from
שָׁפֵל, "to be low ;" signifying when used of the voice, to be,
as it were, depressed, deadened, weak.   The subject in יקום is
"the old man," who is spoken of in the context.   He rises at
the voice of the bird, so soon as the birds begin to sing, that
is, very early in the morning : age has no sleep.*   The men-

* Cartwright says, "summo mane, quum avicularum cantillationes incipiunt,
irrequietus senex, somni expers, membra levabit thoro, ceteræ etiam familiæ

tion of the " voice of the bird" suggests the remark, that the
old man has even lost all capacity for, and pleasure in song ;
a remark which coincides with 2 Samuel xix. 35, where Barzillai says to David—" can thy servant still taste what I eat
or drink, can I hear any more the voice of singing men and
singing women ?"   The term " daughter" is used to designate
that which belongs to a thing : for example, the daughters of
Rabbah, in Jeremiah xlix. 2, are the places which belong to
Rabbah.   Here accordingly the qualities which belong to song,
the singing qualities, are personified as the daughters of song:
Aquila, πάντα τὰ τῆς ᾠδῆς.

Ver. 5. *Also*—to mention this further characteristic of their
miserable condition—*they are afraid of everything which is
high, and terrors are in the way.*   Where there is little strength
every height is dreadful, and defenceless impotence sees terrors
wherever it goes and stands.   *And the almond tree blooms.*
That the almond tree is here used as a symbol of that watch-
fulness with which old age is visited, is suggested even by the
etymology.   שָׁקֵד, originally the name of the tree, not of the
fruit, to which, strictly viewed, it is inappropriate, and can
therefore be only secondarily applied, is a poetical designation
of the almond : the real name in natural history is לֻז.   It is
called properly the "waking tree," because it first awakes
from the sleep of winter.   Theophrastus says in Hist. Plant.
i. 15, of the alum tree, πρωὶ βλαστάνει.†   To this we may
add that in Jeremiah i. 11, the almond tree is in like manner
employed as a symbol of watching :—that passage may be regarded as commentary to the present verse.   Why mention is
made of *blooming,* Pliny teaches us in the Hist. Nat. 16,
25 : according to him, the almond tree blossoms first of all
trees,—"floret prima omnium amygdala mense Januari.o"
According to the explanation just given, which is adopted by the
Septuagint, (καὶ ανθήσῃ τὸ ἀμύγδαλον,) by the Vulgate, (et florebit
amygdalus,) and by the Syriac, יָנֵאץ is the Hiphil form, and
from נוץ, which is used in the sense of "blossom," even in the

---

quietem turbans. Nam uti intempestivus somnus, ita et intempestiva vigilia
comites aut sequelæ senectutis sunt."
   * Gesenius. "שָׁקֵד amygdala arbor, ita dicta, quod omnium arborum prima
e somno hiberno expergiscitur et velut vigil ceteris plantis advigilat."

the Song of Solomon, (see chap. vi. 11 ; vii. 13.) These passages agree too closely with the present verse to permit of a
separation between them. To the blossoming pomegranite
trees there, corresponds the blossoming almond tree her.. We
need not be surprised at the א which has been interpolated :
it is found elsewhere in the usage of a latter period, (see
Ewald, § 83 c.) Objections which have been raised, do not
touch the explanation in itself, but only the false turn given
to it when the blossoming almond tree is made to represent
the grey hair of old men. In such a case, there is of course
the plain objection, that the blossom of the almond tree is
not white. According to others, יִנְאַץ is the Hiphil future of
נאץ, "to despise :" the toothless old man despises the pleasant
tasted almond. But even as regards the form, there are difficulties in the way of this explanation ;—for example, the
vowel point Kametz ; and the Hiphil, which occurs nowhere
else :*—besides, the meaning of the verb נאץ does not suit, for
נאץ is not a simple refusal, but one connected with scorn and
contempt. To this we may add, that the thought is rather
too far-fetched. *And the locust shows itself troublesome.*
סבל, "to press heavily on any one," in Piel, (which does not
occur,) "to lay a burden on any one;" (Pual is used in Psalm
cxliv. 14,) and in Hithpael, "to show oneself burdensome, to be
troublesome," (compare Gesenius' Thesaurus.) Locusts must not
be taken here, as Gesenius and others take them, in their proper
sense, viz., in the sense of an excellent species of food, which the
old man must renounce because he is no longer able to bear it.†
For locusts were in any circumstances but poor nutriment, taken
only by those who either had no other, or wished to mortify themselves ; and then the expression, "become burdensome or
troublesome," would be out of place. The locust must rather be
employed figuratively, in correspondence with the predominantly

---

* Hitzig is obliged to confess that the form as it here lies before us cannot be derived
from נאץ—"the pointing is without doubt not intended for the Hiphil of נאץ,
(that is for יַאֵץ instead of יְנָאֵץ) which never occurs elsewhere, but for the
Hiphil of נצץ, to wit, יָנֵץ, as was also the view of the authors of the versions
led astray by שָׁקֵד itself, (compare Numbers xvii. 23.)"

† Molesta est seni locusta, quia ægre ab illo manducatur et concoquitur, quamquam grati saporis

symbolical character of the entire description. If this is the case, there can be no doubt as to the sense. The most prominent characteristic of locusts, is " devouring ;" compare 2 Chronicles vii. 13, " I command the locusts, (הגב, as here,) to devour the land." For this reason, wherever locusts are alluded to in a figurative sense in the Scriptures, they designate hostile ravages and destruction. Here accordingly we must understand by them, the forces hostile to life, which consume it especially in old age. *And desire faileth :* Luther gives the sense accurately as follows, " an old man has pleasure in nothing." אביונה from אבה, " to wish, to will," occurs nowhere else, but still the derivation is quite legitimate. To be rejected, is the limitation to one particular kind of desire.* The explanation, " caper," although widely spread, must still be characterised as without foundation.† The fact that some old translations have hit upon it, (the Septuagint, for example, which was followed by the Syriac and the Vulgate,) offers no sure support for it. It has been sought, but in vain, to draw confirmations of this usage from the Talmud and the Rabbins.‡ " Appetitus, concupiscentia," which is the simplest explanation, suits the context admirably, and is recommended also by the parallel expression of Barzillai,—" can I still distinguish between good and evil, can I taste what I eat and drink, etc. ?" The Hiphil form of פרר signifies elsewhere always " to reduce to nought, to destroy," and must not therefore here without further reasons be rendered, " become nought." *Desire* refusing its services, reduces the enjoyments to nought, which it might have afforded us. *For man goeth to his eternal home ;* and of that all these things are forerunners—they are symptoms that life is shortly to cease.‖

The *eternal house* can only be the grave, out of which there is never a return to this earthly life : compare Job vii.

* So the Chaldee, " prohibeberis a concubitu;" correctly on the contrary the Greek Venet., παύση ἡ ὄρεξις. Abulvalid renders, " cessabit concupiscentia;" Rabbi Parchon explains the word by תאוה.

† Gesenius, " et irrita erit capparis, *i. e.*, vim amplius habebit capparis, neque in cibi desiderio movendo, neque in Veneris concupiscentia provocanda."

‡ Compare for a contrary view, Winzer's Comm. on xi. 9,—xii. 7, in the " Comm. Theol." of Rosenmüller, Fuldner and Maurer i. 1, p. 95.

‖ Geier, " nec mirum est omnem evanescere appetitum, quia abit et magis magisque sensim occidit ejusmodi homo."

10, "he will not return to his house, nor will his place know him again." We find the same expression used of it in Tobias iii. 6, also. *And the mourners go about in the streets.* סבבו is the *pret. proph.* That which is impending in the immediate future is anticipated in spirit. What is said here is equivalent to, "they will soon go about in the streets." The reference is to the mournings which took place at funerals, (compare Amos v. 16.)

Ver. 6. *Before the silver cord be removed.* The words are connected with the admonition at the commencement of the chapter, "remember thy Creator." The *cord* denotes the *thread of life,* the continuity of existence. That the cord is of silver is a sign that life is a noble possession: compare chap xi. 7, "sweet is the light, and pleasant is it for the eyes to see the sun."* The Niphal form of רהק "to become far" is never used. As invariably happens in such cases, the vowels belong to the marginal reading. We must read ירהק, "removed afar off, departed," (longe recessit, discessit.) The Masoretic conjecture is the less to be trusted as the meaning, "be broken," ascribed to נרתק, is by no means certain. The verb which signifies "to bind, to enchain," cannot, in Niphal, which otherwise never occurs, mean "to be unchained, torn loose," as Ewald would have it. רהק, "to remove," and רוץ "to run, to haste away," correspond admirably to each other.— *And the golden bowl haste away.* Many interpreters consider that רוץ here stands for רצץ, "till the golden bowl be broken," Septuagint, καὶ συντριβῇ τὸ ἀνθέμιον τοῦ χρυσίου. Elsewhere, however, the spheres of both the verbs רצץ and רוץ remain distinct. Even in Isaiah xlii. 4, רוץ retains its meaning "run," (compare my *Christology* on that passage.) The former of the two verbs always signifies elsewhere "to break," never "to be broken." רוץ "to run, to escape," forms quite a suitable parallel with רהק "to become far;" so also in the second half of the verse נרץ "to be beaten to pieces" with נשבר "to be broken." The use of נרץ immediately after shows that תרץ may not be referred back to רצץ, for the recurrence of the same verb would be awkward. גלה means properly

---

* Jerome says, "funiculus autem argenti caudidam hanc vitam et spiramen quod nobis de cœlo tribuitur, ostendit."

"source," and is equivalent to גַּל in the Song of Solomon iv.
12.　It is used in the same manner in Joshua xv. 19,
and Judges i. 15.　Then in Zechariah iv. 3 it denotes the
reservoir out of which the oil flows into the seven lamps of
the candlestick, (the masculine form גַּל in chap. iv. 2 is chosen
only on account of the suffix.)　On that passage in Zechariah,
is based, as it would seem, the one now under notice.　Corresponding with the "cord," life, now, as the ground and
source of all particular manifestations thereof, is represented
under the image of an oil-bowl.　Four figurative designations
of life are connected together in this verse.　In the passage
adduced from Zechariah the remark was made, "that the
candlesticks being entirely of the noblest metal, namely of
gold, indicates the glory of the church."　Here also we are
taught that the life which God has adorned with such noble
gifts, and to which he has appointed such high tasks, is a
noble possession, in that the oil-bowl is described as being
golden.　*And the pitcher is broken to pieces at the well.*　The
pitcher is the image of individual life, the well is the image
of the *general* life.　Hitzig justly compares with this the
drawing of breath, although that is not the whole, but only
one single act, by which we take to ourselves something out
of the great general treasure from which all individuals are
supplied with that which is necessary to their subsistence.
And the wheel is broken to pieces at the cistern.　The cistern,
or fountain, is the world.　Life is represented under the image
of a wheel because of its rapid motion.*　In James iii. 6 it is
said of the tongue, ἡ σπιλοῦσα ὅλον τὸ σῶμα, καὶ φλογίζουσα τὸν
τροχὸν τῆς γενέσεως·　The first words are based on chap. v. 5 of
this book, "Let not thy mouth make thy flesh sinful:" the
second clause, referring back to the present verse, represents
life under the image of a wheel, (γένεσις, Bengel, "constitutio
naturalis," i. 23 et vita, compare Judith xii. 19; πάσας τὰς
ἡμέρας τῆς γενέσεως μου, Schneckenburger on the passage.)　If
the pitcher is one day inevitably to be broken at the well,
and the wheel to be beaten to pieces at the cistern, it surely
behoves us to seek earnestly and betimes for such a founda-

---

* גַּלְגַּל, Gesenius, "res volubilis, quæ cito et continuo volvitur."

tion of our life as shall not be subjected to such changes.* The fear of death is legitimate so long as we have not reached this aim. The Berleburger Bible says, "the author having described here the accidents which precede death, and at the same time death itself: in the following verse he informs us what will become of body and soul after death."

Ver. 7. *The dust,* that is, as the Berleburger Bible remarks, "this earthly body, which is so called in order to show partly its origin, and partly also its weakness and littleness." Allusion is made to Genesis iii. 19, "till thou return to the earth, for from it wast thou taken, for dust thou art and unto dust shalt thou return." This passage contains only part of the truth. Its design was to humble man to the dust, who wished to be equal with God: hence, of the two sides of which his nature is constituted, only the one, the earthly side, is specially mentioned. According to Genesis ii. 7, there is in man a divine element, a breath from God, alongside of the earthly. Chap. i. 26 teaches that man is created in God's image, in distinction from all the rest of creation. In this aspect of his being he cannot be subjected to destruction, he must participate in the imperishableness of God. When the author says, that the spirit returns to God who gave it, he advances nothing new, he does but complement Genesis iii. 19 from the two passages just adduced. That the spirit of man does not perish with the body is here, in agreement with chap. iii. 2, (compare also chap. iii. 11,) most decidedly taught. Conscious, however, of the boundary lines separating the productions of "wisdom" from the outpourings of prophecy, he does not enter further on the question.† An earnest mode of looking at sin and guilt, such as is characteristic of the entire Old Testament, and especially of this present book, does not tolerate the notion of a pantheistic diffusion and absorption of the soul, which rationalistic interpreters find in this passage.‡ Such foolish thoughts can only be cherished by

---

* Cartwright, "danda igitur opera ut ipse salientem in se et perennem aquam habeat, quæ illum recreet, cum nec hydria, nec rota sibi consulere possit."

† These limits are mistaken by Winzer when he remarks, "si spes, quam nos foremus lætissimam, Ecclesiastæ, adfulsisset, non obiter ipse tetegisset et verbis ambiguis notasset rem maximi momenti."

‡ Hitzig, "That this particle of the divine breath poured out by God into the world and separated to an individual existence, will be drawn back again to its

those who think lightly of sin. Those terrible words in Deuteronomy xxvii. 26, "cursed be he that keepeth not all the words of this law to do them," should effectually prevent them rising within us. The doctrine of the Old Testament is that righteousness and sin stamp an indelible character on the soul. It is impossible that the distinction between the righteous and the wicked, so emphatically insisted on, should at once be reduced to nought in the moment of death. Against such a view is decisive, moreover, the piercing seriousness with which the future judgment is announced everywhere, and especially in this book. On all these grounds, and on the ground, finally, of the emphasis laid on that retributive work of God with whose mention in verse 14 the whole book terminates, the return of the soul to God can only be such an one as that of which the apostle speaks in 2 Corinthians v. 10, "for we must all appear before the judgment seat of Christ, that every one may receive the things done in the body, according to that he hath done whether it be good or bad;" compare Romans xiv. 10, "for we shall all stand before the judgment seat of Christ;" and Hebrews ix. 27, "it is appointed unto men once to die, and after death the judgment." After its departure the soul must present itself before Him from whom it had its origin, to receive from him its judgment. The Chaldee paraphrases the Hebrew as follows, "et spiritus animæ redibit, ut stet in judicio coram deo, qui dedit illum tibi." That is the Israelitish view. The other is a Japhetism of Bunsen's. Only on the view adopted by the Church, not on that of the Rationalists, has the passage the significance which is called for by the context. No other meaning than this, "that the soul must one day return to God as its judge," is fitted to prepare the way for the admonition, "remember thy Creator," which is the main feature of this entire section. Remember thy Creator, in order that thou mayest not have to bewail a misspent earthly existence when it is too late for remedy, and then after death come into judgment.* The Berleburger Bible says, "precisely for this

source and so be united once more with God's breath, which is the soul of the world."

* Cartwright says, "illud juvenes cautos et consultos reddat, quod illico ex hac vita migrantes apud judicem suum sistentur, ibi accepturi prout se gesserint."

reason should a man consider well how he lives and acts here,
seeing that, do what he will, he cannot avoid appearing before
God. Souls come out of eternity into this world as on to a
theatre. There they exhibit their persons, their affections,
their passions, that which there is of evil and good in them.
When they have as it were acted out their parts, they are
forced to retire, to lay off the person in which they presented
themselves, and to go naked, just as they are, before God for
judgment. All men are convinced enough in their conscience
that they cannot remain thus in their own nature, and that
they cannot escape from, or pass by, God when they die, as
the ungodly would fain do, being anxious even for the mountains and hills to cover them, if they can but remain without
God. But, willing or unwilling, we shall all infallibly fall
into the hands of our Creator. And one may see clearly that
the greatest labour and anxiety of dying men arises from
their feeling that they are on the way to God. How the
whole man trembles and shakes! Especially when he dare
not comfort himself with the hope of a reconciled approach!
There is no exception to the declaration, that all men must
return to God, but still there is a great distinction amongst
them. Most men return to God as to their insulted Lord:
some, however, as to a gracious and compassionate friend and
father. Inasmuch, then, as our coming to God is certain and
unavoidable, we should make it our first, as it is our most
needed care, to see to it every moment that we be able to
come unto God in a right manner." Much importance has
been attached to this verse in connection with disputes concerning the origin of the soul. If the soul returns to God,
such was the conclusion drawn by the advocates of Creationism, it must owe its origin to God and not to its human
parents.* The defenders of Traducianism answer, that the
return of the soul to God has relation to the creation of the
first man.† This reply, however, can scarcely be regarded as

---

* Jerome says, "ex quo satis ridendi, qui putant animas cum corporibus seri,
et non a deo, sed a corporum parentibus generari. Quum enim caro revertatur
in terram et spiritus redeat ad Deum, qui dedit illum; manifestum est, Deum
parentem animarum esse, non homines."

† Cartwright, "hoc dico, eos qui ex hoc loco conantur traducem evertere,
fundamento parum firmo niti. Nam liquidum est Ecclesiasten ad protoplasti

satisfactory. The return of the individual soul to God is only satisfactorily accounted for on the view of Creationism, that it owes its origin directly to God. As far then as this passage is concerned, Creationism is in the right, although, an examination of the weighty reasons advanced in favour of Traducianism must convince us that it only gives a part of the truth. The right course is to combine and reconcile the two apparently opposed theories.

CHAPTER XII. 8-14.

We have here the Epilogue of the book. At the commencement (ver. 8), and at the close (ver. 13, 14) the sum and substance of the book is set before us in a very condensed and vigorous form. This epitome serves at the same time as a standard and test for the interpretation of the previous portions. In the middle a recommendation is given of the book as containing wisdom offered by God to the Church, and as sharing, along with the other sacred writings, that all-pervading power which proceeds from inspiration (ver. 9, 11); then we find an admonition to the faithful use of those edifying truths and considerations which are set before men in this and the other sacred writings, together with a warning against a too deep study of worldly literature (ver. 12).

Ver. 8. *Vanity of vanities, said Koheleth, all is vanity.* Ver. 9. *And there yet remains, that Koheleth was a wise man, he taught also the people wisdom, and gave heed and sought out and set in order many parables.* Ver. 10. *Koheleth sought to find out acceptable words, and uprightness was written, words of truth.* Ver. 11. *The words of the wise are as goads, and as nails driven in are those who take part in the collection : they were given by one shepherd.* Ver. 12. *And further, my son, receive instruction from them : of making many books there is no end, and much eagerness is a weariness to the flesh.* Ver. 13. *Let us hear the conclusion of ̓e discourse, the whole matter: fear God and keep his comma for this (is the duty of) all men.* Ver. 14. *For every*

formationem respicere, cum Deus animam inspiravit Adamo, sicut ex ͮcorporis figmento apparet, quod ex terra exstitisse dicitur."

shall God bring into the judgment on every secret thing, whether it be good or whether it be evil.

Ver. 8. The correspondence between this verse and the commencement of the book (chap. i. 2) shows that it is not to be connected with the preceding section, but is to be set at the head of the conclusion.   There is, however, of course a certain connection between it and the close of the preceding section.   If our earthly existence comes to the end described in ver. 7 it is vanity, and true good may not be sought in it.*   This one sentence does not give us the quintessence of the entire book, for it contains many things which cannot be classed under such a head, and Knobel is quite wrong in saying that " the theme of the whole book is the assertion of the vanity of human life and struggles."   What we have here is a single thought of prominent importance, which, as being such, it is the purpose of this concluding repetition to bring to notice.   Verses 13 and 14, which are expressly announced as the true summary of the book, form the complement to verse 8.   What is said in the latter leads and prepares the way for that which is said in the former.   The knowledge of the vanity of earthly things conducts to the fear of God afterwards recommended.   Since all things are vain, man, who is subject to vanity, should do all in his power to enter into a living relation to Him who is the true absolute Being, and through fellowship with him to participate, himself, in a true eternal being.   All being vanity, man should not further vex himself about a "handful of vanity,"—he should not care much whether he have to suffer a little more or a little less, but attach importance alone to that which either hinders or favours his fellowship with Him who is the true absolute, personal, Being.

Ver. 9. יוֹתֵר signifies generally "more" (chap. vi. 8, 11, vii. 11), here it means "remaining," as in 1 Samuel xv. 15.

---

* Jerome—"post descriptionem interitus humani pulchre exordium libri sui repetens, ait, vanitas vanitatum, dixit Ecclesiastes, omnia vanitas.   Quum enim cunctus mortalium labor, de quo in toto volumine disputatum est, huc perveniat, ut revertatur pulvis in terram suam, et anima illuc redeat unde sumta est, magnæ vanitatis est, in hoc seculo laborare et nihil profutura conquirere."

Rambach says, "Patet igitur ex haetenus dictis atque imprimis etiam ex·vita hominis naturali tam brevi et misera, quod recte ab initio adfirmaverim, omnia quæ soli subjecta sunt, vana, misera et caduca esse."

'There remains," that is, "it remains yet to be said." Luther,
who renders, "This same preacher was not only wise, but he
also taught," and others, take יותר in the sense of "besides;"
compare יותר ממני "besides me," in Esther vi. 6. The title
Koheleth did not belong to Solomon as such, but as *Salomo
redivivus*, as the ideal author of this book. (Compare what
has already been said on this matter in chap. i. 1.) This is
evident from this verse alone. Of Solomon himself it was
superfluous to say that he was a wise man, and taught the
people wisdom. After what had been said about Solomon's
wisdom in 1 Kings v. 9-11, such praise would sound rather
cold. A *wise man*, of the kingdom of God; not in the sense
of the world, not of his own making, but of God's, (compare
v. 11): this passage consequently does not contradict Proverbs xxvii. 2, "let another praise thee and not thine own
mouth, a stranger and not thine own lips." He was an organ
of that heavenly wisdom, of which it is said in the Book of
Wisdom vii. 27, κατὰ γενεὰς εἰς ψυχὰς ὁσίας μεταβαίνουσα φίλους
θεοῦ καὶ προφήτας κατασκευάζει.* Koheleth did not limit himself to being wise for himself, but he *further* (עוד) taught the
people wisdom. The title Koheleth of itself indicates this
practical popular tendency. On the side of the readers there
was the corresponding duty, to hear and to take to heart what
was taught. The Piel of אזן, which only occurs here, is most
simply explained by "listen, hearken," after the example of
Aquila, the Syriac and the Chaldee. The comparison of the
Hiphil form is less remote than that of the noun מאזנים,
"scales," from which several have been disposed to derive the
meaning, "to weigh, to consider." To attain to the truth of
things we must listen; especially shall we succeed in this pursuit if we possess a hearing ear for God and his revelations:
compare Psalm xlix. 5, "I will incline mine ear to the parable." תקן is separated from אזן and חקר by the accentuation
and by the want of the copula. The two latter verbs designate the means by which the תקן comes to pass. The verb,
which occurs in chap. vii. 13, in the sense of "to make

---

* Rambach,—" Ex numero scil. illorum sapientium quos Spiritus S. singula-
riter ad docendum scribendumæque instruxit, coll. v. 12, unde non verendum
est, ut aut inutilia ac falsa hactenus monuerit, aut deinceps v. 13, 14 moni-
turus sit."

straight," describes here not merely "the making complete," but at the same time also the skill or ability of the work.—If Koheleth is Solomon only in so far as he is the speaker in this book, then the " many parables," or proverbs, cannot be those mentioned in 1 Kings v. 12, of which a great part is contained in the Book of Proverbs, but must be those contained in the present book, which it is the aim to recommend. The book contains two hundred and twenty-two verses, which may be regarded as so many מְשָׁלִים. There is of course a reference to 1 Kings v. 12: the ideal Solomon follows in the footsteps of the historical.

Ver. 10. *Koheleth strove to find out acceptable words :*—naturally not for the earthly, but for the heavenly minded ; words which should go to the hearts of the true members of the Church of God. Schmidt remarks : " Quæ jure meritoque desiderari et placere debent, tanquam divinæ virtutis et certitudinis." Cartwright says, "Verbi Dei encomium celebratur ab adjuncta dulcedine s. delectatione. Sunt etenim homini pio melle dulciora, Psa. xix., ut cibus famelico ut potus sitienti." *And uprightness was written, words of truth.* The relation of the two halves of the verse to each other is wrongly estimated by Elster, who says, " his representation unites therefore artistic grace of form with inner truth of thought." Words are rather acceptable, because they are upright and true, as in Luke ii. 52, χάρις is a consequence of *Wisdom.* יֹשֶׁר, " uprightness," denotes everywhere that character or condition which is adequate to the idea or standard. Wherein this consists is more carefully described by the addition, " words of truth." Truth is the quality which perfectly corresponds to the norm. The adverbial view of יֹשֶׁר (Luther, " and wrote rightly the words of truth") can scarcely be justified. The fundamental passage in this connection is Proverbs viii. 6-10, where wisdom says, " hear, for I speak noble things, and the opening of my lips is uprightness. For my mouth speaketh truth, and wickedness is an abomination to my lips. All the words of my mouth are in righteousness, and there is nothing twisted or perverse in them. They are all plain to him that understandeth, and upright to them that find knowledge." That which is said there in regard to the Proverbs holds good also of this book, inasmuch as it is a production of the same "wisdom from above," and not of weak, erring natural reason.

Ver. 11. From the praise of his own book, the author passes to the praise of the great whole, of which his work was destined to form a part, to wit, of the canonical books of the Old Testament. *The words of the wise*, of the organs of the ἄνωθεν σοφία, of the authors of the sacred books : to the number thereof the author of this book must be reckoned according to what has preceded.* The Berleburger Bible says, "in ver. 11 the reason is given for that which had been first affirmed : because, namely, he is one of the wise who are driven by the Spirit of God (2 Peter i. 21), whose words, therefore, have a deep meaning and importance." Hitzig observes, "an external connection is established between verses 10 and 11, by the fact that the words of truth in verse 10 proceed from one of the חכמים (ver. 9 a). Hence, *such* words of the wise."† *Are as goads.* דרבן, from דרב in the Arabic "to be pointed," denotes goad in general, and not specially "ox-goad." The point of comparison is only the power of piercing, penetrating deep : Gesenius ; "aculeorum instar alte descendunt in pectora hominum iisque manent infixa." We should be led to this view also by the parallel comparison of *Nails*. Knobel says, quite incorrectly, "just as the ox-goad teaches the ox manners, and causes it to go rightly." *And like nails driven in are the participators in the collection.* נטע means strictly "to plant ;" it is used in Daniel xi. 45, in the sense "to drive in." The plural משמרות is here treated as a masculine : for remarks on feminines in ח which are changed into masculines, see Ewald, 174 g. The plural מסמרים occurs in Isaiah xli. 7, with which

* Correctly Rambach, "Nam verba sapientium, atque ex illis maxime scriptorum θεοπνεύστων, Mosis, Samuelis, Josuæ, Davidis, ex quibus et Ecclesiastes fuit, coll. v. 9." Incorrectly Elster, who says—"By the words of the wise are meant gnomic or didactic poems, which being brief and precise both as to thought and expression are specially fitted to have such a lively, stimulating effect." According to the parallelism, "the wise" are the authors of the entire canonical books ; and that the excellence is not to be sought in the *form*, but in the substance, in the thought, is clear from the fact that their origin is traced to the One Shepherd, or, in other words to Inspiration.

† Schmidt and Rambach, "Ratio hic redditur ejus quod, ver. 10, dictum est scriptam esse ab eo rectitudinem et verba veritatis h. e. firma et infallibilia. *Ratio* nimirum est quia ipse sit ex illis sapientibus, Spiritu Dei actis, quorum verba sint sicut stimuli, etc."

compare 1 Chronicles xxii. 3. The expression בעלי אספות has been most variously explained. It is therefore of the more importance to renounce all attempts at guessing, and to seek a solid groundwork. The form, אספות, does not elsewhere occur, but the masculine form, אספים, does: this latter, therefore, must be our guide, more especially as it is in use amongst the writers of the post-exile period, to whose usage that of Koheleth everywhere bears resemblance. אספים, "that which is collected, collectæ, collectanea," is used in 1 Chronicles xxvi. 15, 17, and Nehemiah xii. 25, of the stores of the sanctuary, in reference to which it is said, in 2 Chronicles xxv. 24, "silver and gold and all the vessels which were found in the house of God."* Now אספות here has quite the same meaning as this אספים :—both signify, "collected things," "that which is collected." The sphere to which what is collected belongs, the nature of that which is collected, is more precisely defined by the foregoing expression, "the words of the wise," to which בעלי אספות corresponds. Accordingly, the reference can only be to the national library : and the Baale or Associates of that which is collected can only be those who have taken part in the contents of the collection, to wit, the authors of the individual books contained therein. בעל is any one who takes part in a matter : thus בעלי ברית are the associates of the covenant, (Genesis xiv. 13) ; בעלי רשע are those who are participators in wickedness (compare Eccles. vii. 12) ; בעלי עיר are the associates of a city, that is, the inhabitants : בעלי תלמוד, are the authors of the Talmud. The two clauses correspond exactly to each other : to the "words of the wise," correspond the "associates of the collection," and to the *goads*, the *nails* driven in. Only in the second clause is the position of the words an inverted one, and the object of the inversion is to connect נתנו immediately with בעלי אספות. All explanations different from the one given by us split on the meaning of אספות just established. So for example that by which even Luther rendered the two difficult words—"as nails fastened in are the 'masters of assemblies,'" namely, the

---

* Lightfoot, opp. i., p. 560, busies himself ex professo with these Asuppim, and under Nehemiah i. c. défines them as "certæ apothecæ, in quas thesauri et oblationes templi colligebantur et recondebantur, et quidem h. l. tales quæ erant ad januas sitæ."

teachers who preside over the assemblies of the people, or that
of Gesenius—"the associates of the (learned) assemblies."
Apart from the fact that this meaning is unsuitable—teachers
or learned men are quite out cf place here—אספות does not
signify "assemblies." In the opinion of others בעלי אספות is
not the subject, but is put in opposition, and describes *nails*
more particularly : "qui ipsi clavi sunt domini collectionum,
i. e., instrumenta v. media firmiter res combinantia," (Geier).
This is thought to suit the expression, "the words of the wise,"
very well : since they not only enable the wise to collect their
distracted minds, but also keep a whole Church together,"
(Berleb. Bible).* But even on this view a doubtful meaning
is thrust on the word אספות; the thought drags, and the impression of the simple image of goads and nails, which was
meant only to represent the piercing, deeply penetrating
power, is destroyed, or else the *nails* are without reason
separated from the goads ; and finally the correspondence between the sentences, which requires that בעלי אספות, corresponding as it does to דברי הכמים, must be the *subject*, is over-
thrown. Hitzig refers the term, "the collected ones," to
"collected proverbs or sayings." In that case, however, בעלי
is unsuitable ; besides, the parallel expression, דברי חכמים, has
a wider signification ; and further, this book does not at all
contain a "collection of sayings." According to the well-
founded interpretation advanced above, the sense of the two
clauses is the following—that the sacred writings of Israel are
endowed with a deeply penetrating power, in distinction from
all worldly literature, which can only produce a superficial
impression, and is incapable of stirring the deepest depths of
the mind and heart. A parallel passage is Revelations i. 16,
which represents a sharp and two-edged sword as going out
of the mouth of Christ. By this we are to understand in the
first instance, not the power which the word has of penetrating to, and healing the heart, but rather the destructive
power it derives from the omnipotence which is its source.
This is clear even from chap. ii. 12, as compared with chap.
ii. 16, where the two-edged sword is said to be directed against

* Following the example of Cocceius, Vitringa says ; " habent virtutem ecclesiam continendi ir eodem sensu, quemadmodum clavi asseribus firmiter impacti
ædium partes a; consertas minime vacillare et hiare sinunt."

the false seed which is in the Church ; and from chap. xix. 21, where it is said to bring down ruin on the anti-christian power of the heathen. But the power of the word to destroy, and its power to penetrate the heart with salvation, have one root. That root is the energetic life it draws from God, who is the fount of all life and of all strength. We may say the same thing of the second parallel passage from the New Testament, Hebrews iv. 12 : "for the word is living and powerful, and sharper than a two-edged sword, piercing even to the dividing asunder of soul and spirit, of joints and marrow, and is a discerner of the thoughts and intents of the heart." There also, "the living energy of the word from which it is impossible to escape," (Delitzsch), is directed in the first instance against its enemies and despisers, as is evident from the warning reference made to facts of the time of Moses, when disobedience to the word was followed by death. Hand in hand, however, with this aspect of the energy of the word goes the healing and redemptive one specially mentioned in the passage now under notice. A canon whereby to judge sermons has been justly drawn from this verse. They ought to have the characteristics of the Scriptures themselves : they are worth nothing if they cannot stand the comparison with goads and nails.* Here also have we a rule for the conduct of hearers towards sermons :—" they must not feel vexed if they leave their sting in the soul."† The words, "they were given by one shepherd," give the reason why such qualities are ascribed to the "words of the wise," and of the "associates of the collection ;"—it is as if the writer said—"and indeed they are such because they were given."‡ Analogous is 2

---

* Jerome, "Simul et hoc notandum est, quod dicuntur verba sapientium pungere, non palpare nec molli manu attrectare lasciviam sed errantibus et tardis poenitentiæ dolores et vulnus infigere. Si cujus igitur sermo non pungit, sed oblectationi est audientibus iste non est sermo sapientis. Verba quippe sapientium ut stimuli.—Hoc stimulo, necdum Paulum, sed adhuc Saulum puto in via confossum erroris audisse ; durum tibi est adversus stimulum calcitrare."

† Cartwright, "Hoc nos admoneat tranquillo animo Ministrorum asperiores et acriores adhortationis morsus placide ferre, et eosdem ad Deum tanquam autorem, non autem ad ministrorum morositatem (quod fieri solet) referre : denique hinc liquet scripturam et sanam doctrinam non assentari hominibus, aut corruptam naturam nostram blandimentis delinire."

‡ Cartwright, " Omnium antem verbi encomiorum nullum majus est, quodque omnium aliarum lau latissimarum virtutum *fons et causa est*, quod postremo

Timothy iii. 16, πᾶσα γραφὴ, θεόπνευστος, καὶ ὠφέλιμος πρὸς διδασ-
καλίαν, πρὸς ἔλεγχον, etc., where the deeply penetrative influence
of the Scriptures is traced to their divine inspiration. The
subject of נתנו is firstly, "the words of the wise," and then
"the associates of the collection:" in regard to the latter,
compare Ephesians iv. 11—"and he gave some apostles, etc."
(see Stier on the passage). The "Shepherd" can only be the
Lord. God is first designated the Shepherd of Israel in
Genesis xlviii. 15 ; xlix. 24 : in the last quoted place He is
simply called "the Shepherd." Further in Psalm xxiii. 1,
where not the individual believer but entire Israel says, "the
Lord is my Shepherd:" (see also Isaiah xl. 11 ; Jeremiah
xxxi. 10 ; Ezekiel xxxiv. 11, 12.) Israel the flock, the Lord
the shepherd—this is a common image, especially in the post-
exile writings. On any other mode of explanation we lose
ourselves in a region of guesses. As a shepherd, as the lov-
ing support of his Church, God has given it the Holy Scriptures.* In contrast to the plurality of the writers, which
gave occasion to the words, "the associates of the collection,"
emphasis is laid on the oneness of the primal source of the
Sacred Scriptures.

Ver. 12. *And for the rest.* The offer is complete ; it now
only remains that what has been offered be appropriated. *My
son :* "dear reader, whoever thou art, whom I have sought to
admonish as a father," (Berleburger Bible.) *Take instruction
from them.* מהמה refers to the preceding verse in which the
entire scriptures are spoken of. Elster's view consequently is
incorrect ; "in verse 12 Koheleth advises his readers to be
content with the simple truth contained in his own book."
His own book is mentioned only as part of a comprehensive
whole. נזהר was used in the sense of "to let oneself be
admonished" in chap. iv. 13. We find it employed with the
same force—"to let oneself be admonished by the Word of
God," in Ezekiel iii. 21, xxxiii. 4, 5, 6. In Psalm xix. 12,
to which there appears here to be a very distinct allusion, it

---

loco ponitur: nempe quod omnes Dei sermones, utcunque per varia Prophetarum organa et instrumenta ad nos perveniant, ab uno pastore Christo nobis
donati sint."

    * Cartwright, "Est enim verbum dei pabulum et veluti tenera herba, qua
pascuntur pii ad vitam æternam."

is said of the revealed commands of God, "moreover, by them is thy servant *warned.*"* Luther translates, "guard thyself, my son, against others more:" and this explanation was approved by Gesenius. For the understanding of מן יותר ־ppeal may be made to Esther vi. 6 ; for the meaning of the verb, to the Chaldee. But it is simplest to understand יותר as in verse 9 ; and the parallel passages are too decidedly in favour of the meaning assigned above to נותר. The meaning, "to guard oneself," does not occur in Hebrew usage. After the exhortation to the right use of the sacred Scriptures, follows a warning against the study of the literature of the world.† *Of making many books there is no end.* It is the nature of the wisdom of this world never to arrive at a conclusion concerning the very highest questions, with which we have alone here to do ; never to come to certain results, never to get rest. It is ever learning and never coming to a knowledge of the truth. There is consequently no consolation for him who devotes himself to this literature with the expectation of finding in it the solution to the enigma of this earthly life : *and much desire is a weariness to the flesh.* להג occurs only here. The verb signifies in Arabic "to be desirous." The reference to the thirst for *knowledge* lies not in the word but in the context : "much desire for that multitude of heathen books." It is not in the interest of *laziness* that this warning against "weariness of the flesh" is uttered. One may meditate day and night on the law of God (Psalm i.) without experiencing this "weariness of the flesh." But one should subject oneself to such weariness only when some positive actual result is likely to be gained. In connexion with the literature of heathendom there was weariness of the flesh and nothing else ; it was a mere Sisyphus labour ; it brought no true gain to the God-descended spirit.‡ Some have maintained that the words, "of making many books, etc.," imply "that at this time the simplicity of the wisdom revealed by God had already begun

---

* "Unde et pater ejus hanc laudem doctrinæ Dei tribuit Psa. xix. quod Dei servus eadem cautus et commonitus redditur."—Cartwright.

† Jerome—"Exceptis his verbis quæ ab uno pastore sunt data, nihil tibi vindices. Alioqui, quærenti multa, infinitus tibi librorum numerus occurret: qui te pertrahat ad errorem et legentem frustra faciet laborare."

‡ Cartwright—"Quorum ex lectione præter tædium et tui ipsius fatigatimem, nullum fructum percepturus es."

to be spoiled by an unfruitful and prolix school-learning."
But that the writer's attack is not directed against the native
Hebrew literature, is evident from the fact that for centuries
long the dogmatical wisdom of the Rabbins was handed down
solely by oral tradition ; and it is quite certain that at the
date of this book, however late we set its origin, there existed
no extended Rabbinical literature.   From chap. vii. 26, as
well as from the contrast drawn between Israelitish and
heathenish wisdom even in the Book of Proverbs, it is evident
that the author's polemic is with that false wisdom which was
threatening to pass from the heathen world to the Jews.
Others, who rightly refer the words to heathen literature, draw
from them the conclusion that the book was not composed till
the time of the Persian dominion.   But it is impossible to
prove that the heathen were more addicted to writing many
books at the end, than at the middle, of this period,   Recent
investigations have put beyond doubt that, in earlier times.
Egyptian literature was both comprehensive and vain and unfruitful.   According to Diodorus, i. 49, over the sacred library
at Thebes was the inscription, "pharmacy of the soul," ψυχῆς
ἰατρεῖον.

   Ver. 13. The saying *here*, corresponds to the commencement of the Epilogue in ver. 8.   There, all things earthly are
represented as vain : here, our connection with God is set forth
as the great essential.   "the conclusion of the discourse, the
whole, let us hear."   The word, סוף is never used by the
writers of the pre-exile period, and indeed, as a Hebrew word,
never occurs except in this book, in Joel, and in 2 Chron. xx.
16 : it frequently occurs in the Chaldee portion of Daniel.
Its meaning is not " the sum," but, " the whole."   At the same
time, only a thought of thorough importance is put at the end
when expressly described as the end ; and we are afterwards
distinctly told that the end is also the sum.   דבר is undoubtedly the particular discourse set before us in this book.   The
article may be omitted, whenever " the context may be pre-
sumed to define more precisely what is meant, and when therefore, the article is considered superfluous," (Ewald,) כל being
strictly a noun, it should not be rendered, " of the whole discourse :" הכל is rather set in opposition, and informs us that in
the termination of the discourse the whole is included ;—it

expressly specifies that the closing thought is the main, the
fundamental thought. We may also regard the oft-repeated
exhortation addressed to murmurers, to enjoy life, as comprehended under the last admonition—"fear God." For
what is it but fear of God, willingly to bear what God has
laid upon us, to rise above our trials with the exclamation,
"the Lord gave and the Lord hath taken away," to live in
freedom from care and fear to the present moment, and cheerfully to enjoy what He offers. All murmuring is godlessness.
נשמע is the pause form of the first plural future; compare Joshua
xxiv. 22 ; Jeremiah xlii. 6. "Fear God and keep his commandments, for that is (the duty of) all men. Many commentators explain, "for that is the whole man." Ewald says,—
"for therein consists the whole man, or that, which is truly
simple, which is sufficient for the entire man, and in which
everything else that is human is comprised." Elster says,
"therein lies man's whole nature, thereon depends his whole
fate."* However attractive this explanation may be, we must
still abide by Luther's translation, "For that belongs to all
men." The phrases כל אדם and כל האדם very often occur and
invariably signify—"all men ;" never, "the whole man."†
Against this consideration the harshness of the ellipsis, "that
(should) all men," is not at all worthy of mention. Such
harsh modes of expression occur not unfrequently in the later
form of the language, in which this book is written.‡ To fear
God and keep His commandments is the duty of all men,

* The saying of Lactantius forms a good commentary on the words as thus
viewed : he says in the Instit. vi. 1, "Id enim est hominis officium in eoque solo
summa rerum et omnis beatæ vitæ ratio consistit : quandoquidem propterea ficti
et inspirati ab eo sumus, non ut cœlum videremus et solem, quod Anaxagoras
putavit; sed ut artificem solis et cœli, Deum pura et integra mente coleremus."

† כל אדם Leviticus xvi. 17 ; Job xxi. 33; xxxvi. 25; xxxvii. 7 : Psalm
xxxix. 6, 12 ; lxiv. 10: Jeremiah x. 14 : etc. כל האדם chap. vii. 2 ; Genesis
vii. 21 ; Exodus ix. 19 ; Numbers xii. 3, xvi. 29-32 ; Judges xvi. 17 ; 1 Kings
viii. 38.

‡ Jerome, "aiunt Hebræi, quum inter cætera scripta Salomonis, quæ anti-
quata sunt nec in memoria duraverunt, et hic liber obliterandus videretur, eo
quod vanas asséverit Dei creaturas et totum putaret esse pro nihilo, et cibum et
potum et delicias transeuntes præferret omnibus, ex hoc uno capitulo meruisse
auctoritatem ut in divinorum voluminum numero poneretur, quod totam dis-
putationem suam et omnem catalogum hac quasi ἀνακεφαλαιώσει coarctaverit
et dixerit finem sermonum suorum auditu esse promtissimum nec aliquid in se
habere difficile, ut scilicet Deum timeamus et ejus præcepta faciamus."

because all bear His image, and can have no true life or
growth except in connection with the primal source of their
existence : they must also be punished with destruction if
they criminally and violently break this connection. This
latter consideration is expressly and emphatically alluded to in
ver. 14, where the motive of the admonition is given. " Into
the judgment on every secret thing." על is very frequently
used of the substratum or object: hence " on" is equivalent
to " concerning, in respect of." That the judgment here is
principally the *future one*, is clear from the corresponding
ver. 7, where the appearance of the spirit separated from the
body before God, in order to receive recompence for its works,
was spoken of: (compare 1 Cor. iv. 5 ; 2 Cor. v. 10 ; Acts
xvi. 31.) Still there is no reason for confining our thoughts
entirely to the future judgment : we should rather think of
judgment in its widest compass, as it is begun in time and
perfected in eternity. The mere mention of " secret things"
does not compel us to limit the words to the future judgment.
For in Psalm xc. 8, it said of the judgment which is pronounced and executed by history—" thou settest our iniquities before thee, our *secret sin* in the light of thy countenance."
Even Luther saw how comprehensive was the application of
the expression : he remarks, " the author does not speak here
only of the judgment at the last day, but, according to Scripture usage, of judgment in general. There is a judgment and
an hour for everything with God, and no one can escape.
Wherefore Arius and all heretics are already judged. But at
the last day it will be made still clearer in the presence of all
creatures, angels and men, that even now in the day of visitation, God the Lord has laid bare their sin and disgrace, that
in a word, there is no more concealment."

  " O how exceeding necessary is it that our light and
thoughtless nature should at all times remember, and be
reminded of, the strict and unavoidable account awaiting us, so
that we may never forget it ! How easily one or another
may be called upon to render his account ere he is ready !
Should we not therefore be ever preparing, if we do not desire
to be put to confusion, but to receive such a sentence as we
desire and can count blessed."